THE LITTLE GUIDES

DOGS

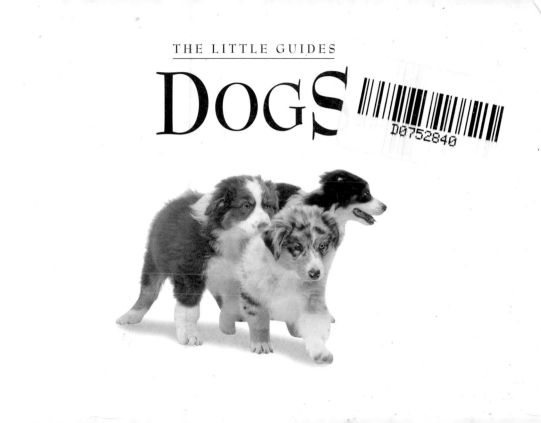

THE LITTLE GUIDES

DOGS

CONSULTANT EDITOR
Paul McGreevy
B.V.Sc. Ph.D.
M.R.C.V.S.

FOG CITY PRESS

Published by Fog City Press
814 Montgomery Street
San Francisco, CA 94133 USA
Reprinted in 2000

Copyright © 1999 Weldon Owen Pty Ltd

Chief Executive Officer: John Owen
President: Terry Newell
Publisher: Sheena Coupe
Associate Publisher: Lynn Humphries
Art Director: Sue Burk
Senior Designer: Kylie Mulquin
Editorial Coordinators: Sarah Anderson, Tracey Jackson
Production Managers: Helen Creeke, Caroline Webber
Production Assistant: Kylie Lawson
Business Manager: Emily Jahn
Vice President International Sales: Stuart Laurence

Project Editor: Stephanie Pfennigwerth
Designer: Katie Ravich
Consultant Editor: Dr. Paul McGreevy

A catalog record for this book is available from
the Library of Congress, Washington, DC.

ISBN 1 875137 63 7

Color reproduction by Colourscan Co Pte Ltd
Printed by LeeFung-Asco Printers
Printed in China

A Weldon Owen Production

CONTENTS

PART TWO
DOG BREEDS

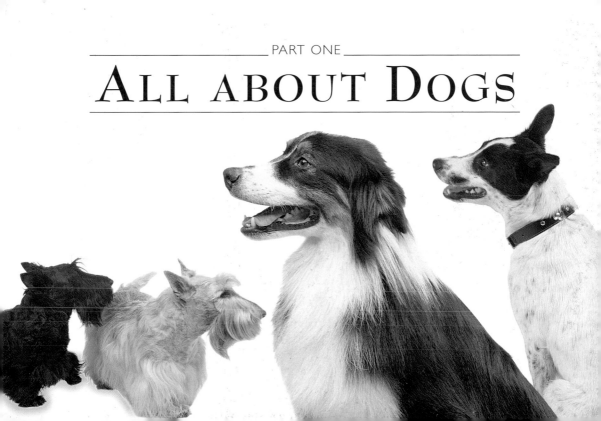

PART ONE

ALL ABOUT DOGS

THE
CANINE STORY

The evolution of the domestic dog is intertwined with the development of human civilization. From the scavengers on the outskirts of the first settlements to the treasured pets of today, dogs have provided thousands of years of companionship and protection. As different human cultures took shape, so too arose a wide variety of domesticated dogs. Different types of dog became invaluable aids in hunting, guarding, herding or draft work. Changing social and economic conditions led to the emergence of toy dogs, prized by nobility and commoners alike. In recent times, the proliferation and refining of breeds to kennel club standards have taken dogs even further from their ancestor, the wolf.

EARLY DOGS

Domestic dogs, along with coyotes, jackals, wolves and dingoes, make up the genus *Canis*. Although the fossil record is limited, the first members of this genus may have appeared about 10 million years ago in North America before migrating into Asia or Eurasia. Due to a number of similarities, both physical and behavioral, it is believed that the domestic dog evolved from the wolf. They have the same number of teeth and display similar behavior when in packs.

First contact By the time humans and wolves began to interact, probably more than 15,000 years ago, there were two distinct types of wolf in the northern hemisphere: those from the north, which were large with long, pale coats; and those from the south, which were slimmer with short, darker coats. These variations were simply natural adaptations to climate and habitat, but once the bond was established between humans and wolves, the gradual evolution of the domestic dog was largely dictated by selective breeding.

Anubis, Egyptian god of the dead, was often portrayed as a jackal, or as a man with a jackal's head.

The Arctic peoples traveled through their hunting grounds with the help of hardy malamutes and huskies.

New partners The domestication of the dog probably began around the time our ancestors became hunters and gatherers. Wild dogs would have scavenged on the outskirts of camps and the hunters would have appreciated the warnings they gave of approaching danger. Hunters may have killed them for food occasionally and used their fur for clothing. Puppies may have been kept with human families, tamed, and used to help the hunters. As settlements became more permanent, dogs would have become increasingly useful as guard dogs, and eventually for herding and pulling or carrying loads.

Purpose-built Dogs were created to perform specific tasks by breeding together those animals that exhibited particular traits, such as stamina and aggression. Gradually, through this process of interbreeding, dogs with distinct types of form and temperament were developed and maintained.

Ancient breeds Mastiff-type dogs and greyhounds are the oldest recognizable breeds of which there are historical records. Depictions of greyhounds have been found on 8,000-year-old fragments of Mesopotamian pottery, and there are records of mastiffs that are nearly as old as this. In ancient times, greyhounds were used primarily as hunting dogs while large, aggressive mastiffs were used in battle and as guard dogs.

An ancient African breed, today's basenjis of Europe and North America descend from dogs brought from Zaire in the 1930s.

WILD DOGS

The genus *Canis* dominates the family Canidae, which originated in North America 57 million years ago. Cousins of the domesticated dog, members of Canidae include foxes, raccoon dogs, maned wolves and dholes. Like domesticated dogs, some wild dogs have had a long association with humans. But not all contact has been positive, and many species are now endangered.

Gray fox

Raccoon dog

Family traits Today 35 species of wild dogs live throughout the world. They evolved to chase prey across grassland, and almost all have lithe builds designed for speed and stamina. Other adaptations, such as interlocked bones in the forelegs (to prevent rotation during running), reflect the sustained strength these animals require to pursue prey. While most foxes are considered solitary hunters, the larger dogs and wolves are social animals that live in packs. All rely on their keen hearing and smell to locate prey, and use their sharp, scissor-like carnassial (molar) teeth to tear flesh.

Bat-eared fox

Varied diet Wild dogs are mainly carnivorous, but their adaptable digestive system allows them to also eat fruits, insects, snails and worms. Some foxes eat fish, and dingoes, descendants of Indian wolves that arrived in Australia about 4,000 years ago, eat everything from grasshoppers to kangaroos.

ALL PART OF THE FAMILY
The large ears of the bat-eared fox help it to detect prey and to keep cool in its African habitat. The gray fox of North America even climbs trees in search of food. The unique raccoon dog of East Asia and Europe prefers to forage in dense forest undergrowth.

Friend or foe? Many cultures have legends associated with wild dogs. Opportunistic and resourceful, foxes and wolves have a universal reputation for cunning deception. However, in North American Indian legends wolves and coyotes are benefactors as well as mischievous tricksters. Stories such as that of Romulus and Remus, founders of Rome, also credit wolves with caring for humans. Nevertheless, wild dogs are regarded by many farmers as a threat to their livestock. Predator control programs, combined with habitat destruction, now threaten the survival of some wild dog species.

Strange relations Some wild dogs' looks make them stand out from the pack. The bush dog's tubby body, short legs, small, rounded ears, broad face and a short tail make it the least "dog-like" in appearance. The maned wolf of Brazil—so-called for the crest of hair across its shoulders—looks more like a fox on stilts, so suited are its legs for roaming tall grass prairie.

Bush dog

African hunting dog

One-of-a-kind Named because of its black face mask, the raccoon dog is unique among wild dogs because it hibernates in winter. It is also the only dog that does not have any kind of bark. Its distant cousin, the bat-eared fox, is not only one of the most peculiar wild dogs—it is unique among carnivores. Entirely insectivorous, it has four to eight extra molars, providing more chewing surfaces for feeding on prey such as termites.

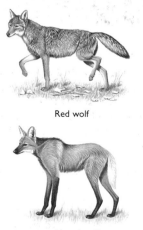

Red wolf

Maned wolf

DOGS IN DANGER
The bush dog of Central and South America is listed as vulnerable; the red wolf of North America and the African hunting dog have also suffered from human intervention and are now endangered. Some people believe that parts of the maned wolf's body, such as its left eye, have medicinal and magical properties. As a result, maned wolf numbers are dwindling.

IN THE WILD

While some wild dogs lead relatively solitary lives, others live in cohesive, highly structured societies called packs. Cooperative behavior, demonstrated most effectively while hunting prey, gives pack dogs an advantage in the struggle to survive. The behavior of pet dogs shows that they haven't lost touch with their heritage.

Solitary existence Wild dogs such as foxes are thought to be solitary animals, since group hunting is not advantageous for dogs that rely on tiny prey such as mice. But recent studies have revealed that some foxes live in small groups, although they hunt alone.

Pack animals Wolves, African hunting dogs, coyotes and dholes are the most social species, living in packs of up to 20 members. Pack life has its advantages: it is easier to hunt large prey; it is easier to find a mate; there are more helpers to care for the litter; and there are more guards to defend against intruders and predators.

Top dog To maintain harmony within the pack—and to ensure its survival— wild dogs such as wolves have rules that establish leadership and control social interactions. Packs are organized into hierarchies centering on the dominant breeding pair, known as the alpha male and female. Each wolf knows its place and defers to the authority of the alpha male, the top dog.

Spreading the message The top dog lets others know of his status by scent-marking his territory. He may also threaten his subordinants by using low aggressive growls. Lower-ranking wolves growl less, instead using barks and whines to communicate. Wolves also howl to locate each other, to pass on an alarm and to communicate with other packs across long distances.

In their first year African hunting dog pups rely on their pack to provide food.

Cooperative skills The top dog decides when the pack should rest or hunt. Using their acute hearing and smell, the wolves locate a victim and sneak up on it until, sensing danger, the prey flees. The pack then rushes to attack, slowing and weakening its quarry by harrying it before biting its flanks and rump. The top dog darts forward to seize its nose while others rip its throat. The feasting then begins.

Old instincts Although domesticated dogs are now far from their ancestors, old habits die hard. Dogs still rely on hearing and smell to understand their world. Like wolves, which bury meat to provide future meals, dogs also bury objects to prevent others from stealing them. Their love of rolling in dung traces to the way wolves use the smell to camouflage themselves when hunting. And dogs use the same pack rules of communication and behavior during encounters with other dogs and within their own close-knit group—their human family.

The howl of a wolf pack can be heard for miles and warns other wolves to keep their distance.

THE DOMESTIC DOG TODAY

Dogs developed and diversified as human needs changed. The evolution of hunting dogs is an example. The greyhound was swift and powerful, but hunting methods were refined and prey became more varied. By the 1800s, dogs had been bred not only to chase game but to sniff it out (scenthounds), to point to it (pointers and setters), to flush it out (spaniels), to fetch it (retrievers) and to dig it out of burrows (terriers).

Saint Bernards may be related to mastiffs, called Molossi, brought to the Alps by Roman armies almost 2,000 years ago.

Aesthetic appeal Since dogs were originally bred to perform specific tasks and to behave in certain ways, their appearance was largely irrelevant. However, this was not always the case. As early as 5,000 years ago, Chinese emperors were breeding tiny ornamental dogs as palace companions and lap dogs. This process of miniaturization led to the development of toy dogs, many of which became favorites with royalty and fashionable wealthy citizens. They remain popular pets to this day.

Pugs were popular in the homes of the wealthy.

The Industrial Age Increasing urbanization and mechanization in the eighteenth and nineteenth centuries played an important role in the domestication of the dog. People now had more time to devote to hobbies, and by the mid-nineteenth century, breeding and showing of dogs were popular pastimes. As a result, the focus of breeding shifted to the dog's appearance and the variety of breeds grew. Then in 1867 the book *The Dogs of the British Islands* set out for the first time the defining characteristics of 35 breeds. This introduced the concept of a breed "standard"—an ideal against which a breed could be compared and judged.

Standards set In 1873, Britain's newly formed Kennel Club established stud books and published its own standards for 40 breeds, as well as stipulating that for a breed to be recognized it had to be registered with the Club. As other clubs, including the American Kennel Club, followed suit, this rule became more influential on the future selective breeding of dogs than any other factor.

Sad legacy There may now be as many as 500 breeds worldwide. However, the constant refining of breeds for appearance and kennel club standards over the last century has led to inbreeding, leaving a legacy of genetic diseases even in hardy breeds. Today, responsible breeders and kennel clubs strive to avoid breeding dogs with traits that jeopardize their well-being.

Dogs today come in all shapes, sizes and colors.

GETTING A DOG

A dog is wonderful, loving, entertaining and loyal. Whether he comes with a pedigree or from a pound, a dog is just about the perfect friend. However, he will demand a lot of you, because he relies on you for nearly everything—food, water, shelter, veterinary care, exercise, training, grooming and protection. While it is important that you choose the right dog for your needs, it is equally important to ensure that you can meet his. You need to prepare your home for his arrival, and make him a welcome and well-behaved member of your community. The responsibilities of ownership are great, but the love and friendship you'll receive in return are priceless.

CHOOSING THE RIGHT DOG

The bond between you and your dog can be one of life's most rewarding experiences. To give this relationship the best chance of success, choose your pet carefully. Too often, a dog does not live up to an owner's expectations— with heartbreaking consequences. Consider your lifestyle, your home and your family needs—and what your dog will need from you.

Family matters Before you get a dog, consider your family as it is right now. Are you single? Do you have children? How old are they? Do you already have a pet? Think about who else might join your family in the next 10 to 15 years, because that's the time commitment you'll be making.

Dog or cat? Feeding, play, exercise, training and grooming are all essential canine needs and take time. If you get a puppy, you will need to house-train him, too. If your family does not have this time, a smaller animal might be a better choice of pet. Also, make sure that no one is allergic to dogs.

Financial burden Consider the cost of owning a dog. You could pay more than $1,000 for a purebred dog. Take into account the cost of food, leashes, bedding, grooming tools, toys, veterinary care and obedience training. You may also need to build a fence.

What kind? Learn as much as you can about the characteristics of different breeds so you can choose the one that best suits your needs. For example, the sporting breeds were bred for long hours in the field and need a lot of exercise. Therefore, a retriever may not be the best choice if you live in an apartment.

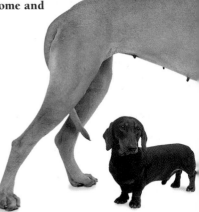

Gentle giants, Great Danes love kids and adapt well to city living. Dachsunds are also suitable for apartments, but they can be snappish around young children.

Coats How much hair can you bear? Some dogs, such as Chow Chows, have thick coats that require daily brushing. Short-coated dogs, like Labradors, require less grooming, but tend to molt all year round. Poodles and other breeds that don't shed need to be clipped regularly—an extra expense if this is done professionally.

Climate If conditions where you live are extreme, choose a dog whose coat type permits adaptation. Arctic breeds such as huskies tend to be uncomfortable in hot, humid climates. On the other hand, greyhounds get very chilled in cold climates.

Gender While dogs of either sex make great companions, first-time dog owners or families with children might want to look for a female first. In general, males have more behavioral problems and are more aggressive than females.

Dogs for kids If you have little kids you could consider getting a big dog, as they tend to be more patient. Small dogs can also be happy companions for kids, as long as the children know how to behave around them. Be aware that children under three may be unintentionally rough with their pets. Dogs, too, can be rowdy with youngsters.

Make it mixed? While it isn't easy to predict the behavior or adult appearance of a mixed breed, they can make the best pets. For more information, see pp. 30–31.

GROWING UP TOGETHER
While playful, friendly breeds such as collies, retrievers, standard poodles and this Australian kelpie can make wonderful companions for children, don't buy a dog in the belief that it will teach your child responsibility. You must be willing to accept responsibility when necessary.

23

PUPPY OR OLDER DOG?

Few things in life are cuter than a puppy, but chewed shoes, puddles on the floor and the other rigors of puppyhood are not for everyone. Puppies and adult dogs have different needs and make different demands of their owners. Many of the same issues you thought about when you decided to get a dog are also the ones you must consider when deciding what age she should be.

Clean slate If you get a puppy, you can make her what you want her to be. You will have more control over her learning during those crucial first few months of life, and if you have children, your puppy will grow up with them, learning to be tolerant and unafraid of children in general. The drawback is that her training has to start from scratch, including her house-training. She will need small amounts of food at regular intervals, she will make messes constantly and she'll chew everything within range.

Time and patience Your puppy will also sleep a lot, but not necessarily to your schedule. Destructive when bored, she'll require a lot of exercise and supervised play. In short, your puppy is a baby, and she'll need more of your time and patience than an older dog. Do you have enough of both to train her, as well as a sense of fun and adventure to play with her?

What about work? An ideal match for puppies is a family where one adult is home for much of the day. If you work from home, you can also adjust your schedule to accommodate house-training trips and some playtime. If all members of the household have to go to work, plan to get your pup during vacation time. Spend that time bonding with her and establishing a feeding and exercise routine. Also include repeated short periods of isolation to teach her how to cope when left alone.

Adopting an adult If your house is empty for much of the day, you might consider getting an older dog. A mature dog will be better at keeping herself entertained, and she won't need your undivided attention when you are home. A dog aged nine months or older is a wise choice, because you can tell what size she'll be and how clean she is. You'll also get an idea of her social skills and temperament. She may already be house-trained and know basic obedience commands.

Raising pups like these papillons requires time, energy—and a sense of fun.

Hidden problems Although many adult dogs up for adoption make wonderful companions, they will already be shaped to some extent by their life experiences. As a result, adult dogs may have behavioral problems that might not be obvious. However, any dog can be taught new tricks, even if she has to unlearn the old ones.

Questions to ask Don't adopt a dog, whether from a shelter or a family, just because you feel sorry for her. Take the time to make an informed decision, finding out as much as you can about the dog's history before committing yourself. You need to know why the dog was given up, where she came from, how many homes she's already had, whether she is house-trained and neutered, and whether she is used to children, men and women. Check that she

NEW HOME, NEW TRICKS
You can form an impression of an adult dog's personality by observing her at the animal shelter. You can ask shelter staff for their opinion of her character. Even if the dog needs retraining to fit in with your lifestyle, you may have found a true friend.

is friendly, calm, obedient and healthy. If you choose carefully, an adult dog may be perfect for you. In addition, you'll have adopted an animal that really needs a home.

A HEALTHY PUPPY

If you have decided that you have the time and patience for a puppy, you want to make sure you choose a pup that's going to be fit and healthy. While there's no way to guarantee that he will never fall ill, you can reduce the chances by checking for certain signs when making your choice.

This mother teaches her cavalier King Charles spaniel pups to respect authority.

Socialization Try to get your puppy between six and eight weeks of age. Since this age is the "period of socialization," it's vital for the development of social behavior that he stays with his mother and littermates until this time. You should also start to bond with him now and introduce him to the world.

Pick of the litter Watch how the puppies interact with each other, and play with each one. Try to avoid the most bossy and shy pups. The runt of the litter might be the cutest, but he is also the one most likely to have medical and behavioral problems.

Early influences Choose your pup from an alert, active and well-fed litter. Try to meet the parents and other relatives to see how your pup is likely to appear and behave when he matures.

Genetic disorders Responsible breeders make great efforts to ensure that the dogs they sell are healthy and not prone to long-term problems. They carefully match the parents based on their genetic backgrounds to reduce the risk of inherited diseases being passed along to the puppies. Make sure that your pup's parents have been checked for heart problems, and ask if any of the pup's close family members or more distant relatives succumbed to any of the diseases or conditions common to the breed. Consult your vet for information about these breed-specific disorders.

COAT
His coat should be glossy and clean, without excessive oil or dandruff. It will feel shorter and thinner than the coat of an adult dog. There should be little or no shedding when stroked. His belly will usually be hairless.

EYES
His eyes should be bright, shiny and expressive, with little or no discharge, watering or redness. The eyelashes should not touch the eyeball.

NOSE
His nose will be moist and cool. It should not be running.

EARS
His ears should be free of discharge, excessive wax and odor.

MOUTH
Pull back his lips to see that his gums are either pink or pigmented, with around 23 white teeth (depending on his age). He should also have clean-smelling "puppy breath."

ANUS
Make sure his anus is clean and dry, not red or irritated.

SKIN
Pull apart his hair to check that his skin is smooth and free of parasites. Its color will range from pink to black to spotted, depending on what type of dog he is. Check that there are no scabs, lumps or pimples.

LEGS
Check that he moves freely when he walks and runs. He should put even weight on all four legs.

PUREBRED DOGS

Although all dogs vary from individual to individual, purebreds tend to have distinct appearances and are genetically predisposed to behave in certain, predictable ways. Their breeding has been monitored for centuries, and their ancestry has been recorded and studied. All that history means that when you decide on a purebred, you'll have a good idea of the looks, character, eventual size and behavior of the dog you are getting.

Bearded collies are hardy working dogs.

Purebred groups Purebred dogs are classified according to the breed's original purpose. Although most modern purebreds are kept as pets, they still retain certain characteristics of their ancestors.

Hounds These dogs were bred to use either their noses to track small game (scenthounds, such as beagles) or their keen sight and speed to run down prey (sighthounds, such as borzois). They tend to have enormous stamina, although they differ in their exercise requirements. Most enjoy room to run and sniff.

Sporting dogs Also known as gun-dogs, members of this group, such as setters, pointers, retrievers and the larger spaniels, were bred to work with hunters in the field. The Vizsla and the Weimaraner also belong to this group. Alert and intelligent, they love lots of energetic, outdoor exercise.

Working dogs This diverse group includes guard dogs (the mastiff, for example), sled or cart dogs (the Samoyed and the Bernese mountain dog), rescue dogs (the Saint Bernard), and well as dogs that serve the military (the Doberman pinscher). They are capable and quick to learn, and make dependable companions. Because of their size and strength, it is important that they be properly trained.

Terriers Most terriers were developed to dig burrowing animals from dens. While much of their aggression has been bred out of them, they remain playful, exuberant and brave.

Herding dogs Used for thousands of years to protect livestock and to prevent them from straying, breeds in this group, including sheepdogs and collies, tend to be very nimble and intelligent. Their instinct to herd is strong, however, and sometimes they can't resist rounding up your children.

Toys Traditional lap-sitters favored by nobility, dogs such as Pekingeses and Japanese Chins are ideal for apartment dwellers. Cute because of their diminutive size, they can have quite determined personalities.

Non-sporting dogs This group contains breeds that don't fit neatly into any of the other categories. The bulldog, Dalmatian, Tibetan terrier and Lhasa apso are included.

Scottish terriers can inherit a blood-clotting disorder called von Willebrand's disease.

Friendly advice It's a good idea to get advice from impartial experts when looking for the breed that suits you best. Ask owners, breeders, trainers and vets for their invaluable opinions. To see various breeds in action, visit obedience trials or dog shows.

Health problems Creating breeds involves concentrating genetic material to obtain certain traits. Sadly, a smaller gene pool can increase a purebred dog's inherited predisposition to certain illnesses. Most large breeds, for example, are prone to hip dysplasia, a joint disorder. A blood-clotting disorder called von Willebrand's disease has shown up in breeds including Dobermans and Rottweilers. Respiratory problems are common in breeds with pushed-in faces, such as pugs. Others are troubled with heart defects, kidney problems, eye ailments and deafness. To reduce the chance that your pup will suffer from a genetic disorder, buy from a reputable breeder and get him checked by a vet.

MIXED BREED DOGS

The mutt is a lovable hybrid whose ancestry sometimes remains a mystery. Because mixed breed puppies are almost by definition unplanned, a disproportionate number of them tend to wind up in shelters or for sale from cardboard boxes for a low cost—or none at all. But despite your lower initial investment, you're not sacrificing quality. Your mixed breed dog will make a devoted companion, and he can be trained to behave as well as any purebred. He'll also be unique.

She may not win any ribbons, but this kelpie-Labrador cross will win plenty of hearts.

Missing link A mixed breed is truly his own dog. No other dog will look quite like him. But this sense of individuality has some drawbacks. In many cases, you won't know who the pup's parents were, let alone his grandparents, which means his ancestry will be hard to trace. It could be especially difficult to predict the puppy's eventual size. One method is to observe him at four months of age, when he will be roughly half his adult size. Predicting his adult build by the size of his puppy

paws will not guarantee accuracy; some breeds, such as collies, have tiny feet in relation to their body.

Surprise element Even if you can predict how large your mixed breed puppy will grow, you will have a harder time predicting his personality, behavior and grooming needs. These factors are determined by his genes, but the way in which his mixed bag of behavioral characteristics are manifested will not be as obvious as they would be if he were a purebred.

Trainability The "good" traits of your mixed breed's lineage may be prevalent, such as the playfulness of the shih tzu. Or the "bad" traits may surface, such as the dominance of the Alaskan malamute. However, the odds are good that your mutt will become a great companion. His personality and manners mostly depend on the dedicated and consistent way you train him. If you teach him to love learning, there are no limits to what he can achieve.

Hardier hybrids? People tend to think that mixed breeds are hardier and healthier than pure-breds. Mixed breed pups may have had to be tough to survive in a world without all the refined care and knowledge lavished on a purebred litter. Also, the blend of genetic material in your mixed breed will certainly lessen the likelihood of him developing the hereditary problems and diseases associated with purebreds. However, mixed breeds can still get sick from the non-hereditary illnesses that can affect any dog. Choose your dog because you like his personality and looks, not because you think he'll be free from genetic disorders. Remember, mixed in any dog's genetic pool will be an assortment of genes—the good and the not-so-good.

A friend for life It is unlikely that the price of a mixed breed dog will come close to that of a purebred; in fact, you may have acquired your new friend from a cardbox box marked "free to a good home." How-

ever, all the ongoing costs of owning a dog—and the responsibilities—will be exactly the same as those for a dog with a pedigree. And just like pure-breds, mixed breeds are wonderful, loving and loyal. They're all dogs, after all.

Regardless of her pedigree, this German shepherd mix needs to be loved, valued and cared for in the same way as a purebred.

WHERE TO GET A DOG

There are many ways to acquire the dog of your dreams. Whether it's a show quality shar-pei or a Heinz-57, you want to maximize the chances of him being a perfect match for both of you. Some ways are better than others. If you're looking for a purebred, it's a good idea to visit several reputable breeders before making your choice, so you'll have plenty of comparison points. But an animal shelter is often the first choice for would-be dog owners. This way you can give an existing dog a good home, rather than add to the overpopulation of dogs.

INFORMED CHOICE
Make sure you know what kind of dog you are looking for before you visit the shelter. Many of the dogs are there because their previous owner did not choose wisely.

Reputable breeders If you want a purebred dog, find a reputable breeder. Your vet, local breed club or national kennel club may be able to direct you to the right person. Responsible breeders are aware of the problems of their breed and work to improve the quality of that breed with every litter.

Breeders to avoid Reputable breeders breed for love, not money. Backyard, or hobby, breeders breed pups as a way of raising cash. They are less likely to be knowledgable about the breed, and they may not understand how to prevent undesirable traits from occurring.

Pet stores Most pet stores are supplied by "puppy mills," which breed large quantities of purebred dogs of questionable lineage for profit. Mill conditions may be poor, with female dogs being bred every time they come into season. Puppies are often taken from their mothers and their littermates too early, before they have received the socialization they need. Buying a sad-eyed pup from a pet store may seem like a humane act, but it just provides revenue to the puppy mills and encourages them to continue to breed indiscriminately.

Your money's worth A puppy from a good breeder may be more expensive than those from other sources, but you are also paying for that breeder's years of experience with the breed, plus her ongoing help and advice. When you consider that you will have your dog for 10 or more years, it's a good investment.

Shelter dogs The best place to find a mixed breed dog is at your local animal shelter. Many dogs there are young adults that outgrew the cute puppy stage and became a handful for their owners, who were unaware of the time needed to care for a dog. Often associated with humane organizations, shelters are run by city or town councils. Many shelters are well-organized and supervised by trained staff. Others, however, are poorly run.

Always check out the shelter yourself. The animals should look healthy and well cared-for. The staff should also be able to answer your questions about the individual animals.

DOING IT FOR LOVE, NOT MONEY
Reputable breeders, like the breeder of these West Highland white terriers, will screen potential buyers carefully, turning down those whom they feel will not provide the pups with the right environment. Don't take offense if a breeder suggests you think about another breed; she has both the dog's best interests, and yours, in mind.

Rescue leagues Shelters are not the exclusive domain of mixed breed dogs; purebreds show up as well. To give them a second chance, breed rescue clubs provide foster homes to purebreds that have been surrendered to a shelter or abandoned. Volunteers evaluate them for obedience, health, temperament and house-training, often working with them if they fall short of the requirements to make a good pet. Rescue leagues are wonderful places to find a young adult purebred dog—and at a less prohibitive price.

PREPARING FOR A NEW DOG

Dogs don't err on the side of caution. They happily investigate all the exciting things life has to offer with never a thought to the consequences. To a dog, the average house and yard are full of fascinating attractions, and they can get themselves into a lot of trouble. This is particularly true when you get a new dog, since she'll be eager to explore—and taste—her new surroundings. Before your dog moves in, make sure your home is safe for her.

Dog-proofing your home Dog-proofing is a lot like child-proofing—it means removing anything that may be a danger to your pet, or at risk of being broken. For example, a dangling cord is an irresistible temptation to a pup. To prevent electric shocks or a bump on the head from a heavy appliance, unplug electrical cords and coil them, or tuck them out of sight.

Strange tastes Toxic substances taste great to dogs, so keep all solvents and cleaning compounds in a safe place. An elevated shower caddy will keep fun-smelling shampoos out of harm's way, and a closed toilet lid will

A ROOM OF ONE'S OWN
Large dogs, such as mastiffs, might find living indoors uncomfortable. If your dog will be spending a lot of time outdoors, either in a yard or an enclosed pen, provide a kennel for shelter from the elements. The kennel should be sufficently large for your dog to move around inside freely. It should have plenty of ventilation and also be well-insulated to keep out extremes of temperature.

A NOSE FOR TROUBLE

Dogs are constantly using their noses and mouths to explore the world around them. They also have surprisingly agile paws, so it's important to store cleaning supplies and solvents where they can do no harm—perhaps on a high shelf. You could even install child-proof locks on kitchen cabinets. Baby gates can also restrict your dog's access to certain areas.

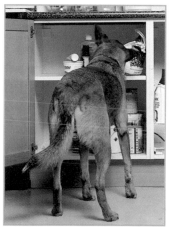

stop your dog from drinking a cocktail of bacteria or poisonous additives. Stash your trash in a can with a tight-fitting lid. Keep medications out of reach, and secure your chocolate—it contains a stimulant, theobromine, which can make her seriously ill.

Maximum security If you have a yard, check that the fencing is secure enough to keep your dog inside. For a small dog, a fence that is 4 feet (1.2 m) high should be adequate, while a 6-foot (1.8 m) fence will hold most large dogs. Remember that dogs such as terriers can dig under a fence, so make sure it is well-secured. If there are any holes, fix them. Check that the gate shuts firmly and that your dog will not be able to squeeze under it. Swimming pools should also be fenced or covered to prevent drowning.

Out of bounds Garages are filled with oil spills, sharp objects and other accidents waiting to happen. Insect sprays, fertilizers, rodent and slug baits

The leaves of the dumbcane can be toxic to dogs.

and paint can all poison your dog. She will be particularly attracted to anti-freeze, so make sure that you store it safely, and that it is not leaking from your car. It's best to keep your dog out of the garage while you're not around to supervise her.

Garden gourmet? Your garden offers your dog a smorgasbord of smells, but some of the tastes can turn her green. Take care to remove all toxic plants, including poinsettia, rhu-barb, apricots, oleander, potatoes, fox-gloves, azaleas, rhododendrons and tomatoes. Also keep your yard free of sticks that, when chewed, could per-forate her palate, throat or intestine. Tempt her with chew toys instead.

ACCESSORIES FOR YOUR DOG

There are a few things that will make life easier and more comfortable for you and your dog that you should buy in advance of your new pet's arrival. These aren't optional extras; they're essential items that will keep her happy and healthy. Make sure that you are ready from the outset to be the best owner your dog could hope for.

Bedding The first thing that your dog will need is a warm, clean, comfortable bed. For a puppy, a box lined with soft, washable bedding is perfect. If she's still being house-trained, you may opt for a crate lined with paper and made cozy with a towel or blanket. She can graduate to a crate pad or a piece of carpet in the bottom once her bladder control is more reliable. A mature dog will appreciate a durable bean bag type-bed or a soft blanket.

Collars The range of collars available can be mind-boggling. Flat leather or nylon collars with plain buckles are

WALKIES!
An extendable leash (above) allows your dog to explore while remaining under control. Attach an identification tag to her collar, whether it's leather (below) or nylon.

good everyday collars for most dogs. However, rolled (round) leather collars with buckles work better for dogs with long hair or thick ruffs, because they don't matt the hair beneath the collar the way flat collars tend to. As puppies continuously outgrow their collars, the nylon varieties are more economical. Check your pup's collar each week to make sure that it has not become too tight—tight collars are uncomfortable and dangerous. Attach your dog's rabies vaccination tag (if required) and identification tag inscribed with your name, address and telephone number to her collar to ensure that you will be contacted if she gets lost.

Leashes The wide variety of leashes available are generally made of leather, cotton or nylon. Leather leashes are the most expensive, but they can last longer and are gentle on your hands.

GROOMING GEAR

Every dog needs some sort of a brush, a comb, some thinning scissors (above), a toenail trimmer, shampoo and a soft toothbrush. The type of grooming tools will depend on your dog's coat. Match the size of the brush to the size of your dog.

Thick nylon is strong and inexpensive, but is less flexible than leather. Short, lightweight nylon leashes are the best choice for puppies. Because they're inexpensive, they'll cost less to replace if they're chewed.

Muzzles If your dog needs a muzzle, get one that allows her to pant and drink water but not to bark and bite. Some muzzles are meant for grooming purposes only, so make sure that what you buy fully covers your needs.

SOMETHING TO CHEW ON

Find bowls (left) that are designed for your dog's breed, so that she can eat and drink without submerging her nose and ears. Solid rubber or nylon chew toys (above) will ease her teething pains and save your belongings.

Pooper-scoopers come in many varieties and are available at pet supply stores.

Canine couture Dogs that spend a lot of time out in the elements often need extra protection. Pet supply stores sell a variety of jackets, rain slickers and cordura-soled booties that can keep your dog warm, dry and protected in rugged terrain. Some dogs may be reluctant to wear clothes, especially booties, at first. Make sure the clothing is the right size and doesn't rub your dog around her legs and neck. Put the clothing on your dog for a minute or two, once or twice a day, and lavish her with praise. Continue to leave it on for increasing periods of time. She will soon get used to it, just as she got used to her collar.

SETTLING IN

When you first bring your new dog home, she will probably be confused and apprehensive. It can take a shelter dog a few weeks to adjust and feel secure enough to relax. Give your dog a little time and a gentle, reassuring approach. The early days of your new relationship may require some effort and, at times, a lot of patience. But once your dog has settled in you'll wonder how you ever got by without her.

Spend time with your dog to get her used to you and the other members of her family "pack."

A warm welcome Like all dogs, your new dog needs to feel that she's part of the pack. From now on, her pack is you and your family, so don't segregate her from other family members. Instead, keep her with you, and play with her as much as you can.

The arrival Take her to the place that will be her permanent toilet area straight after her first food and water. Don't be upset if she doesn't get the message just yet. House-training takes time and patience (see pp. 80–81).

New territory Once indoors, take her to a room where she'll be likely to spend a lot of time, such as the kitchen. Let her familiarize herself with her surroundings. Introduce her to her bed and food and water bowls. Leave her leash on but let her drag it around; this way, if she tries to gnaw a table leg, you can gently distract her. Don't speak harshly to or punish your dog—she needs to trust, not fear you. You'll have plenty of time to teach her the rules of the house after she adjusts to her new environment.

First nights Your dog will probably be homesick and lonely for the first few nights. She may whimper and cry, but try not to go to her every time she makes a noise. If you have a puppy, she may settle down if you imitate her mother's companionship by wrapping a ticking clock and hot water bottle in her bedding. Bringing her bed into your bedroom might also help her.

Dinnertime Changing your dog's diet right away can upset an already nervous stomach, so feed her what she was fed by her breeder or animal shelter. If you want to change her food, wait a week or two before gradually introducing it into her diet.

Other pets Introductions to your other pets should be made gradually and under supervision. Many cats and some older dogs resent the arrival of a puppy, so never leave them alone together unless your pup is inside her crate. Always give them the most attention, never allowing them to feel that they are being replaced. To prevent "food wars," feed the animals separately until they are comfortable with each other.

If your new dog is mature, it's best to introduce her to your other dogs on neutral ground, such as a park. Let them get acquainted before bringing the new dog into the others' territory. The dogs may play-fight as a way of establishing the pecking order.

Other people Resist the temptation to show off your new dog to visitors until she has settled in. Get her used to you and your family first, before letting her meet strangers.

Teach your children to be gentle and quiet around her, especially if she's a puppy. They must learn how to approach her and handle her properly so that no one gets hurt. Always supervise them when they are playing together. If your dog is an adult and you're unsure of her background, keep her on a leash whenever she's around children until she exhibits consistent positive behavior. If she shows any signs of aggression, call your vet. She may just be overwhelmed, but you need to be sure.

Teach your children to be gentle with their new pet. Dogs are playmates—not toys.

39

PUPPIES' SPECIAL NEEDS

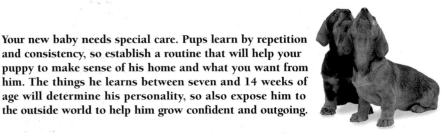

Your new baby needs special care. Pups learn by repetition and consistency, so establish a routine that will help your puppy to make sense of his home and what you want from him. The things he learns between seven and 14 weeks of age will determine his personality, so also expose him to the outside world to help him grow confident and outgoing.

Frequent feeds Growing puppies have greater nutritional needs than older dogs and must be fed more often. Until your puppy is about four or five months of age, feed him three times a day with a reputable brand of dog food. Remember, you get what you pay for—and the quality of the proteins, fat and other nutrients is important. (For more about nutritional needs, see pp. 114–115.) Be patient with table manners and minimize your cleaning chores by buying a food dish that doesn't tip over. Place it in a corner so your pup won't have to chase it all over the floor.

Accidents happen Your young pup won't have the muscular control to hold his urine and bowel movements, and you'll have to anticipate his needs. But his control will gradually improve, and by three or four months old, he should be quite dependable—just be patient and persistent.

Knowing when your pup needs to go is the key to house-training, so establish a routine. Also keep an odor neutralizer and stain remover on hand. An odor-free floor is important; dogs tend to eliminate where their noses tell them they went before, so quick clean-ups prevent repeat performances. For more on house-training, see pp. 80–81.

Pups like this Norwegian elkhound are naturally curious creatures— and born comedians.

Play-time As soon as your pup has had his vaccinations and has learned to walk on a leash, take him out on exploratory walks and play chasing games. Most puppies try to play with their owners as they'd play with other dogs. They jump up, growl and bite. Play is necessary for the proper social development of puppies, but they need to be taught how to play with people. If your pup bites you, squeal like a pup. Since this is the sound his littermates would have made during rough play to signal pain, it will teach your pup bite inhibition. If he gets uncontrollable, either leave him alone in a room or confine him in his crate until he calms down.

Chewing blues When puppies are between three and six months of age, their new teeth begin to emerge. Giving your pup a nylon chew toy or a wet towel that has been left in the freezer overnight will relieve some of the discomfort of teething and help his baby teeth to loosen and fall out.

Curiosity will also lead your pup to put things in his mouth. Chewing develops his facial nerves and jaw muscles, but it's best that he gnaws on appropriate items. Invest in some chewies.

Socialization Your puppy needs to get used to people, places and things so he can learn how to live happily with all that goes on around him. Take him out and introduce him to new situations, sensations and experiences. Make everything you do a positive learning experience.

HANDS-ON CARE

Your pup faces a lifetime of grooming, ear exams and all the other hygiene routines. To get her used to being handled, pet all parts of her body. If she doesn't like her feet being touched, stroke her body and feet until she's sleepy. When she falls asleep, gently massage her toes. Soon your pup will relax and let you touch her feet while she's awake, too.

41

RESPONSIBLE DOG OWNERSHIP

A dog's love is a privilege, and with it comes genuine responsibility. Your dog depends on you and deserves the best care you can provide. When it comes to public considerations, responsible dog ownership is a matter of common sense and courtesy.

Local laws Laws regarding dog ownership vary from place to place. It is common for owners to be required to keep their dogs leashed in public places and certain breeds, such as the American pit bull terrier, may also be required to wear muzzles. Familiarize yourself with any local laws and obey them. Allow your dog off the leash only where regulations permit, and never let him loose without supervision.

Always clean up after your dog in a public place. There are numerous products available to help you do this simply and hygienically.

The identifiable dog Most cities in the US require that dogs be licensed or registered, and many also require that dogs be vaccinated for rabies. In addition to being licensed, your dog should always wear an identification tag on his collar. In Britain, rabies vaccinations and registration are not required, although dogs must wear a collar and tag in public at all times. For permanent identification, you can have your dog tattooed or have a vet inject a computer microchip under his skin. Both procedures are relatively painless. In some countries, such as Australia, microchipping is already obligatory.

Clean up When walking your dog in public, always clean up after him. In many US cities, and throughout Britain, it is now an offense not to do so. If possible, train your dog to defecate on your property before the walk.

Good citizenship You must train your dog from an early age to be well-behaved around people and other dogs. All dogs should be taught to obey basic commands and to walk on a leash without pulling. Also avoid tying your dog out in the yard away from people for long periods. Such isolation can lead to barking and aggression problems. If your dog is noisy and likely to disturb the neighbors, don't let him out in the yard between 10 pm and 7 am. If he does bark a lot when alone, consult your vet about ways to curtail it.

Neutering If you're not planning to breed professionally, then it is sensible and responsible to neuter your dog. A safe procedure, neutering addresses the growing problem of pet overpopulation and has beneficial effects on your dog's health and behavior. Neutering reduces the chances of males getting prostate disease and eradicates the risk of testicular cancer. Spayed females are protected against uterine infections and cancers of the uterus, breast and ovaries. Neutering won't make your dog fat and lazy, and your male dog will

Aggressive dogs must be muzzled when in public.

be less likely to urine-mark, pick fights with other dogs and roam. It is never too late for your dog to be neutered.

Happy and healthy It is your responsibility to feed your dog a balanced diet and to provide water at all times. Daily exercise or play will keep him fit and stop him from getting lonely or bored and developing behavioral problems. You must also provide regular medical care. Annual vaccinations and veterinary check-ups are essential and prevent the transmission of diseases to people and other dogs. Washing and grooming your dog will keep him looking good and control skin parasites, which can lead to health problems that can be passed on to people.

UNDERSTANDING DOGS

Even though your relationship with your dog has some "human" qualities, such as mutual respect and affection, there's an inevitable distance between the two of you. No matter how intelligent and alert she may be, your dog has ways of hearing, seeing and thinking about the world that are totally different to yours, and this invariably leads to confusion. The key to a happy life together is to find a way to "talk" to each other, by learning to read your dog's behaviors and becoming aware of how she interprets yours. If you observe and understand her vocalizations and body language you may even get to the point where you can predict what she will do next.

PACK ANIMALS

In the dog world, you are either a leader or a follower. This pack mentality comes from dogs having wolves as ancestors. Wolves rely on their leader for their survival. Even if a wolf is not top dog, he is still an important link in the chain of command. It's the same with a dog. It does not matter how many people or other animals there are in his family, his instinct is to find out where he stands.

Dogs' motivations Talking with dogs involves more than giving commands. It requires understanding why they do the things they do. The most important thing to remember is that your dog's ancestors belonged to a pack. Nearly everything your dog does, from rolling over on his back to grumbling when you tell him to get off the couch, is motivated by his desire to establish his place in his family "pack."

Changing status A dog's rank can be fluid, depending on the situation and how he perceives the other members of the pack. Every dog will act either submissive or dominant in relation to another dog or human, but he can also be submissive around one dog or person and dominant around another. For example, your dog may obey your commands but ignore those given by your child.

Content to follow Most dogs are born followers. They usually seem quite content to please their human pack so they can get plenty of positive attention. But dogs need a social

This boxer looks up to his leader for guidance and reassurance.

structure with a leader and clear hierarchy. If no one in the family takes the role of leader, your dog will fill the vacancy. He may start to display dominant behavior such as ignoring your commands, being pushy or even threatening you.

Training a pack animal Knowing the motivation for your dog's behavior is the key to changing it—or, assuming that it's good behavior, encouraging more of it. Most well-behaved dogs are submissive to some degree. Well-behaved dogs are also happy dogs, because they derive emotional fulfilment from a sense of belonging.

Pack leader Without using force, you can steer your dog's pack behavior in a positive direction. Act like the wolf leader who controls the food and feed your dog after you have finished eating. Wait until he is sitting obediently before you attach his leash and take him out for a walk. This way, your dog will always know where he stands.

Inherited behaviors Ancient traits that your dog still displays, such as licking and play-bowing, were not only techniques used for establishing pack status. They are also used in day-to-day operations to communicate and cooperate with other pack members. By reading and understanding the behavior of other dogs, your pet's wild ancestors took their cues about how to relate to them. By observing your own dog's behavior, you can do the same.

CHOICE LOCATION
Comfort isn't the only reason dogs take over the furniture. In the wild, high sleeping grounds were always taken by the pack leader. Letting your dog on the furniture will get him thinking that he's your equal—or your boss. Getting him off the furniture will reinforce your dog's subordinate position in the family pack.

HOW DOGS COMMUNICATE

Dogs are expert communicators who use an elaborate repertoire of body postures, sounds and scent to get their message across. Unlike humans, dogs have no reason to camouflage their emotions, so watching them act and react together will give you a good idea of what they are saying. You will also be able to understand what your dog is trying to tell you.

THE ROLE OF ROLLING OVER
Play-fighting stems from dominance displays and is one way dogs establish the pecking order. Going belly-up is a classic sign of submission learned in puppyhood. This West Highland white terrier is discovering that he'll be safe if he rolls over and lets his siblings win.

What they say Most of what dogs say relates to their past. As pack animals, they spend time sorting out their status in the social structure. They also talk about defending their territory and their resources, such as food and toys.

Using scent When dogs meet, the first thing they do is establish rank. Since the anal sacs underneath dogs' tails contain glandular secretions that vary in composition from dog to dog, the nose-to-rear-end method of greeting works well for them. With one sniff a dog can learn the gender, age, sexual status, genetic relatedness, attitude and authority of another. He'll know whether they've met before, and what their relationship is likely to be.

Spreading information Like wolves, dogs also pick up and deliver scent messages by urine marking. Dogs often mark places to declare their dominance, or their ownership of territory, to other dogs. They may scratch at the earth around the mark to activate scent glands in their pads, thereby indicating the position of the mark and spreading the scent further.

Body postures Dogs are tactile animals who use their bodies to express affection, possession or rank. As a general rule, submissive dogs contract, while dominant dogs expand. A dog of lesser rank will make himself as small as possible by shrinking slightly and tucking in his tail. He'll carry his weight over his haunches and may even "surrender" by crouching or rolling over. On the other hand a dominant dog makes himself seem larger by raising his hackles, head, ears and

tail. During play-fighting, he may try to dominate another dog with gestures such as pinning her shoulders with his paws.

Appeasement gestures A dog can bring things back to a friendly level by using the same deferential gestures he used as a puppy, such as licking the other dog's mouth or rolling over. Other friendly body postures, such as play-bows—his rear up, his front down and his tail wagging—are used to attract attention or to lighten the mood of other dogs and humans.

Visual communication In addition to body posture, dogs often reveal their emotional state by their facial expressions and the position of their ears, mouth and tail. Eye contact is another way of

This fox terrier's play-bow is an invitation to play to whoever he's talking to—human or dog.

asserting authority, and a dominant dog may stare down one of lower rank. A submissive dog will often avoid eye contact by averting his gaze and exposing his neck.

Speaking with voice Since humans are verbal creatures, we expect barking to be the main way that dogs communicate. To a dog, though, barking is far less important than body language or scent marking. Still, barks, whines, howls and growls all have a place in the canine language. How your dog "speaks" and what he means depends on the context of the message.

After the anal smells are recognized, the sniffer may sniff the new dog's nose and lips.

USING SOUND

Your dog is capable of a variety of noises—barks, growls, whines, yelps and howls—that can mean different things at different times. If you listen, you will soon learn to interpret his vocabulary, and even be able to talk to him in a language he understands.

Terriers like this Jack Russell were bred to alert their owners to the presence of prey by barking.

Bred to bark Domesticated dogs bark more than their ancestors despite, from an evolutionary point of view, having little need to. This is because a dog's alarm bark was probably one of the first traits early humans selectively bred to accentuate.

Perpetual adolescence In the wild, wolves quickly move through adolescence as they begin to take care of themselves. But some domesticated dogs have been bred specifically to retain their puppy-like traits—shared by juvenile wolves—such as gentleness and friendliness. This explains why mature dogs have a behavioral repertoire similar to that of juvenile wolves. And since all pet dogs are dependent on their owners, some might argue that, in a sense, dogs are psychologically immature.

Whining or whimpering Because they perpetually behave like juveniles, dogs make juvenile sounds, such as whining and crying, more frequently than their mature wild counterparts. Dogs also register that these sounds are a good way to get their owners' attention. An excited or lonesome dog will make high-pitched sounds not unlike yawns. A stressed or fearful dog will give repetitive, squeaky whines punctuated with shrill yaps.

Barking Barking is a dog's equivalent of human conversation. The tone of barking changes with the dog's motivation. In general, the faster and

WHY DOES SHE HOWL?

When your dog howls she is following tradition. Like her wolf ancestors, who howl to communicate over long distances, she is saying "I'm here," "Where are you?" or "This is my territory." The pitch of a siren is very similar to that of a howl, so when an ambulance rushes by and your dogs starts up, she's doing what comes naturally: returning the call of the wild. You could perhaps join in, just to be sociable.

higher the bark, the more excited or agitated the dog. A single bark in a regular voice means he's curious and alert, and a low, repetitive bark means he's feeling defensive or protective. But sometimes dogs just bark out of habit.

Growling Growling is an uncomplicated warning sound. Dogs that combine growls with a submissive posture are frightened. However, dogs can also make growl-like moans of pleasure, especially during a good back rub.

All in the tone Your dog is conditioned to equate growling with leadership because in wild packs, it's usually the higher-ranking dogs that growl. Take advantage of this by using a low, growl-like tone to convey authority. You can also teach a pup to inhibit his nipping instinct, for example, by growling at him the way his mother once did. By using the same tones and inflections that your dog responds to, you can communicate with him far more effectively.

WILD DOG COMMUNICATION

Your dog may be completely at home in your comfortable world, but she still displays behaviors inherited from her ancestors. The examples below illustrate how she communicates many of her moods and intentions in the same way that wolves do.

Howling Wolves are quieter than dogs, but the vocal communication they do use is particularly effective. For example, a howling chorus can be heard for about 6 miles (9 km) away and sends a message to neighboring packs: Stay away, or come prepared to fight. Packs also howl to locate members that have become lost during a long chase after prey. They also howl at the end of a successful chase, perhaps as a kind of celebration. This behavior is certainly echoed in the howls of hound packs after a hunt.

Greetings When a mother wolf returns to her pups after hunting they crowd around, licking her

An alert expression and upright ears indicate a happy, playful wolf.

FRIENDLY
A relaxed wolf will hold its ears half-back. There'll be no sign of tension in its eyes.

ATTACKING
As a wolf becomes increasingly aggressive, it will adopt a straight stance with its ears pricked forward. Its muzzle will wrinkle and its lips will curl into a snarl to expose its teeth.

SUBMISSIVE
The wolf in this state will "shrink" to avoid drawing attention to itself. For example, it will press its ears against its head.

DEFENSIVE
A wolf will protect its resources by raising its hackles, snarling and growling.

NO PROBLEM

A calm, relaxed wolf will hold its tail loosely, in a neutral position. Its weight will be evenly distributed on all four legs.

NO THREAT

A submissive wolf, perhaps approaching a dominant member of the pack to greet him or to beg for food, will crouch with its tail close to its body. The tail tip will be curved back.

FEARFUL

A terrified wolf adopts a humble, subservient pose. It crouches with its tail touching its belly or, in a sign of abject admission, may even roll onto its back and urinate.

ATTACKING

A wolf carrying its tail straight out behind it is an aggressive animal planning to attack. It will appear stiff-legged, with its body leaning forward and its weight on its forelegs.

It will fix its opponent with a hard stare.

muzzle in the expectation that she will regurgitate food for them. Low-ranking wolves greet their leader with similar displays of affection. It is believed that the pleasure our dogs take in our return may be a vestige of these rituals.

Submissive urination A conditioned reflex to dominant treatment, this behavior is echoed by anxious pets who may have been corrected too frequently or too harshly. A puppy may urinate while greeting or when being chastized.

A high, fluffed tail, accompanied by raised hackles, is a sign of authority and dominance in both wolves and domesticated dogs.

READING A DOG'S REACTIONS

Dogs don't write poetry or speak in elegant sentences, but they can still be very eloquent. Here are some of the most common ways in which dogs express themselves with body language, and what they are telling you by each particular behavior.

Ears pulled down and back When your dog's brow and skull muscles are tight and tense, and his ears are pulled down and back, he's probably feeling frightened, anxious or submissive. The more intense his feelings, the more extreme the ear position will be. Dogs also assume this position when they are play-fighting with other dogs.

Ears pricked When stimulated by something they see or hear, dogs will prick their ears and point them in the direction of their interest. They will also prick them when they are feeling aggressive. When combined with raised hackles, a stiffly erect stance and a penetrating stare, your dog is demonstrating dominance.

Tail-wagging A wagging tail usually indicates a friendly dog, but not always. Dogs also wag their tails when they are scared, agitated or unsure. For example, dogs often wag their tails in broad sweeps when they're playing or anticipating something good, like food. But they also use this wag when they're throwing their weight around or preparing to launch an attack. Check how your

Sighthounds like this Italian greyhound normally tuck their tail between their legs, but this dog's ears and posture indicate that he is afraid.

The flattened ear position and slight cringe of this terrier cross shows that she is nervous.

his tail low and between his legs as he considers his next move: "Should I flee, fight or go belly up?"

Mounting and humping These behaviors are expressions of dominance. Mounting other dogs isn't limited to males, and it rarely has sexual overtones. However, there is sexual intent in humping behavior, even if the dog doing the humping is neutered. Break your dog's focus suddenly by making a noise or another distraction.

Mouth and lips If your dog repeatedly flicks his tongue up to lick his nose, he is tense. He may be assessing a new situation, concentrating hard on a task, or wondering whether he should approach a guest. Tongue-flicking often precedes bit-

ing, so approach with caution. If your dog's mouth is closed he is either appeasing or feeling uncertain. A dog with curled lips is issuing a challenge.

Eye expressions Direct eye contact usually signals confidence; casual contact means contentment. But each dog is different—your dog might look directly at you whatever his emotional state. To know his true intentions, you need to observe other body signals and the context in which he uses them.

dog has distributed his weight, before being certain that the tail-wagging is welcoming. If he's feeling aggressive, his body will be tense and his weight will be mainly on his front legs.

Tail tales The height of a dog's tail is a barometer of his emotions. While dogs experiencing anger or other "high" emotions will raise their tails, dogs in low spirits will hold their tails below horizontal and wag them only slightly. A frightened dog may wag

This happy Labrador and collie have relaxed mouths and bodies.

COMMUNICATING WITH A DOG

Just as your dog's body language indicates her moods and reactions, your body, face and voice are sending signals to your dog. To avoid misunderstandings, you need to ensure that you are sending her signals that she can recognize. Add your own different tones, emotions and movements, and you're ready to start training.

How dogs read us Dogs' senses are incredibly sharp but their interpretations of human movements and facial expressions are somewhat limited. No matter how attentive dogs are, it's impossible for them to think like a person. They have to draw on their skills in communicating within their own species to understand our movements and patterns of behavior. As a result, they focus mainly on signals that are similar to those used by dogs or those that they think may play a role in their survival.

Improving your relationship through better communication will have long-term benefits for both of you.

Use her language Except for a few vocal commands they understand, dogs mainly respond to intonations and body language. Base your commands on her language, and consider how she interprets your own behavior. Modify it, if necessary, so that you send her the right message.

Watch yourself Too much exuberance can send dogs the wrong signals. Because dogs make stiff, jerky movements when they're preparing for a confrontation, your dog will become anxious if you use similar movements around her. Other gestures, such as opening your arms, are perceived by your dog as being positive because they resemble the spread-eagled position dogs assume when they're relaxed. By using the movements that suit the meaning you wish to convey, you will communicate to her more effectively.

Adjust your attitude Dogs respect those who are self-assured and confident. If you adopt a confident posture and an enthusiastic attitude your dog will know that your commands are right for her—and she'll obey them.

Key to training Your dog will get the idea of what you want her to do from watching your behavior, so think about it logically. If you tell her to "stay" but then move forward, it's likely that she'll move forward, too. The key to making all the right moves is to use all of your skills—body language, tone and attitude—and match them with the right word commands.

Use the tones dogs use themselves. This boxer knows that his owner's serious tone means a reprimand.

TRAINING YOUR DOG

Every dog needs to be taught basic good manners. Not only does it ensure his safety, and give you peace of mind, it also provides the framework for further training, allowing your dog to fulfill his canine potential. When teaching your new dog, it is important to remember his ancestral roots. A dog is a pack animal, and when he comes into a human home, he expects to follow rules and obey a leader. A critical goal of training is to help your dog recognize you as his leader. He needs guidance, so by setting boundaries, and being firm and decisive, you are in fact being kind and caring—and making your dog feel more comfortable, too.

THE WELL-BEHAVED DOG

Dogs are not well-behaved from the start. It is your job to show your pet the correct behavior and to teach good canine manners. Training is easy and rewarding—no fancy tricks or superdog intelligence are required. Just work with your dog on a regular basis, set the rules and stick to them, and before long he will know what is and what is not acceptable.

Why train? A dog that knows the five basic commands—sit, stay, down, come and heel—is a lot easier to be around. He is less likely to be jumping on people, fighting with other dogs or dragging you across the street at a red light. It's easier for you, too, if your dog can take a trip to be groomed, boarded or to receive medical care all in his stride. You want a dog you can enjoy, and a confident, well-behaved dog is a lot of fun. On the other hand, a dog that constantly disturbs the peace and nearly knocks you over can be a challenge to live with.

Training will help you build a bond with your dog. She will learn to trust you and other humans she meets.

Rules of life Dogs also need training because things that, in the dog world, are considered acceptable, such as defending his food with a snarl, are unacceptable in a human family. Training is the only way to make your dog understand what's expected of him and give him clear guidelines for what he should and should not do.

Beating boredom Every dog has an instinctive need to be busy. Most were originally bred for a purpose, such as guarding or hunting, and when they're not doing something they become bored and destructive. Basic training, such as teaching him to sit or to walk on a leash, similarly gives your dog a purpose and a sense of direction. Rather than being bored and frustrated, he'll be excited and fulfilled because he has a job to do.

Sense of belonging When dogs lived in the wild they lived in hierarchies and relied on a leader for survival. Therefore taking orders from a leader,

from a dog's point of view, is part and parcel of belonging; it makes them feel secure because they know where they stand. Training will teach your dog his place in the family hierarchy. By making him respect your authority, it'll also prevent dominant, aggressive behavior caused by feelings of insecurity.

Obedience is freedom Rather than cramping his style, training will allow your dog more freedom than those without any training at all. A well-behaved dog who reliably comes when he is called, for example, will be able to enjoy more off-leash play-time than his less obedient friends. He'll save you a lot of worry, too.

Using "dogspeak" Knowing how your dog communicates, with other dogs as well as people, provides a tremendous edge in training. Like their wolf ancestors who followed the pack leader, your dog will pay careful attention to your expressions, movements and vocalizations to pick up his cues.

By speaking your dog's language—or the human equivalent—you can get your ideas across more effectively. For example, when training, use tones of voice that mimic those used by dogs when they are talking to each other. A firm "bark" is ideal for commands; a high-pitched tone, because it resembles a dog's excited bark, is good for conveying praise and pleasure. If you can speak in a way your dog can understand, you will not only get him to behave better but also form a deeper bond with him.

You may want to think of your pup as a child who needs consistency and practice at the rules of life.

WHEN, WHERE AND HOW OFTEN

It's never too early to start training. Keep sessions short, but don't confine training to specific times. Incorporate exercises into your daily routine so that your dog can practice what she's learned. For example, make her sit before you feed her. By reinforcing her training in this way, her new behavior will become habit.

This pup is learning good manners while she's young—the best time for learning.

When to start Begin training your puppy the moment she comes home. An older dog may already know the basic commands, but you will have to tell her when to do these things. Practice and encouragement may be all

she needs, but if she has developed bad habits, it will take time to change her. Obedience classes that encourage positive handling and reinforcement may help her to obey your commands.

It's a good idea to train before meals or when your dog is relaxed, but not sleepy—perhaps after a good walk.

How often? Some dogs learn commands in hours, while others may take weeks. But all dogs learn best with repetition. A daily routine builds good learning habits. If you practice commands a few times a day, your dog will begin to link the word with the action and the action with the reward.

How long? Keep training sessions short and sweet. Three to five minutes is long enough for a puppy, with at least a half-hour break in between. Judge the length of time by her response. If she initially performs well but

then loses interest, it may be time to stop. Always try to end on a high note, immediately after your dog has successfully performed a task. You want her to enjoy training, not dread it.

Where? A quiet area, with few distractions or interruptions, is a good place to start training. When teaching her to walk on a leash, move outside into a quiet street or park. Once she obeys your commands, gradually add new and more challenging surroundings with plenty of diversions, such as a crowded sidewalk or shopping center.

Who? The person who will be spending the most time with your dog, and therefore needs to be in control of her the most, should be given primary responsibility for training her. That person can then show other family members what your dog is learning and how they can get her to respond to their commands. If your dog is spending equal time with everyone, the whole family can participate. However, only one person at a time will be able to train her, and children should always be supervised by an adult. A well-trained dog will know that the family member who is handling her at that time is the leader.

PAY ATTENTION
Your dog should be taught a "watch me" command. This gets her attention so that you can then give further commands.

1 With your dog facing you, point to your eyes and say "watch me." Maintain eye contact for about 10 seconds.

2 Release your pet and say "good dog!" Repeat frequently at various locations.

TRAINING TIPS

Your dog wants to please you and be rewarded. When she understands that behaving well makes you happy, she'll keep doing it. To encourage her, always use positive reinforcement. Never let good behavior go unnoticed, and be consistent in your commands. If she doesn't know the rules, how can she play the game?

Reward your dog with snacks, pats and plenty of verbal praise.

Consistency counts As leader, you need to set firm rules from day one about what it is that you want from your dog. Make sure everyone else in your household follows your example. When your dog knows what to expect, she will feel safe and secure.

Give consistent commands, in the same tone of voice, and in the same order. Make sure she does exactly what you want and always let her know when she's done well. Inconsistent messages from you will confuse her. Weak leadership may even encourage dominant behavior, as she steps, however reluctantly, into the role of leader.

Positive reinforcement The lessons dogs remember best are those that they associate with pleasurable things. Therefore, good behavior will increase if immediately followed by a reward. This may be food, a toy or simply praise—anything that sends her a clear message of approval.

Tasty rewards Food, coupled with praise, is not only an excellent way to reward good behavior—it gets your dog to focus on the task and gives her the motivation to perform it. However, once she obeys your commands it's important to use food rewards only intermittently. By making them unpredictable, you will maintain her interest—and improve her behavior—since she'll never know when she'll be rewarded.

Punishment Never hit your dog, shout at her or blame her for not obeying a command. Harsh correction can result in fear and aggression, both of which are counterproductive to learning. Instead, correct her with a quick check of her leash, or use a low, growl-like tone to startle her just as she's about to do something wrong. Then give her another chance to do the task. When she gets it right, reward her.

Timing If your dog misbehaves, she should be reprimanded consistently and immediately. A firm, verbal rebuke is enough! If you hesitate for even a few seconds, she'll be interested in other things and your correction opportunity will have gone. Don't rebuke her for doing something you didn't see her do at that moment.

ANOTHER WAY: REWARD THE POSITIVE, IGNORE THE NEGATIVE
Like reward, punishment involves a relationship between behavior and consequence. Dogs perform for attention and praise, so if their bad behavior is ignored they are deprived of what they crave. They'll come to realize that only by behaving well will they receive rewards. In short, if it feels good, they'll do it—but if there's no payoff, they'll do something else.

65

COLLARS AND LEASHES

Before leash training your new dog you should make sure she has a comfortable collar. When you put a collar on your puppy for the first time, she'll scratch, yelp and roll on the ground to try and take it off. But it's not hurting her—it's just a new, strange sensation. She'll soon be used to it and ready to begin her lessons.

Take care with choke chains. Improper use can cause injury.

Nylon leashes are available in single ply, double ply, or braided, for added strength. Don't weigh a small dog down with a heavy leash.

First collar A good first collar for your pup is a nylon or leather buckle collar, or a snap-on type collar. She should start wearing her collar right away. The first time you put it on, give her a favorite treat. She will take a little time to adjust to her collar, so start with short periods and gradually increase the time that your puppy wears her new garb. After a few days, she won't even pay attention to it, and after a few weeks she will miss it if you take it off! However, you may want to remove it when your pup is in her crate. Sometimes, a collar can get caught on the crate wires.

Right size The collar should fit snugly around her neck. Don't buy a collar a few sizes too big, thinking that she will grow into it—a collar that is too loose will slip off easily and be useless. An oversize collar can also catch on things. You should be able to fit two fingers between your dog's neck and the collar. A puppy of a large breed, such as a Labrador retriever, will outgrow several collars before she reaches adulthood.

INCORRECT
When put on backward, a choke chain will not loosen when you stop pulling. It could suffocate your dog.

CORRECT
Check the ring end attached to the leash comes over her neck. The chain will loosen when you stop pulling.

Choke chains When you start training your puppy you can use her regular collar, but when she is six to eight months old your trainer may advise the use of a special training collar called a choke chain. Don't leave the choke chain on your dog when you're not watching her, as the rings can get caught on all kinds of objects.

Pros and cons Your dog's neck is sensitive and she can be controlled by the pressure she feels there. Since a choke chain allows you to vary the pressure exerted on her neck, you can get her attention the first time, instead of having to yank several times if you were using her regular collar. However, improper use of a choke chain can cause serious injury to your dog. If you are inexperienced at training, a safer—and perhaps more humane—alternative is a headcollar, which encircles her muzzle and neck and controls the movement of her head. Where her head goes, her body will follow.

Getting ready Your dog will need a 6- to 8-foot (1.8–2.4 m) leash that fits comfortably in your hand. For a small dog a quarter inch (6 mm) may be wide enough; for a larger dog, choose one that is one-half to threequarter inch (1.3–1.9 cm) wide.

It's standard practice to stand to your dog's right while she is on a leash. Hold the leash in your right hand and use the left as a second grab, or to reach down to her. It's vital to remember that a choke chain will only work if you stay on her right at all times.

From top: rolled collar; leather collars; nylon collar with plastic clasps.

GETTING USED TO A LEASH

Every dog reacts differently when he hears the click of the leash and feels the tug on his collar. Some dogs are willing to go with you, while others can't understand why they want to go one way but their neck is going another. No one likes to be dragged somewhere, including your dog. If you train him correctly, you will soon have him walking politely on a leash.

If your dog associates his leash with fun, he will soon learn to love it.

Familiarization Just like he did when he wore his first collar, your dog may need a bit of time to get used to the sound and feel of being on a leash. Start by putting on his training collar, then attaching the leash to this. Always take off his regular buckle or snap-on collar when you are using a training collar.

Have your puppy drag the leash around the house for short periods so he won't be afraid of it. Keep an eye on him at all times so that he doesn't get it caught up in anything. Every few moments, pick up the end of the leash and gently call your dog

to come to you. When he does, praise him. Once he comes to your side while he's on the leash, you're ready to start taking steps with him.

First steps Holding the leash, walk away from your dog for a bit, then stop and call him to come. When he obliges, reward him with a food treat, or some praise.

Your dog might resist this exercise by trying to bite the leash or by refusing to budge. These are normal reactions. To discourage him from chewing the leash, you can spray it with a pet repellant such as bitter apple. If he digs in his heels, don't scold him or pick him up—this will just reinforce his reluctance. Be gentle and persistent, and try to entice him, with a toy or food, to move with you.

Follow the leader After performing this exercise successfully a few times, move outdoors. When you take him out for his first walks, don't tug him. Get him to chase you while on leash and play "follow the leader" games. Gradually coax him into moving in the same direction and at a regular speed with you. As he begins to accept this, stop and praise him. Keep repeating the exercise, making sure you have his full attention. If his concentration wanders, give a quick jerk on the leash. Your

dog will soon understand that whenever you put his leash on him, you want him to pay attention to you and to walk at your pace beside you.

Who's walking whom? A dog that pulls constantly on the leash can turn an enjoyable stroll into a shoulder-wrenching marathon. Perhaps he's excited, or maybe he has gotten the idea that he's in control, not you. To change this habit, surprise him. If he lunges ahead, immediately turn and walk in the opposite direction. This will teach him to focus on you so that he won't be surprised in future. If he's distracted, you can either give him a verbal warning, or give the leash a quick, gentle jerk across and down without saying anything. Soon he'll be paying attention to you constantly, learning that you are the leader and he has to follow.

A dog who knows how to walk nicely by his owner's side, like this shiba inu, won't pull her down the street.

69

TEACHING "SIT"

There are two ways to teach your dog to sit. One involves placing him in that position using your hands, and the other uses food. Both will train your dog, but the food incentive is probably better to use for shy or very active puppies. Be sure to give your dog plenty of verbal praise. Most dogs learn to sit very easily, but you have to keep them practicing until they can associate the command with the action.

The fact that a dog has an inflexible spine means that if they tip their heads up far enough, they will sit. You can use this to your advantage. Remember, your pet already knows how to sit; what you want to do is to produce the response on command.

METHOD 1

1 Begin by sitting or kneeling next to your puppy. Place one hand on the back of his rear legs and your other hand on his chest.

2 As you command him to "sit," gently push back on his chest with one hand and press on his back legs so that his knees bend inward. When he slips into position, praise him.

METHOD 2

1 Stand in front of your puppy and hold a small piece of food between your fingers and thumb with your palm facing up. Hold your hand in front of his nose. Then raise your hand up and slightly back over his head. Say his name, followed by the command "sit."

2 As your puppy follows the treat with his eyes, he will lift up his head and drift into the sit position. Once he does this, praise your puppy and give him the treat. Repeat this six to eight times, praising him every time he performs the task. Reduce the frequency of the reward once he gets used to the command.

TEACHING "DOWN"

Learning to rest comfortably is one of the most useful things you can teach your dog. If you want to stop and have a chat with a friend, commanding your dog to lie down so she can rest is much better than having her pull on the leash because she wants to get going. A dog must be able to sit before she can lie down, so teach the command "down" after your dog has learned how to sit.

I Command your dog to "sit," then sit down in front of her. Hold a small piece of food in front of her nose. As you command "down," move the food down to the ground so her nose follows it.

2 If she needs help, put your hand on her shoulders and guide them down. When she is lying down, praise her and give her the treat. You can also push the treat between your puppy's front legs. As she tries to follow it, her back end will slide into a down position. Praise her and give her the reward.

If you find that she will not go into the position when you use this method, it may be necessary to take the food and slowly pull it outward. Your pup should follow it down. Once she associates the word with the action you can be less reliable with the food—but keep praising.

TEACHING "COME"

A dog that will reliably respond to a call to "come" will always be safe. This task is often difficult to teach, but a couple of tips will make the command easier to instill. First, never call your dog and then punish him. If you do, why would he ever want to come in future? Also, take care not to call him away from something fun, like chewing a toy. Instead, practice calling him under other circumstances. When he comes, praise him and send him back to play. This way he'll learn that when he comes to you, it does not always mean the end of something good.

It could take months until your dog is trained to come. Until this time, he should not go outside without his leash.

I Teach your dog to come to you indoors first. He will need to wear his training collar and be on a 6- to 8-foot (1.8–2.4 m) leash. With his leash in your right hand, face your dog and slowly walk backward, telling him to "come" in a happy, upbeat voice. When he follows you, continue to walk backward, praising him all the time. You might like to wiggle a small reward in your left hand.

2 After a few feet, stop walking. Tell him to "come." Lean over with your arms outstretched and give him a warm welcome.

When he is right in front of you, praise him lavishly and give him the treat. Then repeat the process.

3 Keep the distances short at first, but gradually make him come further to reach you. Phase out the food reward and try practicing inside without a leash. You can also practice by calling him to you from across the room. Keep your voice inviting—you have to give him a good reason to come to you.

If you want to correct bad behavior, don't call him—go to him instead. This way he will always associate "come" with positive behavior. Once your dog begins to come reliably, add a "sit" to the end of the "come" command. This will get him used to being called and then taken to a new location.

TEACHING "STAY"

Teaching your dog to stay on command may avoid a disaster, especially if you live in a busy urban area. However, getting your dog to stay can be a difficult task, so it will be a lot easier if you aim for small successes, rather than long stays. Initially, reward your puppy with food and praise if she does not move for five seconds. Then gradually increase the duration of the stay. The same applies to the distance between you and your puppy. Do not go too far at first. This will only result in her breaking the stay and failing the task. Instead, you should always plan for success.

I Stand in front of your dog, hold her leash in your right hand and rest it level with your stomach. Raise your left hand so your palm faces your dog. Look at her and in a firm voice, command her to "stay."

2 Slowly walk backward from your dog, all the while making eye contact. Tell her to "stay."

3 Once you get to the end of the leash, drop it on the ground and put your foot on it. If she tries to move before you have given her permission she'll soon realize she can't go anywhere. Quietly praise her while she is keeping the stay. After five seconds, go back to her and reward her with a treat. Gradually build up the stay to a minute, eventually taking your foot off the leash.

If your puppy breaks the stay or if she seems apprehensive, the chances are you have gone too far or have kept her waiting for too long. When this happens, promptly place her back in position and try again—this time for a shorter distance and for a time limit she is comfortable with. Gradually increase the length of the stay again. When she holds the stay, praise her profusely.

TEACHING "HEEL"

There are two ways to teach your dog to heel. The first method is an extension of the "watch me" command (see p. 63). Repeat this command several times and add the command "heel." At first move only short distances, but gradually move farther and for longer periods as your dog learns to stay with you.

The second method also requires you to get your dog's attention.

METHOD 2

1 Have your dog on a loose 6- or 8-foot (1.8–2.4 m) leash on your left side. You should be holding the leash with your right hand so that it crosses your body. Hook your right thumb into the loop of the leash. Keep your right hand at your waist.

2 As you start walking with your dog, say his name and the command "heel." If he doesn't pay attention and follow you right away, use your left hand to grab the leash and give it a quick jerk. Release your left hand immediately.

3 If he starts to pull or lag, turn in the opposite direction. Don't worry if you bump into him; it's his responsibility to stay out of your way. He'll soon realize that it's more comfortable if he keeps a watchful eye on you.

4 When your dog is walking nicely by your side, praise him verbally. You can also reach down and pet him.

Remember, this exercise cannot be practiced inside. Be prepared to spend a lot of time outdoors, away from the distraction of other dogs.

HOUSE-TRAINING PUPPIES

When a puppy enters your life certain training tasks, such as house-training, become a priority. Following in the tradition of their ancestor, the wolf, dogs will not dirty their eating and sleeping areas. If you follow this instinct for cleanliness, and establish a set feeding routine from the outset, your pup can be house-trained with a minimum of mopping up.

Choose a place Assign your pup an area for her toilet spot. In most cases, this will be a place in your yard.

When dogs relieve themselves they release scent chemicals called pheromones which, when smelled later on, will trigger a reflex that makes them want to eliminate again. This is why it's best to take your pup to the same place every time.

Set a routine House-training begins with a good feeding and watering routine. A pup needs to eat several times a day, so this means she will also have to eliminate several times daily. Your pup is most likely to want to go within 10 to 20 minutes after eating. She'll also need to go straight after waking, drinking, leaving her crate or playing. Your training will be most successful if you can take her to her spot at these times.

Encourage her Once she's at her spot, allow her some time to explore. Then use a key phrase to encourage her. When she is successful, praise her verbally, again using your key phrase so that she will begin to associate it with elimination. If, after an hour, your pup still hasn't gone, take her inside and put her in her crate. Since she won't mess where she sleeps, confining her will teach her to wait until you let her out to eliminate. Never use the crate as punishment, and avoid confining her so frequently that she feels isolated. The minute you let her out of her crate, take her to her spot.

Your puppy is an intelligent animal who will soon learn where—and where not—to go.

Paper training This method may be a necessity if you don't have quick access to the outdoors, but use it only as an interim measure. Whatever the difficulties—bad weather, living in a high-rise apartment—your pup should be introduced to the toilet outdoors a few times in her first couple of weeks at home. To teach her where to go inside, spread several layers of newspaper over a large plastic sheet on the floor (not carpet). Leave a soiled paper under the fresh paper so she recognizes it as her spot. As the days progress, make the paper area smaller.

When you take her house-training outdoors, take along one of her soiled papers for the first day or two. The familiar scent will ease her transition.

A watchful eye House-training won't take place overnight and a few mishaps are to be expected at first. When you are home with your puppy, watch her at all times. If you can't supervise her, put her in her crate. If your pup has an accident inside

and you didn't see it happen, don't punish her. Just clean the area and vow to supervise her more carefully in the future. If you do catch her in the act, distract her by making a noise, such as clapping your hands and telling her, "Outside!" Then swiftly take her to the correct location. When she performs, praise her profusely.

You should never yell at your puppy, hit her, or rub her nose in her mess. This is cruel and unnecessary, and it will only teach her to go behind your back.

Training troubles Despite her best intentions, your pup might have a relapse even up to 12 months of age. Just patiently repeat the training process and she should remember. When she's at her toilet spot, don't let her wander around and play. You need to give her the message: go now, play later. It may be necessary to take her to her spot, wait for her to perform and then bring her back in

for a few moments before letting her out to play. If she consistently uses the wrong spots, such as the stairs, ensure they are thoroughly cleaned. Then try feeding her in those locations. She will not soil where she eats.

BETTER SAFE THAN SORRY
A crate can be your pup's own cozy place. Since she won't soil where she sleeps, it's also indispensable for house-training. Get her used to it gradually, and don't confine her for more than three hours straight.

GETTING USED TO TRAVEL

When you're traveling by car with your dog, half the fun is getting to your destination. To ensure your dog—and the rest of the family—have a comfortable trip, get him ready well in advance for his time in the car and for the sights and sounds he will encounter.

Preparation Your dog should be acquainted with the things he'll come across outside your home from puppyhood. Having him meet a variety of people—young and old, thin and heavy, mustached and bespectacled, with canes or in wheelchairs—will help him feel less stressed when he meets them in new surroundings. Also get your dog used to other animals, such as horses and cats. Be sure that he is comfortable stepping on all types of surfaces. Train him to be tolerant of traffic noise. You can desensitize him by taking him on a series of short car rides through heavy traffic or walking with him along a busy street.

Feeling queasy? Dogs can suffer from travel sickness, with disastrous consequences. If you know your dog is likely to succumb, or if it is his first long-distance trip and you are unsure of how he'll react, put a plastic tablecloth on the backseat to protect the interior.

Overcoming anxiety Many dogs get carsick because they are anxious. Get your dog used to riding in the car by first letting him explore the vehicle while it is motionless. Give your dog a treat and praise him. Later, take him on a quick drive around the block, building up to rides of longer duration.

HOME AWAY FROM HOME
A traveling crate is a good investment, especially if you have a puppy. If you buy one large enough for your puppy when fully grown, you can continue to use it for trips throughout his life. Get him used to it well before your planned trip, by feeding him in it and encouraging him to rest in it. Increase the amount of time he spends in it until it causes him no distress to be confined.

On the road Ease his queasies by feeding him a light meal no later than eight hours before the trip. Don't give him anything to drink two hours prior to departure. Once you're under way, small, frequent sips of water can be given. If this doesn't help, increase the airflow in the car, distract him with toys, or pull over and take him for a walk. Ask your vet about medication for future trips.

Exotic eats Try to follow your dog's normal routine. Feed him his usual food at his regular times, but feed less, since he will be less active while traveling. If he's nauseous, feed him at the end of the day. To prevent diarrhea, avoid sudden changes in diet, except on trips longer than seven days. It will take at least a week to gradually introduce him to the local fare.

Take a break Regardless of how he is taking to life on the road, be sure to stop every few hours to allow your dog to stretch his legs and relieve him-

LET'S GO!
When traveling by car, make sure your dog is restrained. Dog car seat harnesses (right), crates and barriers, available at pet suppy stores, prevent him from disturbing you while you are driving and reduce the risk of injury from sudden stops or accidents.

self. If he is excited or anxious, don't take him out for long periods, since this may only aggravate his problem. Make sure he is wearing his collar and identification tags and keep him on a leash at all times—if he gets separated from you, he may panic and become lost.

Safety first Leaving your dog inside the car while you go off sightseeing is the most dangerous thing you can do

while traveling with him. He may get territorial and bite a passerby, or he could be stolen. Worse still, temperatures inside the car can rise within minutes. He could die of heatstroke, even if the windows are open and he has water to drink. Take him with you.

COMMON BEHAVIOR PROBLEMS

No one has perfect manners, and our dogs are no exception. They bark at midnight, chew on furniture, or make messes where they shouldn't. Dogs don't mean any harm when they misbehave. Usually there's something wrong, and their bad behavior is a valuable way of letting you know that they're not happy. The best way to stop bad behavior is to prevent it from getting started in the first place. The key to changing unwanted behavior is to recognize what is motivating and maintaining it. Once you know what is causing your dog to act up, finding a solution won't be difficult—and you'll soon be enjoying a more confident and contented companion.

AGGRESSION

For dogs, aggression is just another form of communication, like wagging their tails. The message it sends, of course, is much more serious. Similar to human insecurity and anger, aggression is a dog's way of setting boundaries. In the wild, dogs depended on aggression to protect their resources—such as food—from other dogs, and also to protect the pack from intruders and themselves from bodily harm. What's acceptable in the wild, however, is not acceptable in your home.

Warning signs Aggression is a potentially dangerous problem and it needs to be stopped quickly before it escalates. It will never go away on its own. Aggression includes many behaviors, including growling, barking, snarling, lunging, snapping and biting. Sometimes a dog will indicate its aggressive intentions by staring and standing tall with its ears and head erect. Unneutered male dogs often behave aggressively toward other males, and fights can break out.

How you approach your dog's problem will depend on which type of aggression he shows.

How to help If your dog is threatening people or other animals, the intervention of a trained behaviorist is advised. But the best way to deal with aggressive behavior is to prevent it in the first place. Establish yourself as leader from the outset. You can do this by setting rules that are humanely but consistently enforced. If you must reprimand your dog, a firm, verbal rebuke is enough. Harsh punishment can cause aggression based on either fear or pain.

AGGRESSIVE INSTINCTS
Territorial dogs, like this German shepherd, must be handled carefully and given firm, but never harsh, training.

Fear of the unknown Early socialization of your pup will prevent him from feeling insecure and becoming aggressive. Obedience classes can also help build the confidence of an older dog and get him used to strangers and other dogs. Since your dog gets many of his cues from you, stay relaxed.

Who's the boss? It's common for a dog to nudge his owner because he wants some attention. But when he starts pushing you around, playing roughly or even threatening you, he is showing dominance aggression. You need to demote your dog. If you cater to his every desire, he may get the idea that he's the leader, not you. Don't give him anything—food, toys, play-time—unless he does something for you first. For example, make him sit before letting him go outside.

Aggressive play In the wild, dogs compete with each other to see who's dominant. Therefore games such as tug-of-war, which spark your dog's competitive instinct, should be discouraged. You are better off playing cooperative games such as fetch, in which your dog is obliged to obey you, but has fun at the same time.

Feeling threatened Dogs are very territorial creatures, particularly if they are confined to the yard a lot. They become so attached to their space that they'll threaten anyone they think is invading their territory. Also, since they have no means of escaping any teasing or other annoyances that may come along, they may resort to aggressive behavior to stop the intrusion.

To curb this aggression, avoid confining your dog for long periods. You can also help him form a positive association with the target of his anger. If your dog goes ballistic when a visitor comes, train him to associate visitors with good things by having the visitor give him a treat on arrival.

Get your dog used to being handled by all members of the family from an early age.

Stop coddling If your dog is frightened and aggressive, don't make a fuss over him. By rewarding bad behavior you will aggravate the problem. Instead, remain relaxed and give him a firm, verbal correction.

Tire him out Exercise and obedience work can help, but keep your dog leashed in public places. These activities will both reinforce your role as leader and tire your dog. A tired dog is less likely to be aggressive.

BARKING

If it's a dog, it barks—to communicate, to indicate excitement or fear, or to warn of intruders. But barking can be annoying for owners and neighbors alike. While you will never stop your dog from barking altogether, you can at least get the behavior under control by using methods such as the "quiet" command. But first you must determine why your dog is barking so much.

A bark-activated citronella collar is an effective way to distract persistent barkers.

Loneliness As pack animals, dogs find being alone stressful—a feeling they combat by barking. You should look at why your dog needs to be left outside. Is it because you can't trust him in the house? If so, then there are other problems that need to be treated first. But if you must occasionally leave him for long periods, try turning on the radio or television when you leave. He may associate this sound with your presence and be comforted and quiet. Also get a friend to drop by your house that day to play with him.

Boredom Like people, dogs need stimulation. If they have a lot of energy and not enough outlets for it, they will often bark out of boredom and frustration. Exercise and obedience training will give your dog a sense of purpose, as well as tire him out. Toys such as Buster Cubes (see p. 93) can also provide enough mental stimulation to send him snoozing.

A NOISY DISTRACTION

Dogs crave approval, so telling him that you don't like his barking is a powerful incentive to get him to stop. But yelling at him won't help—he'll just think you're joining in the fun. Instead, toss a length of chain or a tin half-filled with nails, coins or pebbles in his general direction. The noise will startle him into silence. Once he stops barking, praise him. He'll soon learn that silence brings rewards.

Facing his fears If your dog barks because he's afraid of something, such as the vacuum cleaner or the lawn mower, try counter-conditioning him to those objects. If you feed him next to them, or while the motor is running, he'll start to associate these scary things with the positive act of being fed and won't bark as often.

"QUIET!"

1 To train your dog to stop barking, you must first get him to start. Speak in an excited tone, or ring the doorbell. When he barks, tell him "good bark" and give him a treat. Keep doing this until the command alone sets him off. It's now time to teach him to stop barking on command.

2 Give the command to get him barking. As he pauses between barks, hold a treat over his nose and say, "quiet."

3 He can't bark and chew at the same time, so he'll swap one activity for the other. Keep practicing until he stops barking when you tell him "quiet."

BEGGING

There isn't a dog on the planet who doesn't lobby for extra goodies every now and then, and few owners can resist their dog's pleading eyes gazing up at them at dinnertime. Dogs lust after what we're eating because they see us enjoying it so much; they want to join in the fun. And your dog may beg because you have inadvertently trained her to do so—by giving in and slipping her a morsel.

Table manners Like people, dogs often develop a strange relationship with food. In the world of dogs, food is associated with care-giving and other maternal traits, so they beg because it brings positive attention.

Never give your dog food from the table. You don't want her to learn that pestering you will result in her getting food. If you reward her begging, it will progress to drooling, whining and jumping up on your lap every meal.

Hunger Every dog needs different amounts of food, and it's possible that yours is merely hungry. Weigh her and consult your vet. If she does need more nourishment, don't supplement her diet from your plate. A dog's digestive system is not the same as a human's, so she can get sick from eating too much human food.

If your dog is the right weight, she may feel more satisfied if you move her usual mealtime forward an hour. You could also consider dividing her regular amount of food into small servings and dishing it out more often.

NO MORE MOOCHING
You can train your dog to stop begging by ignoring the behavior. When she doesn't beg, praise her and offer her a dog treat after you have finished eating. If she's merely hungry, feed her before you eat—when she's full, she's more likely to leave you alone. You could also give her a bone or a food-filled toy to play with while you eat.

Stopping the stake-out To discourage your dog, choose a spot where you want her to stay when you're eating. It could be anywhere; just be sure that you can see her while you dine. Put her on a long leash, lead her to the place and give her a treat. Do this daily so that she'll learn that the easiest way to get food is to go to this spot. Once your dog consistently goes to the place on command, tell her to stay. At first you'll want to get up a few times to reward her for staying put. When she understands that food comes to her, she'll be content to stay and less likely to demand food while you are eating.

CHEWING

Dogs get a lot of fun and satisfaction from chewing. It is a natural activity and helps exercise their jaws and clean their teeth. However, dogs who spend a lot of time alone will sometimes chew as a way of dispelling loneliness, anxiety, frustration or boredom. Don't try to stop the activity—just direct the behavior to more appropriate objects, and find ways to relieve your dog's tension.

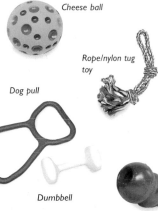

Plush toy (right) and hedgehog squeeze toy (below)

Cheese ball

Rope/nylon tug toy

Dog pull

Dumbbell

Kong toy

What's normal It's normal for puppies to chew—a pup explores the textures and tastes of his world through his mouth. Chewing also eases the pain of teething. However, destructive behavior has no age limits.

Keep him busy Dogs are usually at their most destructive when they're left alone, and they'll chew as a way of relieving tension. To divert your dog from your possessions, give him acceptable alternatives, like chew toys. Avoid giving him discarded shoes—he won't understand the difference between old and new and he'll think that all shoes are okay to chew.

Simple fixes Since chewing is often an outlet for your dog's excess energy, exercise him more often. You can also save your possessions by placing them out of harm's reach. Supervise your puppy while he is indoors, or put him in his crate with something acceptable to chew in your absence.

Deterrents Spraying your dog's targets with bitter apple or citronella will deter him from chewing them again. Or try booby-trapping these targets by putting coins or rocks in a can and tying it to the object. When he starts gnawing, the can's rattle will scare him.

CLIMBING ON FURNITURE

At some point, every dog will attempt to stake a claim on the furniture. A couch is not only comfortable, it's warm and gives your dog a view that she can't get down on the floor. Sitting in your favorite chair might also make her feel close to you when you're not around and she's feeling lonely. But climbing on the furniture is also a mild sign of dominance, and unless you correct your dog firmly and consistently you'll start feeling like a guest in your own home.

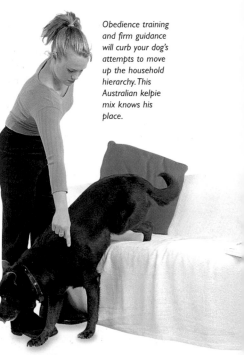

Obedience training and firm guidance will curb your dog's attempts to move up the household hierarchy. This Australian kelpie mix knows his place.

Power play Human comfort zones are positions of power, so keeping your dog off the furniture will reinforce her subordinate position in the family pack. To discourage her from sitting on the furniture, lay plastic bubble wrap on top of it. The next time she jumps up she will be startled by the new sound and feel. For some dogs, that's enough to deter them, but others will learn to detect the bubble wrap and just jump on the couch when it's not there. If this is the case, tuck a bed sheet on top of the wrap and leave it on all the time—or at least until she decides to stay off for good.

Prime location You can also place balloons or lightweight plastic mouse traps under the sheet. These will make a loud snap the moment your dog jumps up and will also scare her into jumping back down. At the same time, provide a comfortable dog bed in the prime real estate—right next to the couch, for example, or near the center of the room, where she can see what is going on.

DIGGING

Dogs love to dig and they do it for many reasons. Some breeds, such as terriers, are genetically programmed to dig. If there are moles or similar animals living underground, they will burrow to get to them. In hot weather, huskies and other Arctic breeds often dig to create a cool spot to lie in. Or your dog may have seen you gardening and just wants to copy your behavior. But many dogs dig to defuse stress and burn off energy.

Know his motivations If your dog is digging to make a cool spot to lie in, then creating a shaded area in the yard might help. A wading pool may also provide him with relief, but if the climate is very hot, it may be better to keep him inside on certain days.

Earth also provides warmth, so let your dog inside in cold weather, or provide a warm shelter in the yard.

Buried treasure If your dog is digging because of his predatory instincts, you will need to get rid of the stimulus. If this isn't possible, consider setting aside an acceptable digging spot in the yard. This spot can be made of different material, such as sand, or can be surrounded with wood. Start burying things there that your dog will enjoy excavating. Put them close to the surface at first so that he can easily smell them. Do this every day until he will reliably go to that spot to dig. Then bury things intermittently.

Make it harder You can sabotage his digging by burying lava rock in areas where you don't want him to dig. The rock will feel strange to him when he hits it. Or try cutting his nails so that digging is uncomfortable— but don't cut them so short that you damage the sensitive quick.

Other options If you catch him digging where he shouldn't, tell him "no!" and distract him with a toy. You can also deter him by placing heavy bricks over that area. Wrap wire mesh around plants you want to protect.

Give him a job Your dog may be digging to expend energy, so take him out for daily walks or runs and give him plenty of attention. A puzzled, preoccupied dog is also less likely to dig, so get him a Buster Cube—a hollow toy with hidden compartments you can fill with dry kibble. The promise of food can keep him happily engaged for hours.

As a dog mouths the Buster Cube, bits of food occasionally fall out.

FEAR

A well-adjusted dog who has been handled by different people and constantly exposed to new things will take unusual situations in her stride. But a dog who was left alone too much or was sheltered from stimuli when young may have a hard time making sense of the world. She may cower, growl, shake or try to run away and hide. Timidity isn't always the result of bad treatment—she may be naturally nervous. But if you don't curb her fearfulness, it can turn into fear biting and aggression.

Socialization Get your dog used to people, sounds and situations between 7–14 weeks of age. Obedience training will also build her confidence.

Act naturally Your dog takes her cues from your body language, so act calm. Rather than comforting her when she's nervous—which may lead her to associate fear with praise—distract her from the source of her fear and praise her when she copes well.

Loud noises Teach her not to over-react to noises such as thunder by rattling pots and pans while she's eating.

Play with her with the radio turned up—if she thinks about play when she hears a noise, she won't be so terrified.

Weird objects Your dog may consider many unfamiliar objects as "monsters." Seeing you touching or using the object will reassure her that it won't attack. Also feed her next to it.

People Get your dog used to the people she'll meet often by taking her to visit a friend. Ask the friend to offer her a treat. If she doesn't want to take it, the friend can toss it to her. Over a period of time these friendly gestures will help to build her confidence.

When the vacuum is used, this collie-cattle dog mix is put in another area of the house where he can only hear it from a distance.

HATES BEING HELD

Your dog likes to be petted, but he may be fussy about having his toenails clipped or his teeth inspected. Or perhaps he is strong-willed and wants to control his own body. It will be difficult to keep a dog who hates being handled well-groomed or have him examined by a vet. Teaching him to be cooperative is a matter of basic obedience training and socialization. The goal is to make him secure enough to accept your authority.

This miniature schnauzer has learned to cooperate through regular handling and training.

Puppies When puppies are not handled much from birth, tactile sensations are new and strange to them. Accustom your pup to your touch by giving him gentle massages from the moment he comes home. Apply very little pressure at first. The more you touch him, the more he'll trust you.

Loving touch Teach your dog that your hands always have a positive intent—such as petting, feeding, grooming and comforting. This way he will be more accepting of hands that have other, less pleasant, duties to perform, such as clipping or bandaging. Never hit your dog to discipline him

or use your hands—or let him mouth them—roughly, even during play.

Don't fight it If your dog struggles and bites your hands to free himself of your grip, tell him sternly, "No bite!" Verbally rebuke him if he continues and praise him when he stops. Resist the urge to hold your dog down or force him to comply. Force will only make him distrustful.

Older dogs Put on your dog's leash and talk softly as you pet him where it feels comfortable. Confidently move your hand to other parts of his body. If

he doesn't like his paws being handled, offer him a treat while gently touching one of them. When he allows you to do this, praise him. If he resists, growl at him to "quit it" and give a quick jerk on the leash. Touch the remaining paws one at a time until you can lift each slightly and are able to gently rub his toes without him protesting. Practice this several times a day.

JUMPING UP

Many dogs jump up when they're excited and pleased to see you, but others may do it to express dominance. You might complain about this behavior, but you might also be inadvertently reinforcing it. A common error is to let your dog jump up in some situations, such as when you're playing ball, and not in others. It's difficult for her to understand when jumping up is acceptable and when it is not when the rules are not enforced consistently.

Ignore her Furthermore, jumping up usually gets attention—even if it's just pushing her away—and this can be enough to reinforce her behavior. For example, your puppy may interpret pushing as a signal for play. Instead, ignore her by turning your back until she obeys the command to sit. Do not give her any attention until she is sitting calmly.

Greeting guests Keep her on a leash when greeting people. When she goes to leap, step on the leash close to where she's standing and say "sit!" When she obeys, praise her. This will remind her of her status within the family pack: She'll only get attention when all four paws are on the ground.

Other tactics Crouching down to greet your dog may stop her jumping. Another technique is to startle her by tossing a soda can full of pennies near her. When she backs away, you can command her to sit before giving her attention. It may be even more effective to rush at her as she comes to you. When she backs off to avoid being stepped on, tell her to sit.

More control Headcollars are helpful for persistent jumpers. If you control where her head goes, you can control her to sit, stay and not jump up on your guests.

When a large dog, like this Newfoundland, jumps up, the effect can be overwhelming.

POSSESSIVENESS

Dogs tend to be possessive of things they see as valuable resources, such as food or toys. This behavior makes sense in the wild, where dogs roam in packs and possession is 100 percent of the law. But even in the wild there's one simple rule: No dog will take something from another dog that's higher in the pecking order. If your dog is possessive he is forgetting that in your family, you are the leader, with all the rights that position confers. Possessiveness is a challenge to your authority, and it can lead to aggression.

This Irish terrier has learned that giving up objects can have its rewards.

Teach him to share Put a collar and leash on your dog and give him a new toy. Immediately ask him to give it back to you by saying "drop it." (See p. 99.) The moment he releases it, even slightly, praise him. If he refuses, ignore the toy and give him a few "sit" and "down" commands. These obedience drills will remind him that you are the leader, and your authority must be respected. Repeat the drills several times, then end the session by taking away the toy. If he still fusses about giving it to you, you may have to resort to curing his obsession by throwing the toy away.

Overwhelm him Devalue the objects your dog considers valuable by providing more of them. Instead of giving him one ball, give him five. He'll be so overwhelmed by his riches that he probably won't object when you take a couple away, even if they are the ones he's playing with.

Win-win You can also give him a toy in exchange for the item he is playing with. As soon as he releases the item, give him the new toy. A few minutes later, return the original toy. By making a game of handing toys back and forth, you'll encourage him to trust you.

Overprotectiveness Toys aren't the only things your dog can be possessive of. A dog who thinks of you as his property can soon turn aggressive. Don't tell him "It's okay" when he growls at someone else—you are just reinforcing his behavior. Instead, start obedience training straight away. This will reinforce your role as leader. Telling your dog to sit, for example, will also give him something to focus on when someone approaches.

STEALING

If your dog doesn't have enough things to keep her busy, then she'll find her own entertainment, however unappealing an activity it may seem to you. If you catch your dog stealing, be careful not to overreact. If you shriek and start chasing her, you might frighten her or unwittingly buy into a game she plays to get your attention. Many dogs love a chase and will flaunt their prize to entice you.

The "drop it" command is also useful for when your dog gets hold of dangerous objects or spoiled food.

Caught in the act The best time to correct your dog is at the moment she steals. Try booby-trapping objects so that they make a noise as she tries to steal them—to startle her and to alert you. Tie a soda can rattle to the object of her desire, or leave a noisy bunch of keys on top of it. Sprinkling Tabasco sauce, pepper flakes or bitter apple is another way to deter criminal acts.

Drop it Instead of chasing your dog, crouch down and ask her to come. If this doesn't work, try running away. If she chases you, you can then stop and praise her for coming to you. Then try to take the object while saying "drop it." If she obeys, give her even more praise. You should teach her a "drop it" command from an early age.

Fair trade If she won't drop the object, offer her a bribe while saying "drop it." Once she surrenders the object, reward her. Practice the command throughout the day and phase out the treat almost completely, so that it becomes unpredictable.

Food thieves If there is food within reach, it is a rare dog that will not attempt to eat it—it's in her genes to wolf down whatever's on offer as fast as she can. Therefore, it is really your responsibility to remove the source of temptation. Sometimes the problem is that your dog has too much freedom. Supervision is a vital part of early training.

Last resorts Baby gates may protect certain parts of your house from pilfering paws. You could also consider motion sensors that will be briefly activated when your dog breaks the field of alarm. For some dogs, the sound of the alarm will be enough of a deterrent.

1 Command your dog to sit in front of you. Give her something she can hold in her mouth. It should be large enough for you to be able to grasp part of it while she has it in her mouth.

2 While your dog is holding the object in her mouth, say "hold" and praise her for a few moments.

3 Grasp the object firmly and guide it from her mouth. Don't yank it. At the same time, use your other hand to hold the leash two feet from her collar and jerk it downward, telling her to "drop it" or "release."

4 Praise her when she drops it. Persist with this exercise until your dog drops the object quickly, then test her with other objects.

EXERCISE

As a species, dogs are naturally very active and playful. Their wild relatives spend most of their day hunting food, defending their territory and playing with each other. Pet dogs, on the other hand, are given all the food they need (usually more), and are often confined to a house or a yard for most of the day. As a result, they tend to get overweight, out of shape and lazy. Lack of exercise can also lead to boredom, which makes many dogs unhappy and destructive. The key to a happy, healthy dog—big or small—is regular exercise. No matter how busy you are, always make time to exercise your pet.

EXERCISING YOUR DOG

As a dog owner, providing your pet with a daily workout is a key responsibility. It could be a two-mile jog, a steady walk, or simply playing chase and fetch around the apartment. Not only is the exercise good for her, but she will also have fun.

Physical benefits Regular exercise is absolutely essential for your dog's physical well-being. It will keep her from becoming overweight, which has been linked to health problems such as heart disease, respiratory failure and arthritis. Since it causes the body to secrete lubricating fluid to the joints, exercise will also

TAKING THE LEAD
A daily jog is enough to keep many dogs happy and healthy. When exercising your dog in public areas, keep her on a leash and under control.

prevent arthritis from getting worse. It stimulates the intestines, helping to reduce flatulence and constipation. Regular exercise also improves blood circulation and will expand your dog's heart and lung function, giving her energy and stamina.

If your dog is young or middle-aged, exercise will help her age more gracefully. Consistent exercise also keeps older dogs fit, stimulated and supple.

What she needs Before buying a new dog, get to know the different breeds and the exercise they require. Many breeds, such as the sporting and working dogs, need regular vigorous exercise. If you are a busy professional, it would be irresponsible to take on one of these dogs unless you can arrange for someone to exercise her. You would be better off with a toy breed or one of the less active dogs.

Conditioning programs Burning off excess calories will not only make your dog slimmer—it will make her fit. But taking her for a quick stroll or letting her spend an extra hour out in the yard won't suffice; she needs conditioning.

Your dog needs a muscular and cardiovascular workout to get her legs, heart and lungs working harder than usual. A conditioning program combining cardiovascular work, flexibility, strength work, speed work and weight control will help her to develop strength and endurance. Overall fitness will also improve your dog's timing, balance and coordination. By strengthening her tendons and ligaments and stabilizing her joints, exercise will also help her to avoid injury.

Getting started Before starting your dog on an exercise program, ask your vet to examine her to find out if she has any medical conditions, such as a heart murmur, diabetes or hip dysplasia, which could mean that certain types of exercise are a problem for her. Even if your dog does have a health problem, she still needs to exercise and be fit. You vet can suggest a regimen that will get her in shape without causing her discomfort.

Keeping fit Keeping your dog fit is an ongoing responsibility, and conditioning an out-of-shape dog takes time. You could try giving her a quarter of the recommended amount of exercise for two weeks, increase this to half the amount for a couple of weeks, then increase it to three-quarters for another two weeks. By the end of six weeks, she should be ready to go the distance.

Working together Exercising by herself is no way for your dog to get the workout she needs. Keeping her confined in your yard will also inhibit her from achieving a full range of motion. And it's simply not safe for your dog to wander about on her own. You should always accompany her as she explores, and keep her on a leash whenever she goes out in public. Your dog should only be allowed off the leash if she obeys commands, and even then only in safe areas where regulations permit.

Besides, if you keep your dog company as she exercises, you might start to feel and see some personal benefits, too.

These Border collies must get plenty of exercise; boredom leads to bad habits.

WHY EXERCISE IS IMPORTANT

Exercise is essential for your dog's emotional health. The well-exercised dog is less likely to get bored and develop troublesome traits, such as persistent barking and destructive digging and chewing. Exercise also causes the release of endorphins in the brain. These chemicals give your dog a great feeling of well-being, and what better way to keep him content than with a natural high?

These Australian cattle dogs are raring to go on their walk.

A healthy highlight Exercise means a great deal to your dog. Apart from dinnertime, going for walks or playing games are the highlight of his day. And endorphins are not the only reason why they make him feel great. Exercise represents an outing with his family pack, plus an affirmation of his bond with you, the pack leader. An adventure beyond the house or yard also provides him with a thrilling cascade of new sights and, more importantly, smells. At the same time, it reacquaints him with a comforting catalog of familiar stimuli.

Walks, jogs and romps in the park are the main events on your dog's social calendar. He can catch up with his canine friends—and enemies—and meet new dogs that may become potential play-mates and, if he is unneutered,

TOY BREEDS

Two 15-minute walks a day is enough exercise for most tiny dogs like this Pomeranian, provided they are also encouraged to play games. Many toy dogs have a strong instinct to retrieve, so if you can't manage long walks, a bouncy ball or a small Frisbee will make the ideal basis for a game.

future sexual partners. He can check on others' scent-markings, plus signal his territory by adding some markings of his own. Exercise also provides your clean-living canine with an opportunity to eliminate away from his "den."

How much? Your dog needs at least 30 to 45 minutes of exercise a day. The kind of exercise

depends of his age, breed (or, if he's mixed, his probable genetic makeup) and state of health.

Active breeds If you can match the exercise needs of your dog to those of his breed, he'll get the maximum out of his daily routine. Sporting dogs, working dogs, herding dogs, hounds and the larger terriers thrive on vigorous outdoor activity. If he's medium to large, start with a brisk 20-minute walk or jog followed by 10 minutes of strenuous play, twice a day. You can also substitute the second round of exercise with a long swim.

Special needs Working and herding dogs are noted for their stamina, so you could consider jogging your dog for up to one hour a day. Sighthounds such as greyhounds and borzois need an opportunity to stretch out and run (in a safely fenced area) for five or 10 minutes after a lengthy walk. Repeat this workout in the evening. If there's no place to let your hound run, set aside 30 minutes for a morning jog and chasing games. Dachshunds and the smaller terriers, on the other hand, only need a 15-minute walk twice a day, plus plenty of indoor games.

Non-sporting breeds The smaller members of this group, such as the Boston terrier, bichon frise and schipperke, need the same amount of exercise as the smaller terriers. The keeshond, standard poodle, Finnish spitz and Dalmatian should be exercised in the same way, and for the same amount of time, as one of the working, sporting or herding dog breeds.

SOME FITNESS FUNDAMENTALS

You want to create an exercise program for your dog that is safe. Start off slowly, be consistent and patient, and you can gradually increase the level of activity when he shows that he's ready for more.

Puppies Pups do need some moderate exercise, but take it easy. Puppies' muscles aren't fully developed and their bones are softer. Don't start your pup on serious fitness training until he is 14 months old, when the last of the growth plates on his bones close. (The growth plates of some giant breeds don't close until 22 months of age.) Increase his fitness program over several months, and give him time to develop his coordination.

Preventing bloat Movement of food in the stomach can accelerate fermentative processes and cause bloat, particularly in large dogs. To give your dog's digestive system a chance to

settle, avoid feeding him immediately before or after a strenuous workout. Give him a quick drink of water before and during the activity, and the same amount once he cools down.

Start slow If your dog is old, unfit or unhealthy, start with a daily 15-minute walk and slowly increase the duration. For healthy dogs, walks may not provide enough exercise; vigorous, off-leash activities (in safe areas) should be added. If your dog enjoys playing with other dogs, organize for them to meet.

WALKING WORKOUT
To build cardiovascular fitness, start slowly, gradually increasing speed and distance.

This fox terrier is being given a few gentle limb bends and stretches before beginning exercise.

Warming up Begin your dog's exercise sessions with a five to 10 minute warm-up. This helps prevent injury by stretching the tendons and ligaments, and getting the blood to the muscles and nerves.

Cardiovascular training When both of you are walking faster and further without panting, try jogging. Break into a short sprint every now and then. The change of pace will get your dog to use his muscles differently, and it will also keep him interested.

Strength training To build his strength, try walking a steep hill when you're out together. Dash up the stairs at home or throw a ball up a slope for him to fetch. Playing games not only stimulates his mind and provides vigorous exercise—it lets you establish your leadership in an enjoyable way.

Speed conditioning Chasing games, complete with sprints and changes of direction, are great exercise. Send your dog after balls or Frisbees thrown on level ground so that he can stretch his body right out. Always stop while he's still raring to go, so that it remains a treat that he looks forward to. But if chasing doesn't appeal to him, get him to run to you by calling to him from a distance away. Just be ready to dodge as he hurtles toward you, and praise him when he arrives.

Cooling down Vigorous exercise should never stop suddenly. A stroll and some stretches at the end of the session are just as important as the warm-ups before it.

Other aerobic exercise Swimming is a great way to exercise him without putting stress on his bones and joints. It is especially good for dogs with joint problems such as hip dysplasia. Splashing around will also increase your dog's stamina and keep him cool in summer.

SPORTS DOGS LOVE

A daily walk will provide your dog with good exercise and keep her mind alert. But just as people enjoy doing the things they have a natural affinity for, whether they be music, sports or art, dogs also enjoy the activities they were designed to do.

Giving chase If full-speed dashes are your dog's delight, create a chasing toy by using a fishing rod with several feet of fishing line attached to a plastic garbage bag. Twitch the bag to make it go in circles and change its direction as she gives chase. Let her catch the lure and rip into it at times, so she knows she has a chance of winning.

Retrieving games Many dogs relish games of catch and fetch. Labrador and golden retrievers especially enjoy dropping field dummies, made for retriever training, back at your feet. If fetch is your dog's favorite, send her swimming after sticks and floating toys.

Aerial aerobics Some dogs prefer Frisbees to balls and sticks, and will perform amazing contortions to snatch them out of the air. Start low and slow, rolling the disk on the ground, before gradually working up to mid-air acrobatics.

Hide-and-seek Many dogs love this game and can be taught with the help of a human friend. Get the friend to hide in a closet with a treat in his hand and the door slightly ajar. Then tell your dog to go find him. When she is successful, reward her with the treat and lots of praise. If she has trouble at first, get the friend to call to her

ORGANIZED ACTIVITIES
If you and your dog are bored by the same old walk, activities such as agility trials may provide inspiration. Trials involve directing your dog through a colorful course of planks, jumps, tunnels and other obstacles. The training required almost guarantees that your dog will be in tip-top condition.

150 mm

200 mm

250 mia

softly. When she understands the game, she'll be ready to sniff out more challenging hiding places.

Swimming Some dogs love to paddle—some retrieving breeds even have webbed feet. To introduce your dog to the water, carry her about 10 feet (3 m) from shore, gently place her in the water and praise her as she swims. If you toss her in deep water, she'll develop an aversion to swimming. Support her rear by placing one hand, palm up, under her tail and back legs until she realizes that she makes better progress using four legs.

Play-killing squeaky Loved by puppies and older dogs alike, play-killing is the closest city dogs get to the thrill of the chase and the kill. Hold a toy with a built-in squeaker in your hand and squeeze it a couple of times to tempt your dog. Then throw it. If she pounces on the toy and shakes it hard enough to scramble her brains, you've just discovered one of her favorite games. Don't leave her alone with her toy, though. She could tear it apart and swallow it, squeaker and all.

WHY WON'T SOME DOGS FETCH?
Many breeds, especially hunting dogs, have a genetic tendency to retrieve. But dogs that have different sets of inherited skills may be less inclined to bring back a toy. Every dog can be taught to fetch, however. Attract your dog's attention by waving a toy in front of her face. Then throw the toy away and tell her to "Fetch!" When she goes after it, encourage her to bring it to you by saying, "Come!" Open your arms wide to welcome her. When she comes to you, praise her, then tell her to "drop it" to make her release the toy. Repeat the exercise several times.

HOW MUCH IS ENOUGH?

During most activities, your dog will run faster and cover more ground than you do. He may have so much heart that he keeps going past the point of exhaustion, just because he thinks you want him to. Use your common sense, practice moderation, and watch him for signs of fatigue or breathing difficulties.

The best time Exercise your dog at any time that suits your schedule and the climate. Avoid summer heat and humidity by taking him out in the morning or at dusk. If at any time your dog starts to drop behind, slow down.

Heatstroke Dogs will happily play as long as you let them, but on hot days their exuberance can get them into trouble. They don't have an efficient way to keep cool—their only sweat glands are on their pads. When they push themselves too hard they can succumb to heatstroke. It's up to you to set limits.

Most at risk All dogs can get heatstroke. Most vulnerable are elderly dogs, overweight dogs, large or heavily muscled dogs, short-nosed dogs and those with a double coat. To prevent suffering, avoid exercising your dog vigorously in extreme temperatures.

Warning signs Dogs with heatstroke pant heavily, drool and feel hot to the touch. Their eyes will become glassy, their inner ears and lips will flush and their lips will stick to their gums. As the condition progresses, dogs can suffer bloody diarrhea and vomiting.

HIGH RISK OF HEATSTROKE?
The coats of these Norwegian elkhounds can insulate them from heat, but other dogs aren't so lucky. Those with thick coats are particularly vulnerable to heatstroke. Short-nosed dogs such as boxers and pugs are also at risk, since their small airways make them less able to exhale hot air.

What to do If your dog is unsteady on his feet, barely or not responsive, or even comatose, you must act immediately. Heatstroke can cause cell damge within minutes and, without fast treatment, can be deadly. Start lowering your dog's temperature by giving him icecubes to lick. If he is unconscious, bathe his pads with rubbing alcohol. The rapid evaporation of the alcohol will help dissipate body heat.

Get him wet Also soak your dog in cool water. (Don't use cold water—it can bring on seizures.) Use a garden hose or, if he is not too heavy, lift him into a bathtub or sink. Using a fan will also speed the cooling process.

Seek medical advice Continue to cool him en route to the vet by placing wet towels on his head, neck, chest and abdomen. Keep giving him ice or putting rubbing alcohol on his pads, and turn on your car's air conditioning. Even if your dog seems to have recovered, your vet will be able to detect any permanent damage to the heart, lungs, kidneys or brain.

Pad problems Heatstroke is not the only problem brought on by exercise in high temperatures. While your dog's pads are strong and sturdy, they are also unprotected from things that you, in your socks and shoes, don't notice. Exercise during the coolest time of the day throughout summer will ensure that his pads aren't burned on hot pavements. Check the temperature of the pavement before you step out by placing your bare hand on it. If it's still hot from the sun, wait a couple of hours, or exercise your dog on grass.

Cold weather precautions Unlike ordinary salt and sand, the road salt and road sand used in winter to melt snow can also burn your dog's feet. (It can also burn his mouth if he bites at his feet, and his belly if he kicks the material onto himself while trotting along.) After your walk, towel off his chest, belly and feet to get rid of any snow or chemical residues on his skin and between his toes.

Frostbite In winter, don't let your dog play outside for too long on ice-encrusted snow or when there is a high wind-chill factor. If he has hairy feet, clipping the hair from between his toes will prevent the formation of snowballs. Also check his pads for cracks or cuts. If his pads become dry, a daily dab of moisturizer or petroleum jelly may soothe them.

KEEPING COOL
No matter where you go with your dog, take water with you. Offer him a drink every 20 minutes and try to keep him shaded.

FEEDING YOUR DOG

Feeding your dog a nutritious and balanced diet is one of the most important things you can do to keep him happy and healthy. Like people, dogs are omnivores and cannot live on meat alone. They require a varied diet that contains protein, carbohydrates, fats, minerals, vitamins and plenty of fresh water. While all dogs need these important nutrients, how much they need depends on their age, health and level of activity. If you aim for quality and balance—and a touch of variety—and feed in the proper amounts, you will see your dog's good nutrition reflected in his health, vitality and sleek condition.

A DOG'S NUTRITIONAL NEEDS

The six basic nutrients required by all living things are water, proteins, carbohydrates, minerals, vitamins and fats. A dog's individual nutritional requirements will determine how much of these nutrients she should have, depending on her age, state of health and lifestyle.

Proteins Dogs don't require proteins as such; they need the amino acids that make up the proteins. They make some non-essential amino acids within their bodies, but dogs must get the rest from animal or plant products that contain protein. These will ensure that your dog's cell-building, blood-clotting, infection-fighting and myriad other bodily processes are functioning properly. Working dogs —those that herd livestock or haul sleds—need more high-quality, animal-derived protein than sedentary dogs.

Carbohydrates Foods containing sugar, starches and fiber help provide your dog with energy. Carbohydrates also keep the intestines functioning so that food wastes pass through her system efficiently. They shouldn't make up more than 50 percent of her diet.

Minerals These either trigger chemical reactions within the body or serve as building blocks for specific bodily systems, such as nerve tissue (magnesium) or skin and enzymes (zinc). Most commercial dog foods will provide your dog with the minerals she needs.

Vitamins Your dog also needs vitamins for chemical reactions and normal metabolic function. There is no need to supplement her intake if you are feeding her a balanced diet. If you feed her homemade food, however, review her diet with your vet to check if any supplementation is necessary.

Fats When properly balanced with other nutrients, fats are essential to your dog's good nutrition and health

FOOD FOR GROWTH
Puppies need up to three times as much energy and balanced nutrients as adults until they reach four months of age.

WHEN TO FEED

Whether you feed your dog at regular times or make food available throughout the day depends on the type of food you feed, your dog's tendency to overeat, her age and health. Most adult dogs can sustain their energy and nutrient levels on one meal a day.

as well as being an important source of energy. Feeding the proper amount of a complete and balanced dog food should ensure that she gets the right amount of fats, but beware too many calorie-packed treats and snacks.

Pregnant or lactating dogs You don't need to change your dog's diet until she's six weeks pregnant, when she can start having three or four small meals a day. During lactation she will have nutrient needs three to four times higher than normal, so give her all the water and protein-rich food she wants. As she starts to wean her puppies, gradually reduce her rations to normal.

Puppies A dog will experience her greatest growth in her first year, so she'll need more high-quality animal-derived protein, such as eggs or milk, and a specially formulated puppy food. Only feed her what she needs to maintain a steady rate of growth. Rapid, disproportionate growth of bones and muscles could lead to joint problems. Consult your vet about your dog's recommended calcium intake—calcium levels in a large puppy should be kept low, since too much calcium can interfere with her bone and cartilage development. Puppies from small breeds, on the other hand, are susceptible to low blood sugar levels and need small amounts of food at least four times a day until they are three months old. When your pup—large breed or small—is mature, she can go on to her adult ration.

TYPES OF DOG FOOD

Commercial dog foods come in three basic types: dry, semi-moist and moist canned. There are also three quality levels: generic, popular name-brand and premium. What you choose to feed your dog is up to you. The difference is in the ingredients, palatability, cost and convenience. To get the balance of nutrients right for your dog—taking into account her breed, age, size and levels of activity—you may need to feed her a mixture of types.

Dogs love the smell and taste of canned food.

Canned foods The palatability and texture of canned food means it is recommended for finicky eaters, for dogs that have trouble putting on weight, and for aging dogs whose teeth are no longer in the best condition.

Canned food contains a variety of meat, fish and cereal-based products. It's also highly digestible, and its nutrients are readily absorbed. However, its energy content is relatively low, so large amounts are needed to satisfy large dogs. (It's best to feed large dogs canned mixed with dry food.) Canned food is also expensive, considering it contains about 70 percent water. It also spoils quickly once it's opened, so you can't leave it out for your dog all day.

Semi-moist foods Like canned food, semi-moist food tastes and smells good, and the popular brands are very palatable and digestible. Semi-moist food is not as messy as canned and doesn't require refrigeration after opening. Packets also come in convenient single-serving sizes.

The energy content of semi-moist food is relatively high, so much smaller amounts can be fed. It contains only about 15 to 30 percent water as well as meat and plant proteins and cereals, fats and sugars. Semi-moist food has such a long shelf life because of the high level of sugar and preservatives. For this reason dogs with health problems such as diabetes might fare better eating canned or dry food.

Semi-moist doesn't spoil as quickly as canned.

Dry foods Dry foods contain only about 10 percent water and have the highest energy content. Unlike mixers or kibble, which are made from cereals and contain very little protein, nutritionally complete dry foods contain adequate sources of protein such as meat, bone meal or soy beans. They are also almost odorless and can be left out all day without spoiling. However, they are not as tasty as canned or semi-moist foods and are often mixed with these to improve palatability.

Quality level Whatever you feed your dog, always be sure it contains high-quality ingredients such as animal protein. Generic foods are low in price, but may also offer the lowest nutritional value. Your dog will have to eat more generic food to get the same amount of energy as she would from a name-brand food. The formulations of generic foods may also vary, causing bowel upsets in sensitive dogs.

On the other hand, premium foods have more high-quality meat protein to plant protein. They also contain a higher density of digestible, absorbable nutrients per volume. Since your dog will only need a small amount to be well-nourished, premium food is more cost-effective. She will also produce fewer stools, and they will be firmer.

Name-brand foods are just as nutritious as premium foods, although they may contain fewer exotic ingredients. The animal–plant protein ratio may also differ. But name-brand foods are cheaper, so if your dog is doing well on one, stick to it.

Homemade food The main advantage of commerically prepared food is convenience. Preparing a homemade diet can be more expensive and time-consuming. However, a homemade diet may be good for a dog with medical problems, allergies or special nutritional requirements. Don't go in for experiments; instead, ask your vet for a recipe that is nutritionally balanced for your dog's needs. The ingredients in a homemade diet should be comparable to what you eat yourself. Make sure that everything is fully cooked.

Dry food is also good for your dog's teeth.

SNACKS AND TREATS

Treats are a great way to reward your dog for learning commands and tricks—or for just being your best friend. But many snacks and treats tend to be high in calories and not nutritionally balanced. Like all good things, they should be given in moderation, especially if your dog is overweight or has another health problem.

What to give There are all kinds of dog snacks and treats; even low-calorie treats for dogs that need to shed a few pounds. If your dog follows a specific diet for medical reasons, ask your vet to recommend an appropriate treat.

Chewy treats Rawhide balls and sticks or jerky are "just-for-being-a-great-dog" rewards. Another treat that will give your dog hours of enjoyment is an artificial bone or a toy with a hollow that you can stuff with peanut butter, cream cheese or soft, semi-moist food.

Biscuits Satisfyingly crunchy, biscuits have the added benefit of helping to scrape tartar off your dog's teeth. Tiny biscuits and soft-moist treats also make good rewards during training sessions because they are gulped down quickly. However, they are also high in sugar and preservatives, so give them sparingly.

Cookies These snacks come in fun flavors, such as pumpkin, peanut butter and liver-chip, and are often made of healthful ingredients such as whole-wheat flour. But that doesn't mean

FRESH IS BEST
Bits of apple, banana and avocado, grapes, strawberries, peeled oranges, carrots and even the odd stalk of broccoli will reward your dog while helping to keep his teeth clean and his breath fresh. Wash the fruit and vegetables and feed him just a few small pieces at a time—you don't want to give him diarrhea.

you can give them to your dog by the handful—cookies contain calories just like any other snack.

Human food Your food can also be good for him, provided you make the right choices. Treats are not leftovers from your table; they're not bones, or the skin off the chicken, the turkey carcass or the fat trimmed off the steak. Treats should be healthful. Try your dog on green beans, low-fat cheese, carrot sticks and bits of broiled, skinless chicken. Unsalted, unbuttered popcorn can also be a favorite. Keep his snacks separate from your food—if he associates treats with the dinner table he may be encouraged to beg at mealtimes.

Dangerous treats Dogs love chocolate, but it's about the worst food they can have. Chocolate contains caffeine and a related chemical called theobromine, stimulants that can raise your dog's heart rate dangerously high. Chocolate can also cause vomiting and

severe, life-threatening diarrhea. Baking chocolate is especially bad for your dog because it contains nearly nine times more theobromine than milk chocolate.

Your dog can smell chocolate from across a room and will go to surprising lengths to get a taste. For his safety, keep it behind closed doors.

Bones The only safe bone for your dog is a raw, fresh, whole beef femur, sometimes known as a marrowbone or shin bone. Any other kind of bone could break his teeth; become lodged in his throat; or cause constipation. There's even a chance of them splintering and puncturing the intestinal tract—an injury that usually requires surgery and is sometimes fatal. Sterilized bones are not recommended either, as they are more fragile than some raw bones. Alternatives to bones that will provide him with the same level of satisfaction and enjoyment are rawhides, nylon bones, pig ears and rope bones.

SNACKS TO SAVOR
Jerky (top), puppy biscuits (left) and dog cookies (right) are all tasty treats for your obedient dog. You can prepare another favorite snack at home. Place a piece of raw sheep's liver on a baking tray or cookie sheet, then oven-bake on low heat until it is cooked and chewy in texture. When cool, cut the liver into strips—and watch your dog's delight!

FEEDING EQUIPMENT

Your dog doesn't need a fork and spoon when he has his dinner, but well-designed food and water bowls will make his meals more enjoyable, not to mention less messy for you. Be sure you keep his dishes clean, washing them out or running them through the dishwasher regularly so that encrusted food doesn't build up and attract insects and contamination.

BEST BOWLS
Separate dishes are more convenient than partitioned bowls. There are many available, such as these weighted, non-slip bowls designed (left) for a dog with a wide muzzle and (right) for narrow-muzzled dogs. If your dog tends to tip his bowls, weighted dishes will keep dinner where it belongs.

What he needs Dog bowls can be metal, plastic or ceramic, and your dog will need one for food and one for water. Metal and plastic bowls have the advantage of being inexpensive, lightweight, easy to clean and unbreakable, but ceramic bowls are often more attractive, with decorative designs. They are also heavier, so it's not as easy for your dog to shove them around the floor or knock them over. However, ceramic bowls may require hand-washing as they aren't always dishwasher-safe.

Raised bowls If your dog is tall or deep-chested, or you've got a puppy who will grow to be that way, consider buying raised feeding bowls. They are more comfortable for him to eat from, and are recommended for dogs that are prone to a dangerous digestive condition called bloat, such as boxers, Weimaraners, Great Danes, Irish setters and Saint Bernards. If he isn't bent over as he eats he will swallow less air, so a raised bowl will keep the gulping and gobbling to a minimum.

An older dog with arthritis can find it painful if he has to bend too far for his food, so he will also appreciate raised bowls.

Floppy ears If you have a dog with long, drooping ears, you may need a bowl that keeps his ears from dragging through his food and water. If he eats from a regular bowl, you'll have to clean his ears after every meal. A dish

FOOD FOR THOUGHT

A good bowl is sturdy, easy to clean, won't tip over easily, and has plenty of room for your dog's muzzle. If you choose a ceramic bowl (left), make sure it was made in North America. Some foreign-made ceramics contain high levels of lead, which can leach into food or water and harm your dog. Other special bowls on the market include those with moats around them (below left) that will keep out ants and other crawling insects.

with an inner rim may solve the problem, or you could make a collar out of a cut-off t-shirt sleeve or similar material (you could even knit one!) and slip it over his head and down his neck during mealtimes. The collar will keep his ears clear of the food.

Automatic systems Dogs are creatures of habit and they like to eat at the same time every day, but it's not always possible to get home right when your dog is expecting his evening meal. An automatic feeding and watering system might be the answer.

You can purchase dishes that work on a timer and pop open at whatever time you specify. They can be filled with either dry food or, if you buy a model that keeps canned food refrigerated, with moist food that won't spoil during the day.

To ensure your dog always has fresh, clean water, you can buy a dish that can be attached to a reservoir, such as a 2-quart (2 l) plastic bottle, or to a garden hose. The bowl will automatically refill as your dog empties it.

Feeding feuds Before dogs were domesticated, they never knew where their next meal was coming from, so they ate whatever they could, as fast as they could, before another dog in the pack took it from them. Although we've been feeding our dogs for a long time now, their age-old instinct tends to re-emerge in the presence of food.

If you have more than one dog, it's best not to feed them all from one bowl. A free-for-all could result, making it impossible to monitor whether each dog is getting his fair share. It's much better if each dog has his own bowl and is fed the right amount according to his size and needs. Separate bowls may also prevent fights from breaking out.

A timer makes the lid open automatically.

THE RIGHT WEIGHT

Don't overnourish your dog. Giving food formulated for an active young dog to a sedentary old one will not make her any healthier—just fatter. Instead, evaluate your dog's needs and adjust her rations accordingly. Whatever her age, metabolic rate and level of activity, the guidelines below will help you ensure that your dog maintains a healthy weight.

If her ribs are not obvious, she's plump.

Catering for individuals The amount of food a dog requires varies with the individual dog. Every can or package label is printed with guidelines. The trouble is, these are written with the "average" dog in mind, but nobody knows what the average dog looks like, let alone how much she needs to eat. A tiny Maltese needs only about 250 calories a day, whereas a fully grown Rottweiler may need 2,400 calories—more than most people! Even dogs that weigh the same can have different nutritional requirements. Different metabolisms,

increased energy output (such as strenuous exercise or during lactation) and even cold weather increase a dog's caloric needs, whereas a sedentary life decreases them. Use the feeding guidelines on the container as a starting point, then focus on the needs, the size and breed of your not-so-average dog.

Evaluation You should only feed enough to maintain your dog's optimum body weight. You can calculate how much food she needs by learning to evaluate her overall body condition. First, take a good look at her

from the back and from above to see if she seems lean or heavy. Fit dogs have obvious waistlines; overweight dogs do not. Then feel her ribcage to find out whether the ribs are prominent or padded with subcutaneous (beneath the skin) fat. Armed with this information, use the guidelines to see how she rates, then gradually adjust her rations until she meets the ideal.

What is ideal? The following descriptions will help you to determine your dog's body condition and the amount of food she should receive.

Underweight

Ribs: Easy to feel beneath her skin, with minimal subcutaneous fat layer.
Tail base: Raised bony structure with little fat under the skin.
Abdomen: Abdominal tuck; marked hourglass shape.

Ideal Weight

Ribs: Possible to feel, with some subcutaneous fat.
Tail base: A smooth contour and perhaps some thickening; possible to feel bony structures under a slight layer of subcutaneous fat.
Abdomen: Abdominal tuck; well-proportioned lumbar "waist."

Obese

Ribs: Very difficult to feel, with a thick layer of subcutaneous fat.
Tail base: Appears thickened; difficult to feel bony structures.
Abdomen: Pendulous, bulging belly; no "waist;" back markedly broadened.

If your dog is too fat, you will need to gradually feed her less. Weigh her every two weeks until she matches the "ideal" weight and body shape.

TOP VIEW

SIDE VIEW

Underweight

Ideal weight

Obese

WATER NEEDS

Although often taken for granted, water is as important to your dog as oxygen. It is necessary to maintain proper levels of body fluids so that nutrients can be carried throughout the body and wastes can be eliminated. A supply of fresh water should be available at all times.

GOOD MEDICINE

Dogs with kidney problems often produce a lot of urine because the kidneys aren't able to recycle fluids as well as they should. By regularly drinking plenty of water, this Labrador mix is helping her kidneys work better.

Vital for life While dogs need all the essential nutrients to survive, they need fresh, clean water most of all. Dogs can go for a while without food, but without water they become dehydrated or suffer heatstroke and perish in a few days.

An adult dog's body is 60 to 70 percent water; a puppy's is more than 80 percent. Make sure your dog has a constant supply of fresh water. A dog of medium size that eats a diet primarily of dry food could require more than 2 quarts (2 l) of water every day.

Clean and fresh If her water isn't fresh, your dog may drink only when very thirsty. It's important to clean her bowl every day, since bacteria in her mouth may proliferate in the bowl and give her diarrhea. Change the water every morning, then check it again during the day, especially in hot weather when your dog will be thirstier and her water will evaporate rapidly. Cover the outside water sources within your yard, and prevent her from drinking from those beyond it—she could get an infection from mud puddles and stagnant pools.

Special needs Fresh water is especially vital for pregnant dogs. Water carries nutrients to the developing fetuses and also helps flush wastes from the mother's body. Plenty of water is also needed during lactation to keep up the milk supply for the litter.

Too much? Your dog can drink as much as she wants, whenever she wants, except when it's time for serious exercise. (Her water should be rationed immediately before and after exertion.) You need never be concerned about giving her "too much" water. However, if you notice a marked increase in her water consumption you should talk to your vet. Diabetes, kidney failure,

Cushing's disease and many other serious health problems are characterized by increased thirst.

First aid Water can help to alleviate the symptoms—and the effects—of many health problems. Dogs prone to urinary tract infections, for example, will benefit from drinking more, since the increase in fluids will help dilute and flush bacteria from the urinary tract. Water can also help prevent constipation.

Dogs with diarrhea or a fever are at risk of becoming dehydrated. However, sick dogs often

feel miserable and not up to drinking. If your dog doesn't seem interested in her water bowl, try tempting her with some beef broth. A little salty gravy added to her food, or some saltine crackers, will also help her work up a thirst.

Keep water bowls full, especially on hot days.

GROOMING

Dogs keep themselves clean by rubbing and rolling on the ground and licking or scratching themselves. However, this is often just not enough to meet the human definition of clean. Moreover, many of the things that dogs choose to roll in may smell unpleasant to humans. Regular grooming will keep your dog looking good and make life around the house more pleasant for everyone. Grooming also keeps the effects of shedding to a minimum and gives you the chance to inspect your dog to make sure her skin, teeth, ears, eyes and nails are healthy. Make grooming sessions part of your dog's preventive health program.

DIFFERENT DOG COATS

To know how best to groom your dog, you need to determine the type of coat he has. All dog coats fit into one of the following categories. If your dog is a mixed breed, he'll also fit into one of these categories, depending on the type of breed that is most dominant in his genetic makeup.

SHORT DOUBLE COAT

Labradors (left) and Rottweilers have this coat, with straight, coarse hair on the outside and a soft, thin coat beneath. Such coats shed constantly and must be brushed at least twice a week.

LONG COARSE COAT

The long, human-hairlike quality of this coat makes it one of the more time-consuming coats to groom. Shih tzus, Lhasa apsos and Tibetan terriers (left) have this coat type. Mixed into the long coarse coat is a softer undercoat.

SHORT SMOOTH COAT

Pugs, basenjis (right) and Doberman pinschers have short, smooth coats. Since there is no undercoat, these dogs are probably the easiest to groom. A weekly brushing will keep shedding under control. A bath with a light conditioner will also be beneficial.

LONG SILKY COAT

The coats of breeds such as Yorkshire, silky and Maltese terriers (right) need to be groomed at least two or three times a week. There is no undercoat with this kind of coat.

HAIRLESS COAT

Since they have little or no hair, dogs such as the Inca orchid and Chinese crested dog (left) don't require regular brushing. However, they do need frequent baths, preferably using a shampoo with an anti-bacterial agent to help ward off the skin problems common in these breeds.

SHORT WIRY COAT

Dogs with short wiry coats have hair that is thick and hard, and somewhat bristly to the touch. Wirehaired dachshunds and most terriers have this kind of coat, including Irish terriers (left). These dogs need to be either stripped or clipped every two to four months. Clipping will make their coat softer.

CURLY COAT

This coat does not shed, so regular brushing and clipping is required to keep the thick, soft curls looking neat. When bathing a curly-coated dog, such as a poodle (left) or bichon frise, apply a conditioner with body-building properties. Dry him with a towel, then use a blow-dryer to fluff-dry him, brushing outward from the skin with a soft slicker brush.

LONG DOUBLE COAT

Samoyeds, Chow Chows (left) and collies all have these coats: A long, straight and coarse outer coat with a very thick undercoat all over the body. These coats shed the most.

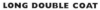

GROOMING TOOLS

To keep your dog looking his best, you will need to have the right grooming equipment. There's a wide range of brushes and combs to choose from. A combined approach—brushing your dog, followed by a thorough combing—will remove huge amounts of excess hair.

Slicker brush

Combined bristle and pin brush

Bristle brush These are best used to remove dirt and loose hair on short-coated dogs, since they don't do a good job of penetrating longer coats. Bristle brushes also stimulate your dog's skin and spread the natural oils that help to keep his skin healthy and his coat shiny.

Pincushion brush This kind of brush has long, straight metal pins attached to a rubber backing. Most pin brushes are oval-shaped and are used primarily on long-coated breeds. Pin brushes are also excellent for fluff-drying dogs with long hair. Note that dogs with either long silky coats or short smooth coats have no undercoat to protect their delicate skin, so be gentle.

Pincushion brush

Slicker brush The most versatile brush, the slicker works with many different types of coats, including the wiry coats of terriers and the short, dense coats of breeds like the Labrador. The brush's bent wire bristles grasp and remove a dog's loose undercoat with every stroke. Slickers come in many different sizes and shapes and with varying degrees of bristle stiffness. Coats that are brushed regularly with a slicker seldom become matted.

Wide-toothed comb

Mat splitter

Combs These come in different tooth sizes, and the spacing between the teeth varies. Some combs have handles, while others are straight with one-half of the comb containing finely spaced teeth and the other half, widely spaced teeth. The larger-toothed combs are used to remove the undercoat of the heavier-coated breeds. Other combs are handy to tease out tangles and to remove any loose hair that may remain after brushing.

Stripping combs Stripping, which involves pulling the dead hairs from the dog's coat, is used to keep the coat stiffer. Stripping combs are commonly used on terriers and other wire-coated breeds. Since proper use of a stripping comb requires considerable skill, they are perhaps best left in the care of professionals. However, you can try stripping your terrier with your hands.

Hound gloves Some people prefer to use a hound glove or grooming glove instead of a brush. As their names suggest, these brushes fit over the hand and feature a cloth base with rubber nubs that capture loose hair. Dogs enjoy being groomed with a glove because it feels just like they're being petted. The loose hair can be washed out or easily removed by hand.

Dematting tools These are combs and splitters designed to saw through mats and burrs in your dog's coat so you don't have to cut them out. Skill is needed to use them, so take care.

Dryers Don't use your own dryer—they get too hot and can burn your dog. Professionals use a special dryer, called a force dryer, designed for use on dogs. They cost between $150 and $500, so you'd have to be a serious groomer to buy one. However, there are some portable models produced for home use that are adequate—and more affordable.

Double-sided grooming glove

Hound glove

131

HOW TO GROOM

There is a basic technique for grooming each of the coat types found in dogs. Each technique is designed to make the dog's coat look its best and the way it is supposed to look for the breed. Even if she's not a purebred, your dog can still benefit from the proper treatment of her coat.

A pin brush is being used to keep this Afghan's coat looking beautiful.

Short smooth coats Using a bristle or slicker brush or a hound glove, brush against the lie of your dog's coat. This will help remove any excess hair from underneath. Then, using the same tool, brush in the right direction to pick up loose hairs on the surface.

Short and long double coats Separate sections of your dog's coat with your hand so there is a parting where her skin is visible. Using a pin brush or slicker brush, comb out the thick undercoat, brushing outward from the skin. The undercoat is thickest on the hindlegs and around the neck, so you may need to work through some mats here.

If you encounter a mat, first try to gently untangle it with your fingers. If you can't untangle it, use a mat splitter to work through the mat. Put your fingers between the mat and your dog's skin so that you don't cut her.

LONG DOUBLE COATS
After brushing, place a wide-toothed comb deep within the coat, parallel to the skin. Comb outward to remove any more loose undercoat.

When the undercoat is finished, use the brush to go over her top coat, brushing with the lie of the coat.

Short wiry coats You'll need a slicker brush, a medium-tooth metal comb and a stripping comb. If the hairs at the very top of her coat begin to protrude along her back, thin the coat by running the stripping comb lightly over it. Then use the slicker brush and the metal comb to pick up any loose hairs. Your dog will also need to be regularly hand-stripped and carded—a technique whereby loose hair is removed by "brushing" your dog with a blade or stripping stone. Take her to a professional groomer when this needs to be done.

Curly coats Use a slicker brush daily to prevent your dog's coat from matting. Since she will not shed, get her clipped every six to eight weeks.

Long coarse and silky coats Difficult to care for, these coats are often clipped to keep matting and tangles to a minimum. An unclipped dog with one of these coats requires a big commitment in grooming time and energy.
Remove any mats, then use a pin brush (a slicker brush on a silky coat), to gently brush the coat in the direction it lies. Then go over it again with a soft bristle brush. Bathe your dog after you have brushed her, squeezing the conditioning shampoo through her coat to prevent tangling. Towel her, blow-dry her, then brush her again.

Hairless coats Give your dog a gentle scrub with a face puff while bathing her to remove dead skin cells. Oil-free moisturizer should also be applied daily. Gently use a slicker brush to groom any tufts of hair on her head, legs and tail. To remove existing light body hair, use a regular safety razor.

SHORT WIRY COATS
After thinning out the overgrown wiry hair, brush your dog's coat in layers, from the skin outward, using a slicker brush.

CLIPPING

Although the mastery of the art of clipping belongs to the professional groomer, you too can use these instruments to groom your dog and make her look good. The extent to which you use clippers will depend on the type of dog you have, but most dogs can benefit from some tidying up with clippers.

This Bedlington terrier requires specialized clipping every six weeks.

Who needs clipping? The breed that requires the most clipping is the poodle. Whether it is one of the large standards or a tiny toy, the poodle coat screams out for clippers. Not only is this because of the stylish of the breed, but also because a poodle's coat grows continuously. Some of the other breeds that are clipped on a regular basis are the bichon frise, Bedlington terrier, Kerry blue terrier, Airedale terrier and bouvier des Flandres. While these breeds don't call for as much clipping as the poodle, they do need shaping to keep them looking the way they are supposed to look.

Keep it simple The finely dolled-up poodles seen at dog shows have their hair clipped down to the skin in some places, and fluffed, shaped and molded in others. Unless you own a show dog, you will be better off keeping your pet poodle (or any other breed that requires clipping) in a simple clip that makes her look good but is relatively easy to maintain.

A CLOSE SHAVE

If you decide to invest in your own clippers, make sure you choose a selection of blades. Different ones are appropriate for the different areas on your dog's body. Be sure to get a number 10 blade for the stomach, feet, face and genital area, and a number 7F blade for clipping the body.

Practice makes perfect If you want to do the clipping yourself, instead of taking your dog to a professional groomer, you will need to practice a lot—it takes quite a bit of skill to clip a dog's coat properly. You may even decide to take a course on dog grooming. This will give you plenty of opportunity to practice before you take the clippers to your pet.

Ask your professional groomer to teach you how to clip, or watch her in action.

Careful clipping One of the most important things to be aware of is that you must always cut with the hair, not against it. Cutting against the lie of the hair can result in burns and cuts to your dog's skin.

Clippers and blades If you decide to invest in your own clippers, narrow your selection down to the two basic types used by professional groomers: small clippers and standard clippers. Standard clippers are used for all-around grooming. Small clippers—ones about the size of mustache clippers—are used on the face, ears and feet of some breeds.

Clipper types
The clippers you find in most department stores are worthless for dogs, because they come with a blade that is designed only to cut clean poodle hair. They will not cut any dog hair that is dirty, and will bind up on cocker spaniels or any other thick-haired dogs.

Ask your groomer to help you buy some decent clippers and blades. The top two brands used by professional groomers are Oster A-5 and Andis. These are available from catalogs and some pet supply stores.

THE "LION" CLIP
The sculpted "lion" clip sported by this standard poodle was originally developed to lighten a dog's coat for swimming while protecting the joints and major organs from chills and penetrating thorns. Such an elaborate clip requires lots of maintenance and is usually only given to show dogs.

EARS AND EYES

Grooming your dog's ears can keep them looking and smelling good. But grooming also has a practical side. When you sit down to groom your dog, you have an opportunity to check his eyes and ears for any signs of problems in their earliest stages and to work at keeping them healthy.

Drooping ears need special care.

When to clean Start cleaning your dog's ears and eyes when he's a puppy. He will become accustomed to having his ears handled if it is part of a regular grooming routine. Your dog's ears could be cleaned once a month, depending on how dirty they are.

Preventing problems Dogs with floppy ears are especially prone to ear problems because the design of their ears prevents air from circulating. The warm, moist environment under a long, drooping ear flap is perfect for fungal or bacterial growth. If you own a Labrador retriever, bloodhound, cocker spaniel or any other dog with floppy ears, be especially diligent about checking and cleaning the insides.

How to clean The best way to clean your dog's ears is to wrap your finger in a soft washcloth or a cotton ball moistened with either mineral oil or a commercial ear-cleaning solution. Rub the inside of his earflap and the ear opening to remove any accumulated dirt and wax. While it's important to keep his ears clean, some wax needs to remain, so don't overdo it. If your dog's ears seem particularly dirty, or there is any sign of discharge, he may have an ear infection. Take your dog to the vet for a checkup.

Hairy ears Dogs with hairy faces tend to have hairy ears, and the more hair in your dog's ears, the more chance there is of dampness and possible infection. Dogs that accumulate

CLEANING EARS
Clean your dog's ears only if they are dirty, waxy or if there is discharge—overcleaning can actually cause problems. Use a cotton ball, not a cotton-tipped swab, since these can pack debris onto the ear drum.

hair in the ear canal, such as poodles, shih tzus and Lhasa apsos, need to have that hair removed. You can pluck the excess hair by grasping a few strands at a time with either fingers or tweezers, and pulling gently. This can be made easier by the use of powders especially marketed for the purpose.

If you don't feel comfortable about plucking the hair, you can trim it with blunt-nosed scissors. This won't necessarily reduce the humidity in your dog's ears, but it may make them look neater. Try to keep the cut hair from falling back into his ear canal. If he won't sit still, take him to a professional groomer—if he's struggling you could hurt him with the scissors.

Clean eyes To keep your dog's eyes sparkling and clear, wipe them with a moistened cotton ball. You might also have to clean under his eyes every day to stop any staining from becoming permanent. Wipe his cheeks with a clean, damp cloth, and use a baby's toothbrush to remove any matter that may have dried into his coat. These soft brushes won't harm your dog if you accidentally touch his eye.

If hair covers his eyes, use a band or clip to pull it back—don't cut it.

Health check If you notice anything unusual about his eyes while you're cleaning them, such as redness, cloudiness, swelling, tearing or pus, contact your vet. It could be caused by an allergy or irritation, or something more serious.

CLEANING EYES
Wipe your dog's eyes from the outside toward the center.

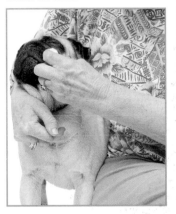

NEAT FEET

Of all his body parts, your dog's feet probably take the biggest pounding. To protect his pads from damage, you can rub vitamin E and juice from an aloe plant onto them before and after exercise. Also remember to inspect his feet after each outing to ensure there are no sharp objects or injuries present. When it comes to grooming, keeping his feet in good condition is not just something you do for his appearance. It's also vital for his health and comfort.

NAIL-TRIMMING
Hold your dog's paw firmly when you are trimming his nails. Using sharp trimmers will prevent the nail from splitting and cracking and make the whole process go smoothly. Avoid cutting the quick (see diagram)—it will make him bleed a little and he will remember the pain, which will make future nail trimmings more difficult.

Neat nails The pain from walking on neglected nails is reason enough to trim your dog's nails about every two weeks. (Dogs that regularly walk on concrete wear down their nails and rarely need to have them trimmed.) Nail-trimming is not as difficult as it may seem, provided your dog cooperates. You can use a sharp hand-held trimmer or an electric grinder.

How to trim A dog's nail is shaped like a crescent. It is widest where it attaches to the skin and narrows to a curved point at the end. You need to cut the nail just at the point where it starts to curve downward. You want to avoid the quick, or nailbed, which runs down the center of the nail and contains the nerves and blood supply.

Avoiding the quick The pink quick can be seen clearly in dogs with white nails. When you trim, clip below this

TRIMMING PAW HAIR
Hair traps dirt and damp, causing foot infections in medium- and long-haired dogs such as Samoyeds, Saint Bernards, golden retrievers, and this Maltese terrier. Regular trimming of the hair keeps the feet drier and healthier. It may also stop your dog from chewing his feet, a hard habit to break.

Using blunt-nosed scissors, cut straight down, not across, following the line of the toe.

clean between the toes with a cotton ball moistened in warm water, but if your dog is medium- or long-haired, a better option is to trim the hair between the toes and the pads.

Cutting the hair The best way to trim the hair is by using a pair of blunt-nosed scissors—the kind used to cut babies' fingernails. Hold up your dog's foot and separate the pads with one hand. Carefully trim the hair as close as possible to the pads.

If the hair on top of the foot is untidy, it can be slicked upward and trimmed carefully with the scissors, a little at a time, until it looks right.

pink line. If your dog has dark nails, finding the quick is trickier. Hold a flashlight up to the nail to see where the quick ends, then go by memory.

Be conservative in your cutting. You will be far away from the quick if you take off only the thin, curved nail tip. If you cut the quick, it will bleed and your dog will be reluctant to let you continue. Scrape the claw through softened soap to pack the bleeding

core, or sprinkle styptic powder over the claw to quickly stop any bleeding.

When you have finished cutting, smooth out any rough edges with a nail file. Also trim the dewclaws (a fifth digit on the inside of the leg).

Hairy toes Hair on your dog's feet traps moisture, dirt, mats, seeds and fleas—even snow and ice—and prevents air from circulating. You can

quick

recommended cut

CLEAN TEETH

An important, but often overlooked, part of your dog's daily grooming routine is the brushing of her teeth. Dogs need to have clean teeth in order to have fresh breath and a healthy canine smile. But there are also some very serious reasons for cleaning your dog's teeth regularly. Poor dental hygiene can lead to a number of diseases in the mouth, as well as infections in the major organs.

Dog toothbrush

Dog toothpaste

"Finger" toothbrush

Avoiding disease If your dog's teeth aren't brushed regularly, plaque builds up on her teeth and under her gums, just as it does in humans. If plaque is not removed, periodontal disease can develop. If untreated, this bacterial infection can transform into gingivitis and damage your dog's gums. Bacteria can also enter the bloodsteam

OPEN WIDE!
Brushing your dog's teeth is not as hard as you may think, particularly if you equip yourself with the specially designed tools shown here. You can also use a washcloth or gauze pad instead of a brush.

and spread to your dog's kidneys, liver, heart or brain. Other problems, such as mouth abscesses and loose teeth, can also develop in dogs that don't have good dental hygiene. And dogs with dirty teeth and periodontal disease will have very bad breath.

How often? One way to avoid these problems is to brush your dog's teeth. Most vets recommend brushing twice a week, although every day is preferable. Your dog's teeth should also be examined once a year by your vet, who may suggest professional cleaning.

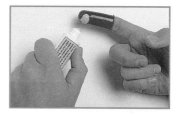

Getting her ready Ideally, you should get into the habit of brushing your dog's teeth when she is a puppy and eager to try new things. But if your older dog's not used to brushing, start out by putting a little beef broth, baby food or canned meat on your finger or a washcloth and rubbing the outer surfaces of her teeth. Once she starts anticipating her "treat," put some toothpaste (see below) on a toothbrush and let her lick it off.

What you need You can either use a piece of gauze wrapped around your finger, a "finger" toothbrush (a nubbly surfaced rubber cap that fits over your index finger) or a soft-bristled toothbrush designed especially for dogs.

Toothpaste You'll also need special dog toothpaste. Don't use human toothpastes—they contain detergents and other chemicals which, when swallowed, will upset your dog's stomach.

Because dogs can't rinse and spit, their toothpaste must be edible. The

better the toothpaste tastes, the more likely it is that your dog will sit still while you brush. The poultry and beef flavors offered in canine toothpastes are appealing to most dogs.

How to brush Start by getting your dog to sit or lie on her side. Lift her upper lip and, using a back-and-forth or circular motion, rub a couple of teeth at a time, taking care to brush where the tooth and gum meet. If she squirms, you may need a helper to gently restrain her.

Work your way around her upper jaw before starting on her lower. Concentrate on the outer surfaces; your dog's mouth is good at self-cleaning the inner side of her teeth.

Brushing doesn't need to last more than a minute, but if you don't have time, rub the outside of the upper teeth with a small towel once a day. This is where the salivary glands are, and where problems are likely to begin.

Relax! Don't be alarmed by a little blood on the bristles the first time you brush. This is normal when your dog's gums are not used to the attention. For more on oral hygiene, see pp. 176–77.

PEARLY BITES
If your dog is small, like this dachshund, pay close attention to her dental hygiene. A smaller mouth means less jawbone for the roots of the teeth. The roots are therefore more shallow, and the teeth less secure. Disease can quickly lead to tooth loss.

Regardless of your dog's size, be sure to clean the back teeth. These are the ones most prone to periodontal disease.

WHEN IT'S TIME FOR A BATH

Dogs don't need baths all that often—which is lucky, given most dogs' lack of enthusiasm for bathtime. But even the most fastidious dogs need regular baths and, depending on their coats, some dogs need them more often than others. Your dog's lifestyle and habits also dictate bathtime frequency. Try bathing at least twice a year, unless your nose and his coat demand more.

Organize the shampoo, towels, scissors and comb before bathing.

Naturally self-cleaning No dog should be bathed more than once a month, unless recommended by a vet. Dogs with thick double coats, such as Samoyeds, rarely need washing—regular brushing is enough to distribute the natural oils, get rid of dirt and loose hair, and prevent matting. Furthermore, the coats of many dogs, such

There are myriad types of shampoos available.

as Saint Bernards and Chesapeake Bay retrievers, have natural waterproofing properties that frequent bathing may damage. It may be best not to bathe these breeds at all. An alternative is to brush dry shampoo through the coat occasionally.

Wash away allergies Baths are necessary, however, when your dog is very dirty or when there is a medical problem, such as parasites, dandruff or infection. Bathing is the best way to remove the dander that causes allergic reactions, such as itching and sneez-

ing, in people and dogs. It will also rid his coat of other possible allergens such as pollens, molds and dust. Rinsing off your dog with clean, cool water will be especially soothing.

He hates baths! Even dogs who love to swim usually hate baths. This is because when your dog is swimming, he is in control. But being bathed is your idea, and you often place him in an environment that is unfamiliar—even scary—to him. There's also the risk of getting water splashed in his eyes and ears, which

142

he hates. (You'll notice that your dog doesn't usually stick his head under water when swimming.) But dogs that are trained early to take baths will often enjoy them. If you have a puppy, get him used to being bathed as soon as you can—and make it fun.

Choosing a shampoo There are enough types of dog shampoo to rival those for humans. An all-purpose shampoo might be acceptable, or you may decide to use another kind.

• Conditioning shampoos work like all-in-one shampoos for people, eliminating the additional step of conditioning. These make it relatively easy to comb through your dog's coat.

FIGHTING FLEAS
A bath will have this beagle's current crop of fleas jumping overboard. But while flea shampoos do kill fleas, most offer little residual protection—it's washed down the drain along with the shampoo. Unfortunately, you can really only regard bathtime as a fairly short-term solution against fleas.

• Oatmeal shampoo can soothe your dog's skin and help reduce itching.
• To combat hair dryness and to promote body, use a protein shampoo—especially if you plan to show him.
• Hypoallergenic shampoo is usually free of perfumes and dye. It is good for dogs who have shown skin sensitivity to other shampoos.
• Medicated shampoos are formulated to combat skin conditions, and should be used only on the recommendation of your vet.
• Flea-and-tick shampoo often contains insecticide, pyrethrin, that kills parasites on contact. However, some of the chemical may stay in the coat and be licked off, so rinse thoroughly.

The finishing touches While not essential, a conditioner can make brushing out a long-haired dog a little easier. Detanglers in particular will assist you if applied after shampooing. Oatmeal conditioner can also be combined with a detangling ingredient to soothe itchy skin.

BATHING TECHNIQUES

Bathtime will go much more smoothly if you're well-prepared. First, make sure you're not rushed. No matter how small your dog, a bath is not a 10-minute job. You must allow time for pre-bath brushing, the bath itself and the drying afterward. For long-haireds, the first and last steps take the most time.

Where to wash Choose a warm, draft-free area for the bath. Very small dogs can be washed in the kitchen sink, although the high sides of the laundry room utility sink will deter any escape plans. Besides, you might prefer dog hair in your laundry rather than in your kitchen.

A bathtub is fine for larger dogs if you use a rubber mat to prevent slipping. However, if you're thinking of bathing your dog frequently, you might consider buying a portable bathtub, available at pet supply stores or through mail order catalogs. Then you won't have to pull skeins of dog hair out of the bathtub drain.

During warm weather, it can be fun to wash him

DON'T FORGET FEET
If water and shampoo are left to dry between your dog's toes, his feet will feel itchy. Get your fingers between his toes to clean them thoroughly, and be fastidious about rinsing and drying there, too.

out in the yard under a hose. Make sure that you don't turn the hose up too strongly or you might scare him.

The brush-off Brush your dog thoroughly before bathing him. For short-haired dogs, brushing is useful because it removes dead hair and loosens dirt, making it easier to wash away. For other dogs, especially those with double coats, brushing is essential to remove any mats. If you can't get a comb all the way through your dog's coat, even around the face, don't get him wet. If you bathe him when his coat is matted, you will never get him clean. You'll also hurt him, since mats pull tighter when they dry, and you risk trapping moisture against his skin, which can cause skin problems. If you can't get the mats out, get a professional groomer to help.

Other preparations When you've finished brushing your dog, clip his nails, pull excess hair from his ears, if necessary, and clean his ears and eyes.

Suds up Getting a reluctant dog into the tub might be a two-person operation. Always use lukewarm, not hot, water—the temperature you'd use for a baby, or even a little cooler for hairy dogs that prefer cool temperatures, like huskies. Use a shampoo formulated for dogs, or a baby shampoo or gentle dishwashing liquid may work.

Wash well Lather your dog from top to toe, being careful to avoid getting soap in his ears or eyes. Massage the suds down to his skin. If your dog has a creased face, wrap a finger in a paper towel or use a cotton-tipped swab to clean the folds. If he has a beard and mustache, wash them free of accumulated food and saliva. A slicker brush pulled through his coat will also remove clumps of molted hair.

Rinse and dry Once the coat is well lathered, rinse him thoroughly—any shampoo left on his skin will irritate him. Apply a conditioner and rinse it off according to the manufacturer's

A PERFECT FIT
Washing your small dog in a bucket or sink will make it easier on your back and knees.

instructions. Then towel off as much water as possible before letting him out of the tub—the less water he has on his coat, the less water he'll shake all over you. Keep him in a warm room for a few hours until he is completely dry. Double-coated or long-haired dogs will also need to be blow-dried (see p. 131) to remove the residual water and to prevent their coats from matting.

HEALTH CARE

Making sure that your dog lives a long and healthy life means providing not only a well-balanced diet and plenty of exercise, but also good preventive health care. This program should begin at puppyhood and continue throughout your dog's lifetime. Learn to observe her behavior and vital signs and make sure she has a vaccination program tailored for her. And because your dog isn't always thinking about how to protect herself, she may at some time get hurt. If her injuries are minor, first aid will allow you to cope with them yourself. Ultimately, knowing what to do in an emergency situation can mean the difference between life and death.

PRACTICING PREVENTIVE CARE

There are some common diseases to which all dogs are susceptible. But vaccines will prevent your dog from contracting many of these illnesses—including rabies, parvovirus, distemper and Lyme disease. Combined with a monthly oral medication to prevent heartworm, these annual vaccinations are a vital investment in your dog's good health.

First visit After obtaining your pup, you should visit a vet as soon as possible. At the first visit, your vet will give your pup a physical examination, administer worming medication and set up a vaccination schedule.

A vaccination program Puppies are susceptible to several life-threatening, contagious diseases that are easily prevented through vaccination. Most vaccination programs start at about six to eight weeks of age. The vaccines continue every few weeks until your pup is 12 to 14 weeks old. They are

A TREAT FOR THE HEART
Heartworm prevention tablets can be fed to your dog like a chewy treat. This boxer has no idea he's taking medicine.

One of the most important things you can do for your dog's health care is to find a vet who suits you—and your dog. Ask your dog-owning friends to recommend a veterinarian or call your local humane society for a referral. The vet should be able to discuss all the issues on a level you fully understand. She or he should also make you feel comfortable about asking questions.

given several times because most pups carry antibodies from their mothers that may interfere with their ability to develop their own protection.

Regular checkups Your pup should also have a dental checkup at six months to make sure his permanent teeth are coming in properly, then another examination and his booster vaccinations when he is one year old. Most vaccines are boosted annually.

What is needed Vaccinations against diseases such as distemper, parvovirus (an intestinal viral disease), parainfluenza, canine hepatitis and rabies (if you're in North America) are obligatory and many are given in a single injection. Depending on your location and your dog's lifestyle, your vet may also recommend vaccines for leptospirosis, a bacterial disease of the liver and kidneys, Lyme disease, a tick-transmitted disease that affects

many body systems, and coronavirus, another intestinal viral disease. An intranasal kennel cough vaccine is often given to dogs who are going to be housed with other dogs, either at dog shows or in boarding kennels.

Heartworm It is easy to prevent this potentially fatal infection, transmitted by mosquitoes. Before starting your dog on a heartworm prevention plan, your vet will run a blood test to make sure he's not already infected. The drug is usually given monthly and comes with additional benefits—some drugs help control parasites such as roundworms, hookworms and whipworms.

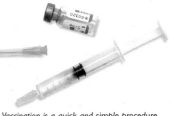

Vaccination is a quick and simple procedure.

A GUIDE TO HOME CARE

The best way to keep your dog healthy is to notice the first signs of a problem before it becomes serious. The best way to do this is to give her a complete once-over every week. Once you know what to look for, you'll know right away whether you need to be concerned. Never hesitate to seek your vet's help if you need it.

This collie-cattle dog mix sits quietly while her breathing is checked.

Regular checkup Dogs are more stoic than people, and they can't tell us when they're sick. That's why home checkups are so important. Of course, your vet can find problems too—but she or he only sees your dog a couple of times a year, and a lot can go wrong in between. Besides, no one knows your dog better than you. If you give her a 5–10 minute checkup every week, little will go by unnoticed.

Lungs The best way to check your dog's respiratory health is to use your ears. At rest her breathing should be fairly slow, steady and quiet; about 20 to 30 breaths a minute. Wait until she is lounging calmly or sleeping and listen to her chest. Counting the rise and fall of her chest as one breath, calculate how many breaths she takes in a minute. If she seems breathless or her breathing is rapid while she's resting, have her checked by the vet.

CHECKING HEART RATE
To take your dog's pulse, gently place your fingers (not your thumb; it has its own pulse) on the femoral artery in the inside of her thigh. Using gentle pressure, count the number of beats in 15 seconds, then multiply the number by four to get the total beats per minute.

Conditions such as allergies and heart disease can cause changes in breathing. If she becomes exhausted after normal exercise and pants excessively, she may have a respiratory illness.

Healthy heart A dog's normal heart rate is between 60 and 150 beats per minute. Generally, larger dogs have a slower heart rate than smaller dogs. Ask your vet what the normal rate is for your dog.

Check the pulse on the inside of her hind leg. It should feel strong and be within the normal range. If it's weak, rapid or erratic, she may have a heart problem.

Fluid levels Dogs that get dehydrated (perhaps from overheating, or from an internal problem such as kidney disease) can go into shock—a real emergency. To check for dehydration, take some skin over your dog's shoulder, then gently pinch it before releasing. If she has enough fluids, her skin will snap back into position in a sec-

ond or two. If she is dehydrated, her skin will "tent" and take longer to slip back. Offer your dog some fresh water, and get her checked by the vet.

Circulation Healthy circulation ensures your dog's heart is pumping blood and nutrients to all her tissues. To check her circulation, lift up her lip and press firmly, but gently, on the gum above her canine tooth. When you stop pressing, there should be a pale spot that becomes pink again within two seconds. If it remains pale for longer than this, your dog has a problem that needs prompt attention.

Temperature Your dog's normal body temperature is between 99.5° and 102°F (37.5–39°C). To take her temperature, put lubricating jelly on the tip of a rectal thermometer and twirl it about 2 inches (5 cm) into her rectum. Don't let go of the thermometer. After two minutes, remove it and read it. Anything over 104°F (40°C) is abnormal and rates medical attention.

THE HEALTHY DOG

Check over your dog on a regular basis. Start by looking at his ears, then move on to his eyes, nose, mouth, body, legs, tail and paws. The exams only take a few minutes, and he'll enjoy the attention.

Warning signs Always consult your vet if something in your home health exam doesn't seem right to you, or if you notice any of the following signs:
• Loss of appetite for more than a day.
• Difficulty eating or mouth pain.
• Sudden weight loss or weight gain.
• Prolonged, gradual weight loss.
• Fever.
• Pain.
• Vomiting more than three times in a day. If the vomit is bloody or dark, call the vet immediately.
• Change in bowel habits and/or stool consistency for more than a day.
• Coughing or labored breathing.
• Sneezing for more than a day.
• Excessive thirst for more than a day.

• Increased urination, sudden incontinence, difficulty urinating (straining), bloody urine or decreased urination.
• Excessive salivation.
• Behavior changes, such as sluggishness or unwillingness to exercise, for more than a day.
• Excessive itching or scratching, including ear-rubbing or head-shaking.
• Lameness that does not improve within a day.
• Seizures or convulsions.
• Eye discharge for more than a day. If your dog is squinting or showing any other signs of irritation, discomfort or pain, take him to the vet immediately.

Nothing to worry about Dogs have some special features which may at first seem peculiar or even alarming. But there's no need to panic if you spot the following:
•Third eyelid: This clears debris from the eye surface and produces some of the eye's lubricating tears.
• Stud tail: Some unneutered males develop a oval, hairless and sometimes scaly or oily patch at their tail base. It's usually harmless, but seek advice if it becomes irritated or infected.
• Penis: Males are always semi-erect due to a bone, the os penis. When erect, a large lump at the base will be visible. It looks odd, but it's normal.

ANUS
Clean, dry and lump-free; no irritation; anal sacs unswollen; fur unmatted; parasite-free.

SKIN
Smooth, clean, dry, pliable, odorless; parasite-free. Colored black, brown, pink or spotted, depending on breed.

EARS
Pink, smooth, glossy, odorless; slightly oily.

NOSE
Cool and moist; free of discharge; not crusty or cracked; no loss of pigmentation.

TEETH
White; no buildup of tartar; no broken or missing teeth.

GUMS AND TONGUE
Bright pink (or tinged with black, depending on breed); moist; never bleeding; no lumps.

EYES
Clear and bright; the pupils equal size; membranes a healthy pink.

BODY
Pain-free; no rigidity or hunching.

COAT
Clean, shiny, unmatted; no excessive shedding; no bald spots.

RIBS
Not too prominent; nor covered with thick padding of fat.

ABDOMEN
A pot belly is normal in a fat dog, but not when dog is underweight.

FEET
No mats, sores or debris between toes.

PADS
No cuts or blisters.

NAILS
Trimmed; just touching the ground.

BREATH
Inoffensive.

BREATHING
Quiet, regular and comfortable. Should pant only when hot, excited or stressed.

LIMBS
Supple; pain-free; no swelling, lumps or sores.

GIVING MEDICINES

Your dog may occasionally need some medication to treat a health problem. Although some drugs are administered as injections by your vet, most will need to be given at home. Always give medications gently and properly—not only to ensure that your dog gets better, but to prevent her from becoming "head shy."

GIVING PILLS

Put the pill between your forefinger and thumb and use your other fingers to push down the lower jaw. Place it in the center of the tongue, as far back as you can.

Hold your dog's mouth shut until she licks her nose—this indicates that she has swallowed. If she's reluctant to swallow, massage her throat to encourage her.

Popping pills Many common health problems respond readily to medication, which may be supplied to you in the form of a pill or liquid. It's important that your dog takes any medication exactly as your vet has prescribed and that the entire prescription is used, even when it's obvious she's feeling a lot better after just a few doses.

How to do it There's no point telling your dog to swallow a pill because it's going to be good for her, however. Dogs don't like being forced to swallow things, so whenever possible, take the easy way out. If your dog has an appetite, try hiding the pill in cream cheese, peanut butter or even a cocktail weenie. But if she's off her food, gently maneuver her into a corner and have her sit up. Point her nose toward the ceiling and follow the procedure as illustrated (left). Most vets follow the pill with two fingers to initiate a gag response and a swallow from the dog, but you might feel more comfortable just closing her mouth. Watch her closely until you're sure the pill has gone down—many dogs will fake a swallow and spit the medicine out when no one's looking.

If your dog is in obvious distress and won't let you handle her muzzle, take her to the vet. It's not worth risking a bite on the hand.

Pouring liquids Since dogs aren't adept at using spoons, you will need a syringe or a dropper to administer liquid medicines and avoid spills. Tip your dog's nose up, with your hand steadying her muzzle. Don't

give the medicine too quickly, or give her too much at a time, because she may breathe it into her lungs.

Eye care Before you try to administer eye drops, enlist a friend's help to hold your dog still and calm her. Pick up your dog's chin so her nose points to the ceiling. (She will automatically look down to protect the cornea.) Gently roll the upper eyelid back and squirt a drop of medication on the surface of her eye. If you're

GIVING A LIQUID MEDICINE
Use a dropper or needleless syringe to draw up the correct dose of medicine. Insert the end of the dropper or syringe in the side of your dog's mouth and gently squeeze in the liquid. Work slowly, giving her plenty of time to swallow.

using ointment, squeeze a quarter-inch (about 6 mm) line directly onto her eye. Massage both eyelids gently together to spread the ointment over the eye surface.

If you are alone and your dog is resistant to the medication, make her sit, then kneel beside her. Extend your arm gently around her neck as if you're going to apply a headlock. Cup her chin in the palm of your hand and point her nose to the ceiling. Use your other hand to apply the drops or ointment.

Ear drops To administer ear drops, put your dog into the "sit" or "down" position and kneel beside her. Pull up her ear flap and hold on firmly to prevent your dog from shaking her head. Then squeeze the required number of drops directly into the ear canal. Fold her ear flap over and massage the base of the ear gently to work the drops into all the nooks and crannies that can harbor infections.

FIRST AID

For minor injuries and ailments, treating your dog at home is not only less expensive and more convenient—he'll be a lot less stressed if it's you treating his cuts and scrapes rather than a stranger in a vet's office. And if your dog is ever seriously ill or injured, first aid is vital to stabilize him before rushing him to a vet.

First-aid kit You will use the contents of your first-aid kit for routine care, such as cleaning your dog's ears, as well as any unexpected mishaps. Don't wait until after an accident has happened to prepare a first-aid kit. It should include:

• Vital Information Card. This should list the name and phone number of your vet; the phone number, address and travel directions to the nearest emergency pet clinic; and the phone number of the local poison control office or the National Animal Poison Control Center.

• First-aid manual

VITAL INFORMATION CARD
Vet name and phone •

Emergency pet clinic phone •
address and travel directions to clinic

Veterinary poison control hotline phone •

USE HOT   USE COLD

SOFT
HOT/COLD PACK
RECHARGEABLE-REUSABLE

• Chemical ice packs and hot packs
• Pantyhose, a necktie or long strip of stretchable gauze (to make a muzzle)
• Blunt-tipped scissors and tweezers
• Rubbing alcohol
• Eyewash (such as contact lens solution)
• Antibiotic ointment or powder
• Milk of magnesia (give if your dog swallows a caustic poison)
• Hydrogen peroxide (to induce vomiting)
• Syrup of Ipecac (also to induce vomiting)
• Soap
• Petroleum jelly
• Antiseptic wash
• Cotton balls
• Needle-nose pliers

- Large, needleless syringe (for giving liquid medications)
- Rectal thermometer
- Bandaging materials: 1–2-inch (2.5–5 cm) stretchable and nonstretchable gauze rolls; and gauze pads in varying sizes
- Packing tape (for taping a broken leg to a firm surface)
- Beach towel, blanket or heavy cardboard (to use as a stretcher)

Wound care Minor scrapes and cuts can be treated at home. Clean the wound very gently, using sterile pads and warm, soapy water. Once it is clean, rinse off all traces of soap and dry it with sterile gauze. (Dry the surrounding hair with a clean towel.) Apply an antibiotic ointment twice a day until the wound heals. If there are any signs of infection, such as redness, swelling, discharge or a bad odor, take your dog to the vet.

If the wound is likely to get dirty, cover it with a sterile gauze pad and wrap it with a gauze roll, taping the end to the layer below. Then wrap it with bandaging cloth. Change the bandage every second day, more often if it gets wet or dirty.

1 A dog in pain may bite out of fear. A muzzle will allow you to help him without being bitten. First, tie a loose knot in the material to create a large loop. Then slip the loop over your dog's nose.

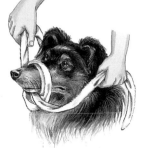

2 Pull the loop about halfway up and draw it tight. Make sure his nostrils are left free so that he can breathe. Then bring the ends of the loop down and pass them under his chin.

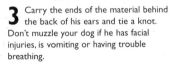

3 Carry the ends of the material behind the back of his ears and tie a knot. Don't muzzle your dog if he has facial injuries, is vomiting or having trouble breathing.

IN AN EMERGENCY

Dogs are lively, curious and adventurous creatures who can get themselves into all sorts of trouble. Knowing how to recognize and react to common emergencies may save your dog's life. But remember, you are not an expert. Your goal should be to prevent further injury and to minimize pain and distress while seeking immediate veterinary care.

MOVING A LARGE DOG
Try to move your dog as one unit. Lifting him as little a possible, slide a firm surface under him. Any sudden moves could worsen fractures, speed internal bleeding or cause paralysis. Bind him to the surface using tape, towels or a coat.

MOVING A SMALL DOG
Carefully lift your dog with both hands to support his whole body. Try to let any fractured limbs dangle. Talk to him throughout the move to reassure him.

Car accidents First muzzle your dog, then check that he is breathing and has a heartbeat. Grasp the fur along his spine with both hands and drag him out of the traffic. Start CPR as necessary (see pp. 160–61) and stop the bleeding. Then place him on a flat surface and take him to a vet.

Heatstroke On hot days, excessive exercise can lead to heatstroke, but it usually occurs when dogs are left in parked cars. Brain damage or death may follow if your dog's temperature is not lowered immediately. See pp. 110–11 for advice on treatment.

Bleeding Always act quickly if your dog is bleeding, especially if the blood is spurting from a wound. This generally indicates a cut artery, which bleeds more rapidly and causes heavier blood loss than a cut vein. Press firmly on the wound with some sterile

Stop the bleeding by applying pressure directly to the wound. Keep pressing firmly until the bleeding stops.

gauze or a clean cloth. If blood soaks through, don't pull off the gauze because this will disturb the clot that has begun to form. Just add more padding to the area. When the bleeding stops, remove the padding and use clean material to bandage the wound.

Pressure points If the bleeding hasn't stopped after five minutes of applying direct pressure, try clamping down on the artery that supplies blood to that area. There are five main pressure points on your dog's body (see illustration, bottom right). If bleeding continues, let up on the pressure slightly for a few seconds every few minutes. While you want to stop the bleeding, you must allow some blood flow to the area so that healthy tissues aren't damaged by being deprived of their blood supply.

If the bleeding continues en route to the vet, or for another 10 minutes, apply a tourniquet as an absolute last resort. Loosen it at five-minute intervals for a few seconds so that blood can circulate.

Poisoning Suspect poisoning if your dog has trouble breathing, has a slow or fast heartbeat, drools or foams at the mouth and lips, is bleeding from the nose, mouth or anus, is behaving erratically, has seizures or is unconscious.

You should consider making your dog vomit. But sometimes it's not safe to induce vomiting—for example, if he's eaten a caustic substance that will burn his esophagus on the way back up. If this is the case—or if he's having trouble breathing, is having seizures, has a slow pulse, has a bloated abdomen, is unconscious, or the product label says not to—take him straight to the vet.

If you think it's safe to induce vomiting, syringe hydrogen peroxide into his mouth: one teaspoon for every 10 pounds (4.5 kg) of body weight. If this doesn't work, give him the same again in 15 or 20 minutes, en route to the vet. Take the tin or label of whatever he's eaten with you.

Upper inside of front legs

Underside of tail

Upper inside of hind legs

PRESSURE POINTS

159

RESUSCITATING A DOG

In the event of an accident, immediate action may be required. Recognizing the problem, then carrying out the solutions quickly and efficiently, are the most important factors in helping ensure that an emergency has a happy ending for your dog.

Life-saving CPR If you know cardiopulmonary resuscitation (CPR), there's a good chance that you can breathe life back into your dog and restart his heart after an accident.

If your dog is unconscious and is not breathing and/or has no heartbeat, administer CPR and call your vet as soon as possible. If, after about five minutes, your dog has not received enough oxygen, he could suffer irreversible brain damage.

CARDIAC MASSAGE
Lie your dog on his right side on a hard surface. Place the heel of your right hand on the ribs over his heart (behind the elbow). Place your left hand over your right and push down with enough force that you press the chest halfway to the ground. Compress 15 times, then breathe into his nose twice. Repeat the process. Ideally, you should compress the heart 80 to 100 times a minute. Count steadily out loud, "One and two and three and four."

A DROWNED DOG
Clear any discharge from his nose and mouth. Then gently swing him back and forth to drain the water from his lungs. If he's too heavy, rest his front legs on the ground as you swing him. If he's not breathing and has no pulse, give CPR and get him to a vet.

MOUTH-TO-NOSE-RESUSCITATION
STEP 1
Lie him on his side and open his airway by swiping the back of his throat with your index and middle fingers. Remove blood, vomit, saliva or any foreign bodies from his mouth. Extend his head back and pull his tongue forward. Also check that his nostrils are unobstructed.

STEP 2
If he's unconscious, hold his mouth closed, place your mouth over his nostrils and blow into them four times with enough force that his chest rises. If your dog is small, place your mouth over both his mouth and nose.

STEP 3
Pause to allow air to exit his lungs, then continue blowing. You should be able to feel resistance and hear air entering his lungs as you blow. Keep blowing until he resumes normal breathing.

How to do CPR Since the three rules of CPR are airway, breathing and circulation, you will need to combine cardiac massage and mouth-to-nose resuscitation. Check the illustrations.

You should continue giving CPR while someone drives you to the vet. If you're not able to get to the vet, continue CPR until your dog is breathing on his own, or for at least 20 minutes.

Choking A choking dog may breathe very loudly, cough, become anxious or gasp for air. If he's light enough to lift off the ground, wrap your arms around him at his groin, just in front of his hind legs. Lift him into the air upside down and shake him to dislodge the object. If your dog is heavier, lift his back legs off the ground as if he were a wheelbarrow, then give him a good shake. If the object has slipped too far down, perform the Heimlich maneuver. Grab him around his belly, just under his rib cage, and give one quick, forceful squeeze. The object will usually be expelled.

HEALTH PROBLEMS

Your dog may seem to be remarkably resilient, but you can't expect him to spend his entire life in perfect health. From coughs to worms to weight problems, he is vulnerable to a variety of health complaints. No one knows your dog as well as you do, so be aware of early signs of disease and seek veterinary advice at the first opportunity. More conditions can be treated at home with lifestyle changes, like altering diets or increasing exercise, and the sooner you tackle any problem, the better. By working closely with your veterinarian, you'll be able to ensure that your dog has the best life possible, no matter what his age or stage of life. Remember, he depends on you.

AGING

Apart from the giant breeds, a dog that is well cared-for can be expected to live for about 12 years. But as dogs age they become more susceptible to a number of health problems. The effects can be minimized by taking a little extra care and being sensitive to your dog's changing needs.

Signs of aging While some health problems are an inevitable part of aging, others are actually illnesses that can be successfully treated. Contact your vet if you notice a loss of energy or appetite; increased thirst and urination; discharges; sores that won't heal; weight changes; abnormal odors; lumps on the skin; and coughing or sneezing.

Arthritis Degenerative joint disease is one of the more common and potentially crippling effects of old age. However, many new medications

ELDER STATESMAN
Your dog may experience problems similar to those caused by senility in people. He may forget his training, or his responses may be slower. New drugs and a retraining program can improve his quality of life.

seem to slow degeneration as well as reduce pain. You can also make your dog comfortable by covering slippery floors with mats and raising his food bowls so that he doesn't have to bend. For more information, see pp. 178–79.

Kidney failure A common disease of older dogs, kidney failure can cause increased urination and increased thirst. A low-protein diet, adequate fluids and good overall care will slow its progression and prolong his life.

Your dog may become incontinent as he ages. Frequent toilet trips could ease the problem, or if it's a case of lost muscle tone, drug therapy may help. Get your vet to check that there isn't a more serious underlying cause.

Dental disease Bacteria introduced to his body through tooth and gum decay can lead to heart, liver and kidney problems. Decay can also make eating painful. Clean his teeth every day (see pp. 140–41) and ask your vet to give him regular deep cleanings.

Diabetes Age-related diabetes can't be cured. But it can be treated if you give him his insulin or oral medications, feed him at the same time every day, and keep his stress levels to a minimum. This requires commitment, but isn't your friend worth it?

Eye disease Older dogs are susceptible to cataracts and progressive retinal atrophy. Contact your vet if you notice changes in the color of your dog's eyes. The cloudiness may be due to nuclear sclerosis, a hardening of the lens protein which, unlike cataracts, won't impair your dog's vision. But if his eyesight is fading, help him by changing his environment as little as possible.

Diet Your dog's metabolism will slow down, so watch his diet. Most older dogs need fewer calories and less protein, but more fiber. A blend of antioxidants containing vitamins A, C and E, combined with fish oil supple-

Cataracts are a common problem in older dogs.

ments, can combat some of the deterioration aging can bring. Check with your vet about dietary requirements if your old dog is under treatment for a specific disorder.

Exercise Gentle daily walks will not only keep his joints mobile and supple—they'll help avoid weight gain and constipation. Exercise also gives your dog something to look forward to, keeping him fit, bright and happy.

COUGHING AND SNEEZING

All dogs cough and sneeze occasionally, but when the odd "eck" becomes hacking, you can assume your dog has a serious respiratory disorder. Conditions such as kennel cough rarely last long, but other coughs may be more serious. If the problem is frequent or persists for more than two days, visit your vet.

Kennel cough Any coughing that appears suddenly in a healthy dog may be due to kennel cough, an upper respiratory tract infection caused by a number of agents including parainfluenza or bordetellosis. The canine equivalent of our cold, it's most common in younger dogs, although older dogs can get it too. Because it's highly contagious, dogs have a higher risk of catching it when they've been in close confinement with other dogs.

A typical kennel cough looks and sounds like gagging, and often brings up a small amount of phlegm. It's rarely serious, but get it checked by a vet if it persists to ensure nothing more serious goes untreated.

Easing symptoms To ease her discomfort, give your dog some juice from an Asian fruit called loquat. Available from health food stores, loquat is rich in Vitamin A, which boosts immunity and strengthens the mucous membranes of the respiratory tract.

A humidifier or vaporizer near her bed will also

EASE OFF ON EXERCISE
While your dog has a cough, her usual collar or choke chain may be uncomfortable and irritate her sore throat, making her want to cough even more. When taking your dog for some gentle exercise, you may prefer to use the type of harness this German shepherd mix is wearing.

fill her airways with soothing moisture, helping her to get some rest. And if your dog eats dry food, moisten it with a little water so it isn't painful to swallow. Also encourage her to drink (see p. 125) to keep her throat moist.

Medicinal relief In mild cases, kennel coughs can be eased with human cough suppressants such as Robitussin. Ask your vet about the correct dosage. Avoid medicines containing acetaminophen, which can be dangerous for dogs. A vaccination against parainfluenza can also be given annually as a standard inclusion in your dog's vaccine schedule.

Older dogs Coughing can occur in older dogs of all breeds, but it is a particular problem for diminutive dogs whose tiny airways are easily blocked. Airways in aged

GASPING FOR BREATH
Some toy dogs, such as this Yorkshire terrier, may cough due to an inherited defect of the windpipe.

lungs can begin to produce too much mucus, and bronchitis often develops. Medications can soothe, if not cure, the problem.

Genetic conditions Young toy dogs frequently cough because of a collapsing trachea, an inherited defect of the windpipe. In severe cases surgery may be necessary to correct the defect.

Heart failure Coughing can signal more serious illnesses, such as asthma, pneumonia or even heart disease. If your dog is coughing constantly, having trouble breathing or has lost her appetite, take her to the vet immediately. When the heart no longer pumps efficiently, fluid builds up in the lungs. Persistent coughing, especially at night or in the morning, may be caused by a failing heart. The cough from heart disease is lower and quieter than kennel cough.

Worms Coughing may indicate an advanced heartworm infection. For more about worms, see pp. 174–75.

Sneezing Persistent sneezing could be due to allergies, but when accompanied by thick, discolored nasal discharge it signals an infection. If your dog has foul-smelling, pus-like discharge from one nostril, she may have breathed in a foreign body or have a nasal tumor. Check by holding a mirror under her nostrils. If the misting on the mirror is uneven, you will need to get your vet to clean out the nasal passages. But you don't need to worry about "reverse sneezing." It sounds like a prolonged, repetitive snort—and it's entirely normal.

EARS

Your dog's ears are intricate and sensitive organs. They are able to hear sounds at frequencies up to three times higher than we can. Since her ears also contain her balance-control center, even minor problems can be very uncomfortable. Without treatment, ear infections can lead to deafness or the need for major surgery.

Think pink Fortunately, most ear problems are easy to detect in their earliest stages. Healthy ears should be pink, smooth, glossy and odorless, with a slight sheen of oil. Reddened tissue inside the ear, or a black, yellow, green or bloody buildup or discharge are signs of infection. Bad smells also signal trouble brewing. On the other hand, a dark, waxy buildup probably just means her ears are dirty. For more about cleaning the ears, see pp. 136–137. Even if you can't see what's wrong, you should suspect

Ear infections thrive in moist, warm, floppy ears.

problems if your dog is frequently scratching or shaking her head, or if her ears seem unusually tender. If she has a head tilt or seems dizzy or deaf, seek help immediately to prevent permanent damage.

Mites Your dog's ears can trap mites: white, crab-like parasites that feed on wax, skin flakes and other debris and produce intense itching. While difficult to see, they leave a visible—and abundant—brown crusty discharge which can be flushed out with a proprietary ear cleaner available from your vet. Soak cotton balls or a gauze pad with the cleaner and gently squeeze it into the ear canal. Use the cleaner once a week for the next few weeks.

However, medicated ear drops will be required to kill all the mites. It can typically take four to six weeks of persistent treatment to cover the mites' entire life cycle. (For instructions on administering ear drops, see below.) An insecticidal shampoo will also be needed to kill mites on the body surface. Other pets will have to be treated to reduce the risk of reinfestation.

Infections Your dog may be prone to bacterial or yeast infections, especially if she has floppy ears or small ear canals, moist hairy ears, problems such as aller-

gies, food intolerance or a hormonal imbalance such as seborrhea (excessive oil secretion). Maintain ear hygiene (see pp. 136–137) and check ears regularly for foreign objects such as burrs and grass seeds. Excessive cleaning efforts and hair plucking can actually increase the odds of her getting an infection, so take care.

Infections should be treated with an antibiotic ointment or lotion available from your vet. To increase the effectiveness of the medication, clean the ears thoroughly before applying. Stand back when she shakes out the excess to avoid getting splattered.

Hematomas Soft swellings on the ear flap formed when small blood vessels rupture, hema-

tomas are common in older dogs. Possibly caused by excessive head shaking, they require immediate treatment to avoid needless pain and deformity.

Ear flap injuries When cut or torn, an ear flap will bleed profusely. To encourage clotting, apply firm pressure to the wound or bind the ear to the head. Stitches may be needed, so take your dog to the vet as soon as possible.

COUNT THE DROPS
Hold the ear flap firmly and squeeze out the required number of drops. Let them run down the underside of the ear flap.

MASSAGE THEM IN
Still holding the flap, massage the ointment into the ear canal. Inflammation in this area can make massage painful, so be gentle.

EYES

Common eye conditions produce discharge, redness and pain—usually signaled by tearing, squinting and holding the eye closed. However, the eyes are surprisingly sturdy and will usually recover as long as the problem is treated quickly. Some problems, however, are genetic and may need surgery.

This Pembroke Welsh corgi has bright, clear eyes— the very picture of good health.

Conjunctivitis The most common cause of eye discharge and redness, conjunctivitis causes the lining of the eyelid to become red and itchy. The discharge may be clear or yellow, thin or thick. It can be caused by allergies, irritants such as cigarette smoke, or bacterial or viral infections. Sometimes the inflammation leads to blockage of the tear ducts, causing tears to flow over the lid and onto the face.

Conjunctivitis is easily treated with ointments or drops from your vet. To clean the discharge from your dog's eyes, wipe the corner of each with a cotton ball soaked in warm water.

"Dry eye" Redness and thick pus are seen in dogs unable to produce enough tears. Known as "dry eye," the problem can lead to permanent corneal damage and loss of vision if untreated. Medication can keep the eyes moist. Surgery, involving the redirection of one of the salivary ducts, is another possible solution.

Glaucoma A red, bloodshot eye, accompanied by pain and discharge, may also signal glaucoma. The disease is caused by increased pressure within the eye. Since it can rapidly lead to blindness, the condition requires immediate treatment.

Cataracts Opacities of the lens make the center of the eye look white. They may be congenital in certain

SOOTHING SORE EYES
When there's debris in the eye, flush it out with a saline solution. (See p. 155 to learn how.) You can also use artificial tears.

breeds, or they may develop with age, and are often caused by diabetes. If cataracts grow large, they can obstruct vision and may need to be removed by a specialist. However, some cloudiness of the lens is a natural part of aging. Called nuclear sclerosis, or hardening of the lens, it doesn't significantly interfere with a dog's vision.

Retinal disease Progressive retinal atrophy is a genetic disease affecting many breeds. The first symptom may be impaired night vision—sadly, total blindness eventuates. There is no treatment, but you can make your dog's life easier by leaving objects where he'll remember them and by protecting him from trouble spots, such as stairways.

Corneal injuries Cat's claws and tree branches often cause corneal injuries. You should suspect such an injury if your dog holds an eye closed, tears excessively and seems sensitive to light. If left untreated, the damaged area can become infected and ulcerated, resulting in blindness. To prevent injury, don't let your dog stick his head out the car window when going for a drive. Long-haired breeds will also benefit from having hair trimmed or pulled away from their face.

Eyelid abnormalities Inherited abnormalities of the eyelids can also lead to corneal damage. Some dogs

may have eyelids that roll abnormally in or out, or have eyelashes that grow toward the eye. Most of these problems are easily corrected by surgery and should be attended to immediately to alleviate pain and scarring.

APPLYING OINTMENTS
Ointments are often prescribed to fight infections. Spread it over the eyeball by gently massaging the eyelids together.

GASTROINTESTINAL PROBLEMS

All dogs vomit and get diarrhea during their lives, and some breeds are more gassy than others. These problems are mostly minor and have commonsense solutions. Maintaining a steady diet, introducing new foods gradually, and keeping water sources clean, trash cans tightly closed and food refrigerated will help prevent upsets. But some gastrointestinal problems are more serious and require professional attention.

Diarrhea Simple diarrhea can be treated by resting the intestines. Fast your dog for 24 hours, but provide water or warm broth to prevent dehydration. Once the diarrhea stops, feed tiny amounts of an easily digestible diet—white rice mixed with boiled chicken—every four hours. Over the next few days, mix in his regular food.

If the diarrhea doesn't improve within a day, or is bloody, explosive or painful, collect a stool sample and see your vet. Severe diarrhea could signal intestinal parasites, viral diseases, ulcers, inflammatory bowel disease, food allergies, digestive disorders, kidney and liver disease and cancer. Even changes in routine can give a nervous dog diarrhea.

Vomiting Like diarrhea, a change in diet or a snack stolen from the trash can cause your dog to vomit. He may also vomit after feasting on grass, a

Diarrhea may be due to infection, or a dog eating something he shouldn't—like yesterday's trash.

favorite delicacy. He may eat it regularly, or he might graze to induce vomiting when he's not feeling well.

How to help As with diarrhea, the best way to settle his stomach is to fast him for 24 hours. Give him small amounts of water or ice to lick so that he doesn't drink too fast and vomit again. Begin feeding him bland food, gradually mixing it with his usual fare.

FIGHTING CONSTIPATION
Cooked vegetables and other high fiber food such as canned pumpkin, beans and green beans can both prevent and treat constipation. Daily exercise will also help this condition.

When to worry If his vomiting contains blood, if he continues in spite of being fasted, or if he looks generally unwell, visit your vet right away. Persistent vomiting may indicate poisoning, inflammation of the pancreas, intestinal obstruction, kidney or liver failure or infectious diseases (such as distemper). Continuous dry retching accompanied by heavy panting is a symptom of a true emergency—bloat.

Bloat This syndrome is most common in large, deep-chested dogs such as Great Danes. The stomach becomes distended with air, then may rotate so that air cannot escape in either direction. If not treated immediately with decompression and surgery, bloat can lead to shock and death. To avoid bloat, feed several small meals a day instead of one large one and restrict exercise before and after meals.

Flatulence Unlike bloat, gas is not life-threatening—although it can make life uncomfortable. Feed your dog

Putting a large rock in his food bowl will make him eat more slowly and swallow less air.

smaller meals, change his diet gradually and keep a lid on the trash. If your dog is very flatulent, try reducing soy-based and dairy products, cauliflower and broccoli and see if it improves. Adding activated charcoal to his meals may help, or try giving him digestive enzymes, available from vets—better digested food means better-smelling air. The acidophilus in live-culture yogurt can also bring beneficial intestinal bacteria (which aids in digestion) back up to healthful levels.

FIGHTING FLEAS AND WORMS

Small, flat, hopping insects, fleas are by far the most common skin parasites that plague dogs. Their bites lead to itching, chewing and scratching, most notably at the base of the tail. Dogs may also get tapeworms from ingesting fleas. Happily, treatments are on hand to combat infestations of both kinds of parasite.

What to look for In addition to tapeworm infection, fleas can transmit typhus and tularemia to your dog. Allergies to flea saliva can also cause severe itching. Check for fleas whenever your dog shows persistent scratching, using either a fine-toothed flea comb or your fingers. Pay attention to problem areas such as behind your dog's ears, on her rump or between her hindlegs. Also look for coarse, black "flea dirt" (a mix of flea feces and digested blood) in the coat. If your dog is black you may find it tricky to spot the evidence, but it's worth persevering.

Treatment Because fleas live both on and off your dog at different stages of their life cycle, eradication can be difficult. Effective treatment requires that you rid fleas and their larvae not only from your dog and other pets, but also from your house and yard. Start by bathing all your furry pets with flea shampoo. When the fur is dry, use a flea comb to pick up any stragglers.

You can also apply a spray or powder to your dog's coat, while medications such as Frontline, applied to her skin once a month, and Program, a monthly pill, also help.

Launder your pets' bedding in hot water and thoroughly vacuum your house, discarding the bag afterward. You should also use an insect growth regulator (which acts like birth control for fleas) in your house and yard, particularly shady places in the garden. Woodpiles and overgrown weeds also provide safe havens for fleas, so even mowing your yard will make it less hospitable for them.

Fine-toothed combs will remove fleas and their eggs.

UP CLOSE AND PERSONAL

Intestinal worms are very common—most puppies are born with worms or get them from close contact with their mother. Adult worms can sometimes be seen in your dog's feces, but your vet may need to do a microscopic examination of the feces to see if your dog is infected with a particular variety of worm.

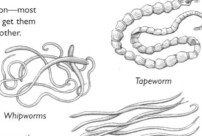

Tapeworm

Whipworms

Roundworms

Other parasites Worms are easily passed from dog to dog. Your dog may catch worms from exercising in places where worms thrive, such as public parks, which are contaminated by the stools of infected animals. She's also at risk if she's in the habit of eating rabbits, mice or other rodents, which carry tapeworm. Fleas are also carriers.

Worm infections place great strain on your dog's immune system. They can cause diarrhea, anemia, vomiting, dehydration and weight loss. In large numbers they will make your dog's coat look dull and give her a pot belly. Worms can also be itchy, and if infec-ted, your dog may scoot on her rear to get relief. Worst of all, they can be spread to people, with unpleasant and sometimes dangerous consequences.

The evidence It's a lot easier—and healthier—to treat worms before they have a chance to get established in your dog's body. Start treatment when she's a puppy—medication is often given at the time of her vaccinations. Also check her stools every other day. Tapeworm resembles short grains of white rice (you'll also see them around her anus); roundworms look like spaghetti. But whipworms, hookworms and other parasites can only be detected with a microscope, so it's worth taking your vet a stool sample or using a monthly broad-spectrum wormer.

Maintain hygiene Inhabitants of the intestines, whipworm and hookworm are usually picked up when your dog ingests the eggs. By cleaning up after her—and other animals—you are also removing the possibility of eggs getting into the soil and causing reinfection.

Extra precautions Coughing, rapid breathing, exercise intolerance, weight loss, or sudden death can signal a heartworm infection. The parasites clog the heart, but their presence can be detected with a blood test and prevented by a monthly tablet. Some treatments can also control fleas, hook-worms, roundworms and whipworms, giving your dog an even greater chance of staying healthy.

MOUTH AND TEETH

Although pet dogs rarely hunt like their wild relatives, they still possess the same set of sharp, shredding teeth. As most dogs' teeth are affected by disease, it's probably fortunate that they don't need to catch their own food. Your dog's teeth should be checked at least once a year.

Dental disease While dogs do not usually get cavities, more than 80 percent get periodontal disease by the age of four. The disease starts with a build-up of bacteria, plaque and tartar on the teeth. The gums and supporting structures of the teeth then succumb to gingivitis, an infection which, if not treated, can lead to tooth loss and even kidney, liver and heart problems.

The symptoms Periodontal disease can be prevented with regular dental care, including tooth brushing, and

This Siberian husky has beautiful clean teeth.

is reversible if treated in its early stages. The first sign of disease is usually bad breath. Other signs may be drooling, reluctance to eat (especially hard food), or a swollen jaw or cheek.

Removing tartar Feeding your dog dry food or hard dog biscuits daily will help to remove the hard brown tartar from her teeth. Nylon chew toys and crunchy snacks like raw carrot or apple are also good for dislodging plaque and tartar. However, if there's significant tartar build-up, the teeth may need professional cleaning, usually done under anesthesia.

Persistent problems If you've been brushing your dog's teeth regularly and her breath still smells terrible, she could have a serious problem. An ammonia odor, for example, can be a sign of kidney disease. Paradoxically, overly sweet breath can be cause for

RINSE AND SPIT
Beat bad breath and disease by cleaning your dog's teeth at least twice a week. Use flavored dog toothpaste on a gauze pad or a specially designed toothbrush. For more on brushing, see pp. 140–141.

concern because it can signal diabetes. Any change in her breath should be investigated by your vet.

Broken teeth Your dog may loosen or even break her teeth by chomping down on a stone or a hard stick. But loose teeth can also be the result of an underlying problem, like an abscess. Don't try to remove a dangling tooth—this can be excruciatingly painful. Instead, feed your dog a soft diet until you can get her to the vet.

Drooling Some dogs, such as Saint Bernards, boxers and mastiffs, drool more than most because the loose skin around their mouths traps saliva that pools and overflows. But a dog that has something stuck in her mouth will also drool heavily. Prop her mouth open with an object too large to swallow, such as a tennis ball, and check her teeth and gums, the roof of her mouth and under her tongue for foreign objects. In most cases you will be able to remove the object yourself with your fingers or a pair of tweezers, but consult your vet if you encounter difficulties.

A dog may also drool heavily if she is in pain—due to a sore tooth, for example—or if she's swallowed something poisonous. If you suspect the latter, try to induce vomiting if you think it is safe to do so (see p. 159) and get her to a vet immediately.

Mouth infections Some breeds, such as spaniels, have extra skin in the lower lip just behind the canine teeth. The extra skin creates a moist fold in the lip that is prone to infection, so clean the area daily. Use a cotton swab to remove accumulated gunk from the fold, then gently cleanse the area with another swab dipped in peroxide, alcohol or chlorhexidine. Don't use alcohol if there are cuts around your dog's mouth.

Chew bones scour debris from under the gums.

177

ORTHOPEDICS

Veterinary surveys suggest that 20 percent of adult dogs will develop osteoarthritis. Also known as degenerative joint disease, it is the most common type of arthritis and may affect any joint. However, genetic defects such as hip dysplasia trouble many breeds at an early age and require a lifetime of care.

Arthritis Osteoarthritis can develop because of an inherited malformation, such as hip or elbow dysplasia, or osteochondrosis, a condition in which bone and cartilage in the joints break down. Old injuries or just normal wear and tear can also lead to arthritis.

The signs Arthritic changes tend to appear when a dog has reached about 75 percent of his estimated life span—around seven years old for a large dog, and up to 11 or 12 years old for a smaller dog. Your dog may seem stiff, sore or lame. He could have difficulty getting up, especially after a rest, but

PRONE TO PROBLEMS
The dachshund's design has made the dog vulnerable to disk disease. Mild slippage of the spinal disks may cause discomfort only, but severe slippage can cause partial or complete paralysis. Severe disk disease requires immediate surgery.

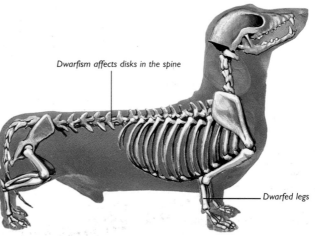

Dwarfism affects disks in the spine

Dwarfed legs

his pain may seem to diminish the more active he becomes. However, he may whimper as he tries to get about.

Home therapy For routine osteoarthritis, a combination of anti-inflammatory medication (such as buffered aspirin) and weight reduction (if your dog is overweight) is usually recommended. Extra weight can put unnecessary stress on his damaged joints.

Regular, gentle exercise is also very important because it improves mobility and strengthens muscles, which will help keep his joints stable. Swimming is a particularly good form of exercise, since water supports the body's weight, reduces pressure on the joints and allows a full range of movement. However, ensure your dog is warm and dry soon afterward.

Dysplasia Elbow and hip dysplasia are genetic defects that cause abnormal positioning of the bones of these joints. The joints don't knit together as tightly as they should, and the movement within them can cause pain and stiffness even before a dog reaches his first birthday. Over time, the "loose" joints can lead to painful osteochondrosis.

Elbow and hip dysplasia are found in almost every breed, but the large dogs are the most affected. Treatment may involve surgery to reconstruct the joint, removal of the heads of the bones or insertion of an artificial hip. Therapy is the same as for arthritis.

Back pain Dogs can also suffer from back problems, and overweight dogs are particularly prone. A reluctance to climb stairs or to jump up onto furniture may signal trouble, or your dog may cry out in pain when touched or lifted. Many problems are due to sore muscles and require rest, muscle relaxants and anti-inflammatory drugs. If he has neck problems, raise his food bowl off the ground so he doesn't have far to bend. However, pain may be the result of a more serious condition, slipped spinal disks, so consult your vet.

LOOSE AND LIMBER
The soft bed enjoyed by this aging Labrador-mix helps to ease his aches. On cold, wet days, a warm blanket or hot water bottle offer him additional comfort. Gentle massage of his sore areas also eases his stiffness by improving blood flow to his joints.

SKIN CONDITIONS

Skin conditions are probably the most common canine medical problems that vets treat. The problem can be as mild as dry skin or as serious as a severe infection. Signs of skin disease include itchiness, dandruff, hair loss, crusting, redness, odors or lumps.

Allergies Severe itching, scratching, rubbing and licking can lead to skin infections. If your dog is scratching, suspect fleas or lice—but if there's no sign of parasites, consult your vet. Some dogs scratch because they are allergic to things they have touched, eaten or inhaled. Allergy-related itching can be soothed with an antihistamine like Benadryl. Check the dosage with your vet. Also keep your house clean to reduce

A cool bath can provide your dog temporary relief from itching.

the dust mites, mold and pollens that might be causing the itching. If you think your dog has a food intolerance, ask your vet about an elimination diet.

Hot spots If licking is confined to one area, a "hot spot," can develop. Bacteria spread rapidly among the hair follicles in the irritated area, causing bald, circular patches of painfully inflamed skin. These will heal on their own if they are kept clean and well-aired.

Ringworm This fungal infection is transmitted by cats, rodents or even moist soil. Once the infection has been diagnosed, you will need to trim the hair around the infected area and rub in antifungal medication once a day for six to eight weeks. Your vet may also recommend a medicated dip or an oral treatment. Wash your dog's bedding and anything else she touches with hot water, detergent and bleach.

CLIP AND CLEAN
Hot spots heal more quickly if they're exposed to the air. Use electric clippers to trim the hair over and around the spots.

Mange Three types of mites—sarcoptes, demodex and cheyletiella—cause mange. Demodex are found in the hair follicles. In humid weather, or when your dog's immune system wanes, they multiply and cause hair loss. Most cases are resolved naturally, but some turn into severe infections.

Unlike demodex mites, sarcoptes (scabies) mites are highly contagious. They burrow under the skin, causing intense itching, crusting and hair loss, especially on the elbows and ears. You may also be bitten by these mites.

Not as itchy as scabies, cheyletiella mites can multiply in such large numbers that it can make skin flakes in your dog's coat appear to move.

Your vet will be able to examine a scraping of your dog's skin under a microscope. Depending on the diagnosis, treatment may consist of baths or an oral or injectable parasiticide.

Dandruff Often caused by dry skin, dandruff may be treated with baths or with supplements of the essential fatty acids. But if the flaking is accompanied by a dull, greasy coat and a bad odor, a disorder called seborrhea may be to blame. Your vet can provide treatment.

Lumps A lump on or under her skin could be a cyst, tumor or abscess. Tumors with an unusual shape or color, or those that grow quickly, could be cancerous. Always get your vet to check any lumps you find.

SUN PROTECTION
A dog with little pigment or a short white coat should have sunscreen put on his ear tips, belly and nose. Avoid creams with zinc or PABA, which can be dangerous if licked.

URINARY TRACT PROBLEMS

There are many causes of urinary tract problems, ranging from infections to prostate disease, and they may signal other conditions, such as kidney failure or diabetes. These problems are serious, so any sudden changes in your dog's habits merit immediate attention.

Cystitis Urinary tract infections can be painful and give dogs an urgent, frequent need to urinate what may be only small amounts. They may also strain to urinate and what they produce can be dark or bloody, with an unusually strong odor.

If you notice these symptoms, give your dog lots of opportunities to relieve himself and try to increase his fluids—about one-and-a-half times his usual intake if possible. Adding salty gravy to his food will make him work up a thirst. The extra water will help to dilute and flush trapped urine—which provides a breeding ground for bacteria—out of his system. Your vet may prescribe oral antibiotics to clear up the infection.

Bladder stones Some dogs develop "stones" in their bladder that can block the urethra and make urination difficult. If left untreated, urinary blockages can be fatal.

To stop any crystals in your dog's bladder from becoming stones, provide plenty

Make sure your dog always has fresh, clean water to drink, and seek help if you notice a problem.

of fluids and opportunities to urinate. Your vet may also recommend feeding him a diet that makes the crystals less likely to become stones. To dissolve the stones already present, your vet will need to determine which type of stone he has (some are more soluble in acidic urine; others in alkaline urine). Once the type is diagnosed, special diets or additives may be recommended to change the pH of his urine, helping to dissolve the stones and making them easier to eliminate.

Prostate problems Located at the base of the bladder, the prostate gland is essential for reproduction because it adds fluid to the sperm. As male dogs age, however, the gland often gets larger and begins pressing on the urethra or the colon. It's also prone to infection, which can make urination painful.

Dogs with prostate problems need to urinate frequently, and they may strain and cry until they've finished. They may also walk a little stiffly to

reduce the pressure on the swollen gland. Buffered aspirin can be given to ease the pain. Due to the pressure on the colon, sufferers may have trouble defecating, so a high fiber diet will make stools easier to pass. Most prostate problems occur in intact dogs—another reason to neuter your pet.

Incontinence Sometimes a dog will lose control without realizing it—some spayed females leave puddles while they are

Diapers help keep fur—and carpets—dry.

sleeping. This type of incontinence responds readily to hormone supplements, along with other medications. Other dogs become incontinent if they are overweight, which places extra pressure on the bladder, or when they are excited or under stress. Older dogs may also become incontinent. In all cases, reduce the stress in your dog's life and let him spend more time outdoors. The more chances for urination, the less pressure on the bladder, and the less likelihood of "accidents."

Specially designed diapers, available from pet supply stores, can improve hygiene. Be sure to change them frequently to prevent skin irritation.

Other problems Bladder control problems are never normal, and a dog that urinates frequently, or without control, may be suffering diabetes or liver disease. Increased urination and thirst may also mean kidney failure or uterine infections, while recurrent cystitis and bloody urine can signal kidney stones. Seek veterinary advice.

WEIGHT PROBLEMS

Obesity is the number-one nutrition-related disease in dogs. Sometimes a metabolic disease, such as hypothyroidism, triggers obesity. Some breeds put on weight easily and require special attention to their feeding needs. However, most overweight dogs simply eat too much and exercise too little.

A big problem In the wild, weight is never an issue because finding food keeps canines fit and lithe. But in domestic situations food is often no more than a room or two away, with predictable consequences—up to 40 percent of dogs in the US are too fat.

It's common for older dogs to get plumper as their metabolic function slows. But whether your dog is five or 14, she should weigh about the same as she did on her first birthday.

Weight worries Regardless of the cause, being overweight can lead to diminished quality as well as quantity

PORTLY POOCHES
Some breeds are susceptible to obesity, including Labrador retrievers (below), basset hounds, bulldogs, beagles, Shetland sheepdogs and dachshunds. Spaniels also gain weight easily.

of life for your dog. Like obesity in humans, the extra weight can cause or exacerbate a number of medical problems, including skin disorders, arthritis and diabetes. Obesity is a common factor of heart disease: Since a fat dog has more tissue than her leaner friends, her heart has to work harder to pump larger amounts of blood over greater distances.

Measuring up Your dog won't get fat overnight. It's important to check her weight regularly to keep it from creeping up— but first find out what her ideal weight should be. If she's a purebred, this information

FETCHING FITNESS
Vigorous games like fetch and Frisbee are great ways to keep your dog in shape.

will be available from a book about her breed. Pick her up and stand with her on a set of bathroom scales. (This is simple if your dog is small, but if she's more than a handful, take care when lifting her. Crouch down to gather her up and rise slowly, using your legs, not your back.) Subtract your weight from the total and check her weight against the breed standard.

An easier alternative, especially if your dog is a mixed breed, is to do a rib test (see pp.122–123). Feel her ribs and look at her body shape. If you can't see or feel the ribs, your dog is certainly overweight.

Diets If you suspect a weight problem, your vet can design an effective weight-reduction program. It may simply be a question of changing her food to meet a lower calorific target. For example, if you are feeding your sedentary pet a premium dog food, which is typically high in fat and animal protein, it is probably providing more calories than she can use. You can either feed her less (usually about 60 percent of her current intake) or initiate a low-calorie, high-fiber diet.

Another tactic Try dividing your dog's daily ration into two or three portions. More frequent feedings will keep hunger pangs at bay and also convince her that she is "full." If she's used to getting snacks between meals, make them low-calorie ones, such as raw carrots or green beans. Replace high-calorie training rewards, such as cereal biscuits, with raw food or with a "social reward" such as a toy or game.

Exercise Regular exercise is a vital part of any weight-loss program. Starting with short sessions of five or ten minutes, try to work up to 30 minutes of active play or brisk walking every day. Monitor your dog's progress by feeling for her ribs and weighing her every week or two. Don't aim for dramatic loss, which can be dangerous—instead, try to have her lose the extra weight over a 12-week period.

Underweight? If your dog's ribs are visible or easy to feel she is probably underweight. Your vet will be able to recommended an appropriate diet. However, if her prominent ribs are accompanied by a pot belly, suspect worms and seek treatment.

Rapid weight loss can be a sign of heart failure, diabetes or liver or intestinal problems. If you notice any sudden changes, seek help immediately.

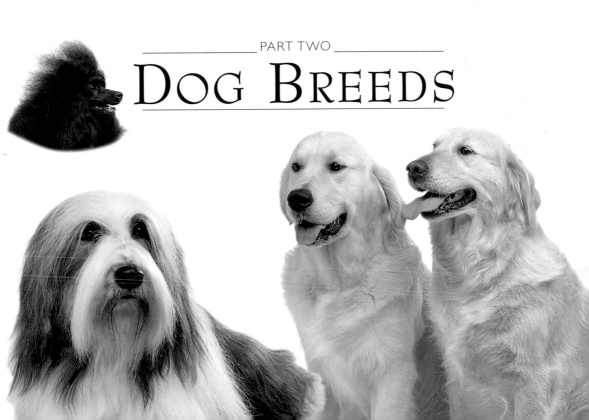

PART TWO

DOG BREEDS

HOW TO USE THE GUIDE

So you want to become the proud owner of a purebred dog!
This guide provides details of more than 90 of the most
popular breeds to help you decide which dog is best for you.

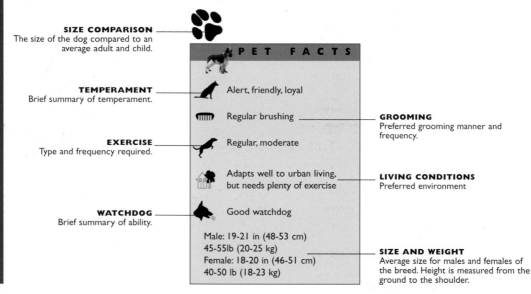

SIZE COMPARISON
The size of the dog compared to an
average adult and child.

PET FACTS

TEMPERAMENT
Brief summary of temperament.

Alert, friendly, loyal

Regular brushing

GROOMING
Preferred grooming manner and
frequency.

EXERCISE
Type and frequency required.

Regular, moderate

Adapts well to urban living,
but needs plenty of exercise

LIVING CONDITIONS
Preferred environment

WATCHDOG
Brief summary of ability.

Good watchdog

Male: 19-21 in (48-53 cm)
45-55lb (20-25 kg)
Female: 18-20 in (46-51 cm)
40-50 lb (18-23 kg)

SIZE AND WEIGHT
Average size for males and females of
the breed. Height is measured from the
ground to the shoulder.

NAME OF BREED
As used by the American Kennel Club.

INTRODUCTION
A succinct overview of the breed.

Sporting Dogs

PET FACTS

Playful, cheerful, loyal

Regular brushing

Regular, moderate

Adapts well to urban living, but needs plenty of exercise

Good watchdog

Male: 19-21 in (48-53 cm)
45-55 lb (20-25 kg)
Female: 18-20 in (46-51 cm)
40-50 lb (18-23 kg)

liver and white

196

ENGLISH SPRINGER SPANIEL

The handsome, robust English springer spaniel excels
in the field at flushing out game, but also makes a
spirited, loyal household pet and companion.

History One of the largest of the
spaniels, this popular breed descends
from the oldest spaniel stock and its
blood probably runs in the veins of
most modern spaniels. Once known as
the Norfolk spaniel, it is an all-weather
retriever and loves the water.

Description This strong,
sturdy dog has a soft, medium-
length, water-repellant coat. It
comes in all spaniel colors, but
mainly white with liver or
black, with or without tan markings. The tail is usually docked.

Temperament A quick learner, it
enjoys company, is patient with children and makes a good watchdog.
However, the breed is prone to the
inherited behavioral disorder known

as Rage Syndrome, so it is advisable
to obtain details of family history
before acquiring a pup.

Grooming Weekly brushing with a
stiff bristle brush will keep the coat
looking good. Take extra care when
the dog is molting. Bathe or dry shampoo when necessary. Check the heavy
ears regularly for signs of infection.

Exercise and feeding The springer
enjoys as much exercise as it can get.
There are no special feeding requirements, but avoid overfeeding this dog.

Health problems A generally hardy
breed, the springer is susceptible to
ear infections. It may also develop an
eye disease, allergic skin conditions
and elbow and hip dysplasia.

MAIN TEXT
Provides a detailed
description of the
breed, including its
history, distinguishing
characteristics and
temperament. It also
details the grooming,
feeding and exercise
requirements of the
breed, as well as alerting
prospective owners to
common health problems
that may afflict these dogs.

♂ = male

♀ = female

MAIN IMAGE
A good representative of the breed.

DOG BREEDS
SPORTING DOGS

With the introduction of firearms to hunting, many breeders turned their attention from the development of swifter breeds, for example, and took a greater interest in nurturing other natural canine traits, such as swimming and going to earth. The result is an intelligent, responsive, trustworthy group of dogs—water dogs, flushing dogs, setters, pointers and retrievers—that combine instinctive ability with a willingness to learn. Although most sporting dogs become noisy and destructive if confined for long periods, they are generally easy to train, almost always patient with children and make spirited household pets.

PET FACTS

Rugged, friendly, energetic

Regular brushing

Regular, vigorous

Adapts well to urban living, but needs plenty of exercise

Good watchdog

Male: 18-21 in (46-53 cm)
30-45 lb (14-20 kg)
Female: 18-20 in (46-51 cm)
30-40 lb (14-18 kg)

○ *orange and white*

BRITTANY

The agile Brittany is admired for its vigorous hunting abilities and for its grace and charming personality. A companionable pet, it prefers an outdoor life.

History Also known as the Breton, this spaniel has a history in its native France going back centuries and a growing following in the US. An excellent tracker and retriever, this dog is also a natural pointer, a trait possibly acquired through interbreeding with pointers. In the field, the Brittany tends to work close to its master.

Description The smallest of the French spaniels, the Brittany is graceful and well-muscled. The medium-length coat is dense and feathered (fringed) on the ears, chest, belly and upper parts of the legs. It comes in white with orange, black, brown or liver, as well as tricolors (three distinct colors) and roans (an even mixture of white and another color). The short tail is usually docked a little.

Temperament Easy to train and handle, the Brittany is a loving and gentle dog, always eager to please—a good choice for first-time owners.

Grooming Twice-weekly brushing of the flat coat will keep it in good condition. Bathe or dry shampoo a few times a year. Check the ears carefully, especially when the dog has been out in rough or brushy terrain.

Exercise and feeding This dog has great stamina and needs vigorous activity to stay in peak condition. There are no special feeding requirements.

Health problems While generally a hardy breed, the Brittany is prone to ear infections, spinal paralysis and eye diseases such as glaucoma.

AMERICAN COCKER SPANIEL

This attractive dog is smaller than its English cousin but retains the lively, friendly personality for which spaniels are known.

History Although derived from the same stock as the English cocker spaniel (see pp. 194–195), the American breed had become so different by the 1930s that it was recognized in the US as a separate breed. British recognition followed about 35 years later.

Description This compact dog has a fine, silky coat, short on the head and longer on the body. It comes in any solid color, particolors (variegated patches of two colors), tricolors and roans. The ears are long and set low on the head. The tail is usually docked.

Temperament Intelligent, responsive and easy to train, the American cocker spaniel is generally friendly and good-natured. However, some dogs may display unprovoked aggression toward their owners, a condition similar to Rage Syndrome in English cocker and English springer spaniels.

Grooming Some owners prefer to leave the coat long, brushing daily and shampooing frequently. Others clip it to a more functional medium length. Either way, it will need regular trimming. Be gentle when brushing to avoid pulling out the silky hair.

Exercise and feeding This dog has plenty of stamina and needs regular exercise to run off its energy. There are no special feeding requirements.

Health problems Prone to eye diseases, the breed may also suffer heart disease, hemophilia, diabetes, spinal problems, epilepsy and ear infections.

PET FACTS

Lively, energetic, playful

Extensive brushing

Regular, moderate

Adapts well to urban living, but needs plenty of space

Good watchdog

Male: 13-16 in (33-41 cm)
25-35 lb (11-16 kg)
Female: 12-15 in (30-38 cm)
20-30 lb (9-14 kg)

♀ particolor

ENGLISH COCKER SPANIEL

An absolute charmer, the joyous English cocker spaniel is still used as a hunting dog, flushing game birds from undergrowth and retrieving their bodies. Its responsive and affectionate personality and sheer good looks have also made it one of the most popular companions and house pets today.

steel blue roan

History The spaniel family originated in Spain—the word may be a corruption of *espaignol*, Old French for "Spanish dog"—and various types became popular gundogs all over the world. References to such dogs appear in writings dating from the fourteenth century, and by the 1800s, the small land spaniels were divided into two groups: springers, whose function was to "spring" game; and cockers, named for their ability to flush and retrieve woodcock from dense undergrowth. Today's English cocker spaniel descends from cocker dogs developed in Wales and southwest England. The breed was officially recognized in England in 1892.

Description This strong dog is slightly larger than its cousin, the American cocker spaniel. While it too has a sturdy body, its back is longer than that of the American variety. The ears, abdomen, short, powerful forelegs and cat-like paws are well feathered. The chest also has an abundant ruff.

The silky, medium-length coat has either straight or slightly wavy, flat-lying hair, with a dense protective undercoat. It comes in solid reds, black, golden and liver, as well as black and tan, particolors, and tricolors, in which the color is broken up with white. Roan coats are also a common sight. The tail is usually docked short.

Temperament Energetic, playful and eager to please, the English cocker spaniel performs with unbounded enthusiasm, wagging its stump of a tail and entire hindquarters furiously. It adapts well to any living environment, enjoys family life and will certainly alert its owner to the presence of strangers on the property.

Intelligent and independent, the breed has a strong personality and should be trained with a degree of firmness. Sadly, some solid-colored dogs may be susceptible to behavioral disorders including Rage Syndrome, which can cause aggression. Before buying a pup, ask to see its parents. If the breeder is reluctant, avoid the litter.

Grooming Brushing and combing about three times a week is necessary to remove dead hair and keep the coat shiny and lying flat. Shedding can be a problem. Bathe or dry shampoo as necessary.

Brush the hair on the feet down over the toes and trim it level with the base of the feet. Trim the hair around the pads, but not that between the toes. The dog will also need some trimming of the head and ruff to keep them looking tidy.

Careful grooming is needed after exercise—brush out burrs and tangles after the dog has been playing in grassy fields or woods. The pendulous, feathered ears also need special attention to ensure they are free from grass seeds, excessive wax and signs of infection caused by poor ventilation. Because the ears will dip into food, be sure to wipe them after meals.

Exercise and feeding Speedy and full of stamina, this spaniel will enjoy as much exercise as its owner can give it. Long daily walks and weekly runs in open areas are a must. Without enough exercise, it may become frustrated. There are no special feeding requirements, but since cockers gain weight easily, take care not to overfeed.

Health problems The breed suffers from genetic eye diseases and skin and kidney problems. It is also prone to diabetes and infections.

PET FACTS

Joyful, affectionate, intelligent

Regular brushing

Regular, moderate to vigorous

Adapts well to urban living, but needs plenty of exercise

Good watchdog

Male: 15-17 in (38-43 cm)
28-32 lb (13-15 kg)
Female: 14-16 in (36-41 cm)
26-30 lb (12-14 kg)

♂ light blue roan

PET FACTS

Playful, cheerful, loyal

Regular brushing

Regular, moderate

Adapts well to urban living, but needs plenty of exercise

Good watchdog

Male: 19-21 in (48-53 cm)
45-55 lb (20-25 kg)
Female: 18-20 in (46-51 cm)
40-50 lb (18-23 kg)

ENGLISH SPRINGER SPANIEL

The handsome, robust English springer spaniel excels in the field at flushing out game, but also makes a spirited, loyal household pet and companion.

History One of the largest of the spaniels, this popular breed descends from the oldest spaniel stock whose blood probably runs in the veins of most modern spaniels. Once known as the Norfolk spaniel, it is an all-weather retriever and loves the water.

Description This strong, sturdy dog has a soft, medium-length, water-repellent coat. It comes in all spaniel colors, but mainly white with liver or black, with or without tan markings. The tail is usually docked.

Temperament A quick learner, it enjoys company, is patient with children and makes a good watchdog. However, the breed is prone to the inherited behavioral disorder known as Rage Syndrome, so it is advisable to obtain details of family history before acquiring a pup.

Grooming Weekly brushing with a stiff bristle brush will keep the coat looking good. Take extra care when the dog is molting. Bathe or dry shampoo when necessary. Check the heavy ears regularly for signs of infection.

Exercise and feeding The springer spaniel enjoys as much exercise as it can get. There are no special feeding requirements, but avoid overfeeding this dog as it gains weight easily.

Health problems This spaniel is susceptible to ear infections, eye diseases, allergic skin conditions and elbow and hip dysplasia.

◯ liver and white

WELSH SPRINGER SPANIEL

Sociable and very intelligent, the Welsh springer spaniel adapts well to any environment but is in its element with space to run and somewhere to swim.

History Less common than the English springer spaniel, to which it is closely related, the Welsh springer is from similar ancient stock. Springers were used to "spring" forward at game to flush it out for the net, falcon or hound and, later, the gun. The tail wags faster as the dog nears its quarry.

Description A hard worker with amazing endurance, this dog is smaller overall than its English cousin. The thick, silky coat is straight and always pearly white and rich red. The tail is usually docked, although some breeders are choosing to leave entire pups intended for non-working homes.

Temperament Its gentle, patient nature and love of children makes it an easily trained and attractive family pet.

Grooming Regular brushing with a stiff bristle brush will suffice. Extra care is needed when the dog is molting. Bathe or dry shampoo only when necessary. Check the ears regularly for debris and infection, trim between the toes and keep the nails clipped.

Exercise and feeding This energetic and lively dog needs plenty of regular, preferably off-leash, exercise. With insufficient exercise it will become bored, fat and lazy. There are no special feeding requirements, but do not overfeed.

Health problems The long ears of this breed makes it prone to infections. It may also suffer from hip dysplasia and eye problems.

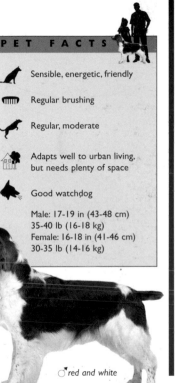

PET FACTS

Sensible, energetic, friendly

Regular brushing

Regular, moderate

Adapts well to urban living, but needs plenty of space

Good watchdog

Male: 17-19 in (43-48 cm)
35-40 lb (16-18 kg)
Female: 16-18 in (41-46 cm)
30-35 lb (14-16 kg)

♂ red and white

197

LABRADOR RETRIEVER

Courageous, loyal and hard working, the Labrador retriever has earned worldwide respect for its dedication to duty. Originally a valued member of every Newfoundland fishing crew, this affable, outgoing and gregarious dog is now one of the most popular and loving of family pets.

○ black

History Early members of this breed originated in Newfoundland, Canada, rather than Labrador as the name suggests. Once known as the black water dog, the lesser Newfoundland or the St John's dog, it was trained to jump overboard as its boat neared harbor and gather the ends of the fish-filled nets in its mouth. It would then haul them ashore, where its human crewmates could empty the catch. It would also retrieve the cork floats of the nets and swim them in to land, so that the fishermen could haul in the catch themselves. The Labrador collected the fish that fell out of the nets and also excelled at retrieving water birds.

By the early nineteenth century British sportsmen, hearing of the breed's reputation, had bought some of the dogs off the ships carrying salted codfish to England. There the Labrador was gradually developed by being bred with other sporting dogs such as water spaniels and the curly coated retriever. It became indispensable as a sled dog, message-carrier and general working dog.

The modern Labrador retriever continues this proud tradition of service. Trained to detect narcotics and explosives, it is used in police work and in the armed forces, where the dog's acute sense of smell and good memory enables it to detect mines buried deep underground. It also enjoys popularity as a gundog, since it is skilled at trailing wounded animals and does not damage game with its "soft" mouth when retrieving. However, the Labrador is perhaps most famous for its work as a guide dog and assistance dog for people with disabilities.

Description This strong, solid dog has a sturdy frame, a broad skull and a powerful neck. The distinctive medium-length "otter" tail is thick at the base and round and tapered along its length. The coat is dense and water-resistant with no feathering. It comes in solid black, yellow, gold, fawn, cream or chocolate, occasionally with small white markings on the chest.

Temperament Reliable, responsive and obedient, the Labrador adapts to almost any living environment. Exceptionally patient and gentle with children, it craves attention and needs to feel as though it is part of the family.

The Labrador is easily trained and accepts any kind of task with a sense of enthusiasm and responsibility. However, to keep its high energy focused the training should begin at an early age. While never aggressive toward people, some (especially the black variety) may fight other dogs. All types will benefit from frequent chances to socialize with people and other animals.

Grooming The smooth double coat requires a comb and brush about twice a week to remove dead hair from the undercoat and to keep the coat shiny. Bathe or dry shampoo only when necessary.

Exercise and feeding This energetic breed is delighted to work and play hard. Its daily, vigorous exercise should include as many opportunities to swim as possible. Given its history, it is especially fond of swimming and will happily retrieve balls, Frisbees—even swimming children—all day long. There are no special feeding requirements, but beware of overfeeding as it can easily become obese and lazy.

Health problems Like other large breeds, this generally robust dog is prone to hip and elbow dysplasia. It may also suffer from epilepsy, diabetes and hereditary eye diseases, such as cataracts and progressive retinal atrophy.

PET FACTS

Reliable, patient, gentle

Regular brushing

Regular, vigorous

Adapts well to urban living, but needs plenty of exercise

Good watchdog

Male: 22-24 in (56-61 cm)
50-60 lb (23-27 kg)
Female: 21-23 in (53-58 cm)
45-55 lb (20-25 kg)

♂ yellow

PET FACTS

Calm, affectionate, gentle

Daily combing and brushing

Regular, vigorous

Adapts well to urban living, but needs plenty of space

Good watchdog

Male: 22-24 in (56-61 cm)
60-80 lb (27-36 kg)
Female: 20-22 in (51-56 cm)
55-70 lb (25-32 kg)

♂ gold

GOLDEN RETRIEVER

This sunny dog gets the seal of approval from everyone who has ever owned one. One of the most popular breeds, it is suitable for families and first-time owners.

History Thought to have been developed in the United Kingdom by Lord Tweedmouth about 150 years ago, the ancestry of this breed is difficult to prove. It has some of the characteristics of retrievers, bloodhounds and water spaniels, making it a very useful gundog with good tracking abilities.

Description This graceful and elegant dog has a lustrous coat in any shade of gold or cream. The hair lies flat or gently waved around the neck, shoulders and hips, and there is abundant feathering.

Temperament A well-mannered, intelligent dog with great charm, the golden retriever is easily trained and almost always patient and gentle with children—an occasional few display Rage-like behavior (see p. 195). While unlikely to attack, it will loudly signal a stranger's approach.

Grooming The coat sheds heavily, but daily grooming will help. Use a firm bristle brush, paying particular attention to the dense undercoat. Dry shampoo regularly.

Exercise and feeding This breed loves to work—the more strenuous the duties, the better. At the very least it needs a long daily walk and a chance to run freely, and it should be allowed to swim whenever possible. There are no special feeding requirements.

Health problems Skin, eye, heart, and orthopedic conditions and von Willebrand's disease are common.

IRISH SETTER

This dog is much admired for its lustrous silky coat. It is a little lighter and speedier than other setters, having been bred to cope with Ireland's marshy terrain.

History The Irish setter, also known as the red setter, evolved in the British Isles over the past 200 years from a variety of setters, spaniels and pointers. Like all setters, this dog was bred to "set," or locate, game birds and then to remain still while the hunter shot or netted the birds.

Description The Irish setter's soft, profusely feathered coat comes in rich shades of chestnut to mahogany, sometimes with splashes of white on the chest and feet. The long ears are low-set and the legs are long and muscular.

Temperament This breed is full of energy and high spirits. It is also very affectionate, sometimes overwhelmingly so. Being easily distracted, it can be difficult to train, but the effort

will be rewarding for both owner and dog. Training must never be harsh or overbearing.

Grooming Daily grooming will maintain the condition of the coat and keep it free of burrs and tangles. Give a little extra care when the dog is molting. Bathe when necessary.

Exercise and feeding The dog needs a long, brisk walk daily, or it will be restless and difficult to manage. Also let it run free off the leash. Since it is prone to bloat, feed three small meals a day.

Health problems Especially subject to epilepsy and skin allergies, this setter also suffers from eye problems, elbow and hip dysplasia and bloat.

PET FACTS

Lively and affectionate

Daily combing and brushing

Regular, extensive and vigorous

Needs space to run free; unsuited to apartment living

Not a good watchdog

Male: 25-27 in (63-69 cm)
55-65 lb (25-29 kg)
Female: 23-25 in (58-63 cm)
50-60 lb (23-27 kg)

♂ mahogany

201

PET FACTS

Intelligent, friendly, loyal

Daily combing and brushing

Regular, vigorous

Needs space to run free;
unsuited to apartment living

Adequate watchdog

Male: 25-27 in (63-69 cm)
60-66 lb (27-30 kg)
Female: 24-26 in (61-66 cm)
55-62 lb (25-28 kg)

ENGLISH SETTER

Reliable and hard-working, this beautiful dog has strength, stamina and grace. It also seems to have an innate sense of what is expected of a gundog.

History Descended from a variety of Spanish spaniels, this breed was also known as the Laverack setter, after Edward Laverack, who played a major role in its development.

Description This elegant breed has a finely chiselled head and large nostrils. Its flat, straight coat is of medium length and comes in white, flecked with combinations of black, lemon, liver, and black and tan. There is feathering along the underbody and on the ears.

Temperament Gentle and high-spirited, the English setter takes its duties very seriously. Friendly and intelligent, it is adept at anticipating its owner's wishes, responding intelligently to each new situation.

Grooming It is important to comb and brush the silky coat every day, with extra care required when the setter is molting. Bathe or dry shampoo only when necessary. Trim the hair on the feet to prevent matting and discomfort. Also trim the hair on the tail and check the long ears for any signs of infection.

Exercise and feeding This breed needs at the very least a long daily walk and opportunities to run free, or it will become restless and may even roam. As it is prone to bloat, feed it two or three small meals a day.

Health problems While relatively hardy, this dog may suffer from hip dysplasia, bloat and eye diseases such as progressive retinal atrophy.

♂ orange belton

GORDON SETTER

Larger, heavier and more powerful than its cousins, the Gordon setter is a natural pointer and retriever which also makes a delightful pet.

History Bred in Scotland as a gundog by the fourth Duke of Gordon in the late eighteenth century, this dog has setter, collie and possibly bloodhound genes.

Description The soft, silky coat is generously feathered and is always a gleaming black with tan to reddish mahogany markings. On the face, the markings are clearly defined and include a spot over each eye.

Temperament Calmer than other setters and more reserved with strangers, the Gordon setter is an excellent, affectionate companion. It is reliable with children and fairly easily trained. Training must never be harsh or heavy-handed, because it is important not to break the dog's spirit.

Grooming Regular combing and brushing of the flat, medium-length coat is all that is required to keep it in excellent condition. Check for burrs and tangles, and give extra care when the dog is molting. Bathe or dry shampoo only when necessary. Trim the hair between the toes and and keep the nails clipped.

Exercise and feeding This breed has great stamina and easily handles tough terrain. It will be difficult to manage if it does not get plenty of vigorous exercise. As it is prone to bloat, feed it two or three small meals a day instead of one large one.

Health problems This setter is susceptible to hip dysplasia, eye diseases such as cataracts, and bloat.

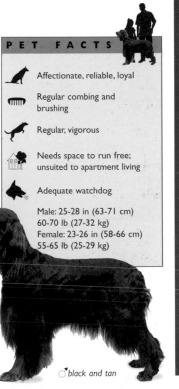

PET FACTS

Affectionate, reliable, loyal

Regular combing and brushing

Regular, vigorous

Needs space to run free; unsuited to apartment living

Adequate watchdog

Male: 25-28 in (63-71 cm)
60-70 lb (27-32 kg)
Female: 23-26 in (58-66 cm)
55-65 lb (25-29 kg)

♂ black and tan

GERMAN POINTER

This versatile, athletic dog is able to track, point out and retrieve game. It searches for game by scent, but on finding its prey stands rigid, nose up and with one foreleg raised and bent, and "points" its discovery to the hunter. The German shorthaired pointer is the older variety, but the wirehaired has the advantage of a durable, hard-wearing coat.

Wirehaired
♂ *liver roan*

History The ancestors of the German shorthaired pointer include Spanish and English pointers, French hounds, Scandinavian breeds and the bloodhound. The resulting array of talents means that the dog is highly prized by hunters. In the search for even greater perfection, it was bred with terriers and poodles in the late nineteenth century. The result was the German wirehaired pointer, with a distinctive wiry coat developed to protect the skin from thorns and other sharp debris while the dog is working in thickets and dense undergrowth. The rugged coat also gives it a more aggressive appearance.

Description This superlative hunting dog is used for fur and feathered game in all types of terrain, including water. Its lean, muscular body and powerful loins give it a useful turn of speed on land, and its strong jaws enable it to carry quite heavy kills. It is also an excellent swimmer.

The short, dense, water-resistant coat of the shorthaired variety comes in solid black or liver, or these colors with white spots or flecks, or roan. The wirehaired has a thick, medium-length, wiry coat, also water-resistant, that comes in solid liver, liver and white, roan or black and white. It has longer hair above the eyes, as well as whiskers and a beard. The tails of both varieties are usually docked to half the length.

Temperament The German pointer makes an affectionate pet. While clean and well behaved in the house, it is better off and far happier with an outdoor life and plenty of work to do. This intelligent dog has a mind of

its own and should never be allowed to get the upper hand. It can be flighty and hard to train and needs an experienced owner. Although both types are generally good with people and reliable with children, the breed can overwhelm younger children. The wirehaired variety has also acquired a slightly aggressive trait along with its wiry coat, probably from its terrier genes, and is inclined to be argumentative with other dogs.

Grooming The shorthaired's smooth coat is very easy to groom. Just brush regularly with a firm bristle brush, and bathe every few months. A rub with a piece of toweling or chamois will leave the coat gleaming.

The wirehaired's coat needs a little more attention. It must be brushed about twice a week with a firm bristle brush to remove the dead undercoat, and thinned during the spring and fall shedding periods.

Check the ears of both varieties regularly for any discharge or foreign bodies. Also check the feet, especially after the dog has been exercising or working.

Exercise and feeding Exercise is of paramount importance for this tireless dog. It is more than a match for even the most active family and should not be taken on as a family pet unless it can be guaranteed plenty of vigorous exercise. With insufficient work, it can become bored, noisy and hard to manage. There are no special feeding requirements for this breed, but always try to measure the amount of food given against the dog's level of activity.

Health problems The German pointer is generally a hardy and long-lived breed, but like other flop-eared dogs it is prone to ear infections. It may also suffer from hip and elbow dysplasia, von Willebrand's disease, genetic eye diseases and skin cancers.

PET FACTS

Intelligent, reliable, keen

Regular brushing; wirehaired more than smooth

Regular, vigorous

Adapts well to urban living, but needs plenty of space and exercise

Good watchdog

Male: 22-26 in (56-66 cm)
50-65 lb (23-29 kg)
Female: 21-25 in (53-63 cm)
45-60 lb (20-27 kg)

*Shorthaired
♂ liver and white*

PET FACTS

Intelligent, affectionate, willing

Regular brushing

Regular, vigorous

Adapts well to urban living, but needs plenty of space

Good watchdog

Male: 22-26 in (56-66 cm)
45-60 lb (20-27 kg)
Female: 20-24 in (51-61 cm)
40-55 lb (18-25 kg)

VIZSLA

Hungary's national dog, the Vizsla was little known elsewhere until after World War II. This agile gundog is now becoming popular outside its country of origin.

History Also known as the Hungarian pointer, the Vizsla was bred for tracking, pointing, hunting and retrieving. A possible descendant of the Turkish yellow dog and the Transylvanian hound, it is more likely to be related to the Weimaraner. A good swimmer, it retrieves just as well in water as on land.

Description This handsome, lean, well-muscled dog moves gracefully either at a lively trot or in a swift gallop. It is also a great jumper. The smooth, greasy coat is short and close, rusty gold to sandy yellow in color.

Temperament Although good-natured, intelligent and easy to train, the Vizsla is somewhat sensitive and

♂ rusty gold

needs to be handled gently. It is reliable with children and quickly adapts to family life.

Grooming Use a firm bristle brush, and dry shampoo occasionally. Bathe with mild soap only when necessary. The nails should be kept trimmed.

Exercise and feeding This dog has great stamina and needs plenty of exercise and opportunities to run off the leash. If bored, it can become destructive and will escape a yard that does not have a sufficiently high fence. There are no special feeding requirements.

Health problems Reasonably hardy, this breed may suffer from hip dysplasia, epilepsy and eye diseases such as progressive retinal atrophy.

WEIMARANER

Given firm handling by a strong, experienced adult, the confident and assertive Weimaraner can make a wonderful companion and working dog.

History Once widely used in Germany to hunt bears and wild pigs, the Weimaraner became prized in more recent times as a gundog and retriever of small game, such as waterfowl.

Description This superb hunting dog has an athletic, well-proportioned body. The sleek, close-fitting coat comes in silver-gray to mouse shades, often lighter on the head and ears. The striking eyes are blue-gray or amber. The tail is usually docked.

Temperament Strong-willed and intelligent, the Weimaraner is happiest when occupied with tasks that engage its mind. It needs firm, thorough training to control its tendency to dominate and be aggressive. It makes a great watchdog and is good with children.

Grooming The coat does not shed much and only needs brushing once a week. A rub with a chamois will make it gleam. Dry shampoo occasionally and bathe with mild soap when necessary. Inspect the feet and mouth for damage after work or exercise sessions. Keep the nails trimmed.

Exercise and feeding The Weimaraner has enormous stamina. It needs opportunities to run free and lots of regular exercise. As it is prone to bloat, feed it two or three small meals a day.

Health problems In addition to bloat, this generally hardy breed can suffer from hip dysplasia and various skin ailments. It is also prone to sunburn on the nose.

PET FACTS

Intelligent, friendly, powerful

Regular brushing

Regular, vigorous

Adapts well to urban living, but needs plenty of space

Excellent watchdog

Male: 24-27 in (61-69 cm)
55-70 lb (25-32 kg)
Female: 22-25 in (56-63 cm)
50-65 lb (23-29 kg)

♂ silver-gray

HOUNDS

Hounds are the most ancient group of dogs. Bred to hunt game, they are categorized according to how they locate and pursue prey. Speedy sighthounds such as the borzoi spot prey from afar and give chase—a style of hunting popular prior to the development of shotguns. Scenthounds such as the bloodhound trail their quarry with their noses to the ground. Bred for stamina, they corner their prey, then signal the hunters. These days most hounds are kept as pets, although old habits die hard. Scenthounds can be vocal, and the mournful howls of a basset hound may not endear it to the neighbors. Quieter sighthounds need regular opportunities to run free. With care and attention, both types make intelligent, lively and loyal companions.

♂ tricolor liver and white

BASSET HOUND

The solemn face of this lovable hound belies its lively nature. A reliable hunting partner, it also makes a delightful pet in homes where there are young children.

History While most basset breeds originated in France (*bas* means "low" in French), the basset hound was developed in Britain only about 100 years ago. Its ability to concentrate on a particular scent quickly earned it respect as a hunting partner.

Description This dog has short, stocky legs on which the skin is loose and folded. The body is sturdy and barrel-shaped. The coat comes in combinations of white with tan, black and lemon. The long ears are velvety.

Temperament The basset hound is good-natured, sociable and gentle with children. However, it can be stubborn and is one of the most difficult breeds to house-train, so owners must be patient.

Grooming The smooth, shorthaired coat sheds only moderately. Use a firm bristle brush, and shampoo only when necessary. Wipe the ears every week.

Exercise and feeding Short daily walks will help to keep it healthy, but discourage it from jumping and stressing the front legs. Since extra weight places too great a load on the legs and spine, do not overfeed. To avoid bloat, feed it two or three small meals a day.

Health problems These dogs suffer from bloat, spinal disk problems, glaucoma and skin infections. The long, heavy ears are susceptible to infection.

BEAGLE

An endearing and engaging dog, eager to romp and play, the beagle loves children and craves human companionship. It is also an enthusiastic hunter.

History Packs of beagles were traditionally used to hunt hares by scent. The name may come from the Celtic word for small, *beag,* or the French for gape throat, *begueule.* The modern dog is considerably larger than those of earlier times, which were often carried in pockets or saddlebags.

Description This muscular little dog has a dense waterproof coat. It comes in combinations of white, black, tan, red, lemon and blue mottle.

Temperament The beagle needs firm handling as it is strong-willed and not always easy to train. Alert and good-tempered, it is rarely aggressive. However, if bored and sedentary it can become destructive. A lonely dog may also bark excessively, or wander.

Grooming Brush the smooth, short-haired coat with a firm bristle brush, and dry shampoo occasionally. Bathe with mild soap only when necessary. Check the ears carefully for signs of infection and keep the nails trimmed.

Exercise and feeding Energetic and possessing great stamina, the beagle needs regular exercise. A brisk daily walk and occasional on-leash running in an open area will satisfy its needs. There are no special feeding requirements, but take care that it doesn't become obese.

Health problems In addition to obesity, it is prone to epilepsy, genetic eye and bleeding disorders, skin and spinal problems and heart disease.

PET FACTS

Alert, joyful, even-tempered

Weekly brushing to remove dead hair

Regular, moderate

Adapts well to urban living

Not a good watchdog

Male: 14-16 in (36-41 cm)
22-25 lb (10-11 kg)
Female: 13-15 in (33-38 cm)
20-23 lb (9-10 kg)

♂ tricolor

DACHSHUND

The unique appearance and lively, cheerful nature of this extraordinary "sausage" dog has made the breed popular as a pet and watchdog. In some parts of Europe, especially in its native Germany, the dachshund is still used for hunting. It comes in a range of colors, sizes and coat types—it seems there's a sturdy little dachshund for every taste.

History The dachshund (pronounced dak sund) originated in Germany many hundreds of years ago—*dachs* is the German word for badger. Bred to hunt and follow these animals—as well as marten and weasel—to earth, it gradually became highly evolved, with short-ened legs to dig the prey out and to go down inside the burrows. Smaller dachshunds were bred to hunt such animals as hare and stoat.

The dachshund has many "terrier" characteristics. It is a versatile and, given its diminutive size, courageous breed which has been known to take on foxes and otters as well as badgers.

Standard wirehaired ♀ brindle

Description

The dachshund comes in two sizes—Standard and Miniature. Both sizes have a low-slung, muscular, elongated body, twice as long as it is tall, with very short legs and strong forequarters developed for digging.

The skin is loose and the coat comes in three types: smooth, short and dense; longhaired (see p. 209), soft, flat and straight with feathering (fringing); and wirehaired with a short double coat, a beard and bushy eyebrows. The wirehaired variety of dachshund is the least common and was developed to hunt in brushy thickets.

The three coat types come in a range of solid colors, such as red, black, tan or brown; or particolored, brindled, tiger-marked or dappled.

Temperament Intelligent, alert and affectionate, the dachshund is a great little character and makes a wonderful house pet. However, it can be slightly aggressive toward strangers. It has a big bark for its size, which might be enough to intimidate intruders.

Although sometimes stubborn and difficult to house-train, the dachshund can be reasonably obedient if carefully managed. It will become destructive if bored—an enthusiastic digger, it will wreak havoc in a garden.

The Miniature variety is perhaps less suited to households with young children, as it is vulnerable to injury from rough handling and can become snappish.

Grooming Regular brushing with a bristle brush is appropriate for all coat types. Long- and wirehaired coats could be brushed and combed several times a week, and smooth-coated dogs weekly. The wirehaired variety may need to be professionally trimmed. Dry shampoo or bathe when necessary, but always make sure the dog is thoroughly dry and warm after a bath. The smooth variety will come up gleaming if rubbed occasionally with a piece of damp toweling or a chamois. Check the long ears regularly to prevent infection from occurring.

Exercise and feeding This active breed has surprising stamina and it loves a regular walk or session of play in a park. However, be careful when pedestrians are about as the dog is more likely to be stepped on than larger, more visible breeds. Prone to spinal damage, it should be discouraged from jumping.

There are no special feeding requirements, but the breed has a tendency to become overweight and lazy. This is a serious health risk, putting added strain on the spine, so take care not to overfeed.

Health problems Herniated disks in the back can cause severe pain and paralysis of the hindlegs. As it is a rather long-lived breed, the dachshund also suffers problems common to aging dogs, such as obesity and heart disease. It has a higher than usual risk of developing diabetes and is also subject to genetic eye diseases and skin problems, including pattern baldness on the ears.

P E T   F A C T S

Brave, curious, lively

Regular brushing

Regular, moderate

Ideal for apartment living

Good watchdog

Standard
Male: About 8 in (20 cm)
20-22 lb (9-10 kg)
Female: About 8 in (20 cm)
18-20 lb (8-9 kg)

Miniature
Both sexes About 6 in (15 cm)
Up to 11 lb (5 kg)

*Miniature smooth
black and tan*

WHIPPET

Affectionate and adaptable, the whippet makes a delightful companion and jogging partner. Clean and obedient, it settles happily into family routine.

History This descendant of the greyhound, perhaps with some terrier blood, was used for hunting rabbits in northern England. It was also pitted against its peers in rag racing, in which the dogs, when signaled with a handkerchief, streaked from a standing start toward their owners.

Description The whippet's delicate appearance belies its strength and speed—it can accelerate to about 35 mph (55 km/h). The fine, dense coat comes in many colors or in mixes. The muzzle is long and slender.

Temperament A docile pet, it is inclined to be nervous around children. Care must be taken not to break its spirit by being harsh or overbearing.

Grooming The smooth, fine, short-haired coat can be groomed with a bristle brush. A rub with a chamois will make the coat gleam. Bathe only when necessary.

Exercise and feeding The whippet should have regular opportunities to run free on open ground as well as have long, brisk, daily walks on the leash. There are no special feeding requirements, but avoid giving it starchy or liquid food.

Health problems Because of its fine coat, the whippet is sensitive to cold and may get sunburned. Its bones are delicate and easily broken. It is also subject to genetic eye diseases such as cataracts and progressive retinal atrophy.

♀ particolor

214

GREYHOUND

Agile and swift, this breed is one of the oldest known, long valued for its hunting prowess. Its elegant lines are often emblazoned on the coats of arms of royalty.

History The greyhound probably originated in the Middle East but also has a long history in Europe, being much sought after as a hunting dog.

Description Lean and powerful, this dog can run at speeds up to 45 mph (70 km/h). The close, fine coat comes in black, gray, white, red, blue, fawn, fallow, brindle or any color broken with white. The dogs bred for racing are slightly smaller than the pet variety.

Temperament Gentle with children, the greyhound makes a surprisingly docile and obedient pet, given its hunting background. It does, however, retain a highly developed chase instinct and should always be kept on a leash in public. Owners must be careful not to be harsh with this sensitive dog.

Grooming A firm bristle brush and a chamois will keep the coat shiny. Shampoo only when necessary.

Exercise and feeding The greyhound loves routine. If kept as a pet, it should have regular opportunities to run free on open ground as well as have long, brisk walks, preferably at the same time every day. There are no special feeding requirements, but it is better to give it two small meals a day rather than a single large one.

Health problems The greyhound is one of the few breeds not prone to hip dysplasia. However, its thin skin tears easily and is unsuited to cold climates. It may be sensitive to some common anesthetics and flea-killing products.

PET FACTS

Docile, loving and sensitive

Occasional brushing

Regular, moderate

Adapts well to urban living if given plenty of exercise

Good watchdog

Male: 28-30 in (71-76 cm)
55-70 lb (25-32 kg)
Female: 27-28 in (68-71 cm)
50-65 lb (23-29 kg)

♀ *fawn and white*

215

PET FACTS

Intelligent, very independent

Weekly brushing

Regular, vigorous

Well suited to urban living

Poor watchdog

Male: 16-17 in (41-43 cm)
25-35 lb (11-16 kg)
Female: 15-16 in (38-41 cm)
20-30 lb (9-14 kg)

♀ tan and white

BASENJI

The handsome basenji is as fastidious as a cat about its personal grooming, even washing itself with its paws. Well known for being barkless, it "yodels" when happy.

History This ancient African breed was used for hunting and valued for its great stamina. It was introduced into Europe and then North America in the twentieth century.

Description This compact, muscular dog has a distinctive trotting gait. Its loose, silky, shorthaired coat comes in combinations of white, tan, brindle, chestnut and black. When alert, the dog's forehead wrinkles, giving it a worried look. The tail is tightly curled over the back. The breeding pattern is unusual, the bitch coming into season only once a year.

Temperament Alert, affectionate, energetic and curious, the basenji loves to play and responds well to training, as long as it is handled regularly from an early age. Provide the dog with plenty of chew toys and a secure fence—the basenji likes to climb and can easily negotiate chain-wire fences.

Grooming Use a firm bristle brush, and shampoo only when necessary.

Exercise and feeding Vigorous daily exercise will keep the basenji trim—it has a tendency to become fat and lazy unless its owner is conscientious about exercise. Green vegetables should be included in the diet.

Health problems This breed may suffer from kidney problems, which must be treated at the first sign of any symptoms. It is also susceptible to progressive retinal atrophy and colitis (inflammation of the large intestine).

AFGHAN HOUND

While undeniably elegant and, when in peak condition, a thing of beauty, the Afghan hound is not an easy-care pet. It requires a great deal of attention and time.

History An agile breed with great stamina, the Afghan hound has been used for many centuries in its native land to hunt gazelle and other large prey, including snow leopards. It was especially favored by royalty.

Description The coat is very long, straight and silky, except on the face and along the spine, and comes in all colors and some combinations. Thick hair on the legs protect it from cold. The tail tip should curl in a complete ring. The gait is free and springy.

Temperament Although it is intelligent, the Afghan hound is not easy to train and, being quite large, it isn't easy to handle either. The dog is not a fashion accessory, and owners need to establish a genuine relationship with their pet. Too many Afghan hounds have been abandoned due to unrealistic expectations.

Grooming The thick coat demands a great deal of attention and must be brushed at least every day. Dry shampoo when necessary and bathe once a month.

Exercise and feeding This hound loves open spaces and must be allowed to run free as well as have long daily walks. There are no special feeding requirements.

Health problems Generally a robust breed, it may suffer from hip dysplasia and eye problems.

chocolate brindle

PET FACTS

Independent, lively, loving

Extensive

Regular, vigorous

Adapts well to urban living, but needs plenty of space

Not a good watchdog

Male: 27-29 in (69-74 cm)
55-65 lb (25-29 kg)
Female: 25-27 in (63-69cm)
50-60 lb (23-27 kg)

PET FACTS

 Gentle, reserved, sensitive

 Regular brushing

 Regular, moderate

 Adapts well to urban living, but needs plenty of exercise

Not a good watchdog

Male: At least 29 in (74 cm)
70-90 lb (32-41 kg)
Female: At least 27 in (69 cm)
65-85 lb (29-38 kg)

♂ blue sable

BORZOI

The borzoi is a dignified dog of grace and beauty. If you want a constant companion and can provide the exercise and love it craves, this may be the dog for you.

History Also known as Russian wolfhounds, pairs of borzois were used by members of the Russian aristocracy to chase wolves. The borzoi is probably descended from the "gaze hounds" of the Middle East, which it resembles.

Description A tall, elegant dog, the borzoi has a lean, muscular body designed for speed. The long, silky, often wavy coat is profusely feathered (fringed), and comes in all colors, usually white with colored markings. The small, pointed ears are well feathered.

Temperament Gentle, reserved and sometimes nervy around children, the borzoi is affectionate with its owners and tolerant of other dogs. However, it needs plenty of attention.

Grooming Brush regularly with a firm bristle brush. Bathing presents problems with such a tall dog; dry shampoo when necessary. Clip the hair between the toes to keep the feet comfortable and to stop them from spreading.

Exercise and feeding To maintain its fitness the borzoi needs plenty of exercise, including regular opportunities to run off the leash. It should be fed small meals two or three times a day. Avoid exercise after meals.

Health problems This large, deep-chested dog is particularly prone to bloat. As it ages, it may also become susceptible to eye diseases. Provide a well-padded bed to prevent calluses and irritation to the elbows.

SALUKI

This breed was used in Arabia for hunting gazelle and other game. While falcons swooped over the quarry, Salukis chased and held it for a mounted hunter to kill.

History Named after the ancient city of Saluk, this dog was traditionally thought of as "the sacred gift of Allah." It was never sold, but could be presented as a gift to an important person.

Description The graceful Saluki is built for speed and is capable of bursts of 40 mph (65 km/h). It has exceptional stamina and can jump very high.

Both the smoothhaired and feathered coat types have fringing on the ears and the long, curved tail, but the smooth variety has none on the legs. The silky coat can be black and tan (see p. 208), white, cream, fawn, gold and red, or combinations of these.

Temperament Intensely loyal to its family, the Saluki may remain aloof with strangers. It can be sensitive and, while easy to train, may become timid if the trainer's manner is harsh or overbearing.

Grooming Take care not to overbrush, as this may break the coat. There is little shedding. Trim the hair between the toes to prevent matting and discomfort. Shampoo only when necessary.

Exercise and feeding This dog needs long daily walks as well as opportunities to run. It can be a light eater and, perhaps due to its region of origin, drinks less than other dogs.

Health problems The breed is prone to cancer, genetic eye diseases such as cataracts and sunburn, especially on the nose.

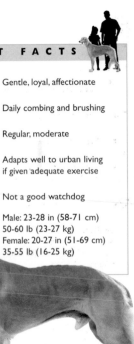

PET FACTS

Gentle, loyal, affectionate

Daily combing and brushing

Regular, moderate

Adapts well to urban living if given adequate exercise

Not a good watchdog

Male: 23-28 in (58-71 cm)
50-60 lb (23-27 kg)
Female: 20-27 in (51-69 cm)
35-55 lb (16-25 kg)

*Smoothhaired
♂ gold*

PET FACTS

 Gentle, sensitive, affectionate

Minimal

Regular, vigorous

 Adapts well to urban life, but needs space and exercise

 Too shy to be a very good watchdog

Male: 25-27 in (63-69 cm)
40-50 lb (18-23 kg)
Female: 23-25 in (58-63 cm)
35-45 lb (16-20 kg)

○ black and tan

BLOODHOUND

Brought to England by William the Conqueror, the mournful-looking Bloodhound has entered literature and legend as the archetypal "sleuth" dog.

History The bloodhound's ancestry can be traced directly to eighth-century Belgium, and it is also known as the Flemish hound. It is able to follow any scent, even a human's—a rare ability in a dog.

Description Large and powerful, the bloodhound looks tougher than it is. The skin is loose and the coat is short and dense. Especially fine on the head and ears, the coat can be tan with black or liver, tawny, or solid red. There is sometimes a little white on the chest, feet and the tip of the tail.

Temperament Sensitive, gentle and shy, the bloodhound becomes devoted to its master. Rarely vicious, it gets along well with people and other dogs.

Grooming Use a firm bristle brush and bathe only when necessary. A rub with a rough towel or chamois will leave the coat gleaming. Clean the long, floppy ears regularly.

Exercise and feeding The bloodhound needs a lot of exercise. It enjoys a run, but if it picks up an interesting scent its owner may find it difficult to get its attention. As this breed is prone to bloat it should be fed two or three small meals a day instead of one large one. Avoid exercise after meals.

Health problems In addition to bloat, the breed is susceptible to ear infections and hip dysplasia. A well-padded bed is recommended to avoid calluses on the joints.

RHODESIAN RIDGEBACK

An all-weather, low-maintenance dog, the Rhodesian ridgeback bonds closely with its adoptive family as a puppy and makes a fun-loving pet.

History The breed gets its name from a peculiarity of the coat—a dagger-shaped ridge of hair that lies along the spine in the opposite direction to the rest of the coat. Although it originated in South Africa, it was in what is now known as Zimbabwe that it became prized for its ability to hunt lion and other large game.

Description This strong, active dog has a dense, glossy coat. It comes in solid shades of red to light wheaten with a dark muzzle and sometimes a little white on the chest. The brow wrinkles when the dog is alert.

Temperament The Rhodesian ridgeback is gentle and friendly, but it can be a tenacious fighter when aroused. It makes an outstanding watchdog and a devoted family pet. Training should begin early, while the dog is still small enough to manage. It should be treated gently so as not to break its spirit or make it aggressive.

Grooming Use a firm bristle brush and shampoo only when necessary.

Exercise and feeding This dog has great stamina; owners will tire long before it does. It also loves to swim. There are no special feeding requirements, but don't overfeed—it will eat all it can get and still act hungry.

Health problems This relatively hardy breed is susceptible to hip dysplasia.

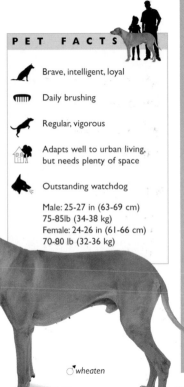

PET FACTS

Brave, intelligent, loyal

Daily brushing

Regular, vigorous

Adapts well to urban living, but needs plenty of space

Outstanding watchdog

Male: 25-27 in (63-69 cm)
75-85lb (34-38 kg)
Female: 24-26 in (61-66 cm)
70-80 lb (32-36 kg)

○ wheaten

221

PET FACTS

 Calm, affectionate and gentle

 Daily combing

 Regular, moderate

 Needs plenty of space. Unsuited to apartments.

Adequate watchdog

Male: 28-38 in (71-95 cm)
90-120 lb (41-54 kg)
Female: 26-34 in (66-86 cm)
80-110 lb (36-50 kg)

♂ fawn

IRISH WOLFHOUND

A true gentle giant, the Irish wolfhound is wonderful with children. It was so successful at hunting that wolves have disappeared from the British Isles.

History After working its way out of a job, the breed was brought back from the brink of extinction about 140 years ago by a British Army officer, Captain George Graham, who saw its potential for rescue work.

Description A massive, muscular dog, the Irish wolfhound is the tallest breed in the world. Its rough, wiry coat comes in gray, brindle, red, black, fawn and white. The paws are large and round, with markedly arched toes and strong, curved nails.

Temperament In spite of being a killer of wolves, this dog is gentle, loyal and very affectionate. It is trustworthy around children, although it might knock them over with its large tail. While disinclined to bark, its size alone should be daunting to intruders.

Grooming Unless the hard, wiry coat is combed often, it will become matted. Clip out any knots. Trim around the eyes and ears with blunt-nosed scissors.

Exercise and feeding Inclined to be lazy, the Irish wolfhound needs a reasonable amount of exercise, but no more than smaller breeds. To avoid joint damage, young dogs should not be taken for long walks. There are no special feeding requirements.

Health problems This breed may suffer from heart disease, hip dysplasia, bone cancer and cataracts.

NORWEGIAN ELKHOUND

Surprisingly, the handsome Norwegian elkhound can adapt to warmer climates than its homeland as its thick coat insulates it from both heat and cold.

History A member of the spitz family, dogs of this kind have been used to hunt bears, elk and moose since Viking times. They would chase and hold the prey until hunters arrived for the kill. They were also used to pull sleds.

Description The elkhound has a shortish, thickset body, with the tail tightly curled over the back. The coat comes in various shades of gray, with black tips on the outer coat, and lighter hair on the chest, underbody, legs and underside of the tail. There is a thick ruff around the neck.

Although it is totally silent while tracking, the elkhound is perhaps the most "talkative" dog of all. Owners soon learn to recognize its vocabulary of sounds, each with a different meaning.

Temperament While gentle and devoted to its owner, the dog needs consistent training that is firm but never harsh. It prefers a set routine.

Grooming The coarse, weatherproof coat must be brushed regularly. When the dog is molting its dense under-coat, extra care must be taken to remove dead hair. Bathing is largely unnecessary.

Exercise and feeding An agile, energetic dog, the elkhound revels in strenuous activity. There are no special feeding requirements.

Health problems Bred for a rugged life, it suffers from few genetic diseases other than hip dysplasia and the common eye diseases.

PET FACTS

Fearless, intelligent, good-tempered

Regular brushing

Regular, vigorous

Adapts well to urban living, but needs plenty of exercise

Good watchdog

Male: 19-21 in (48-53 cm)
45-55 lb (20-25 kg)
Female: 18-20 in (46-51cm)
40-50 lb (18-23 kg)

♂ *gray-black*

223

224

WORKING DOGS

This group includes breeds developed to perform a specific task, be it guarding a settlement, droving cattle, hauling loads or rescue work. Some breeds, once used as weapons of war and as combatants of bulls, bears and other dogs, today provide service to the police and military. Since many modern working breeds—especially the guarding and fighting dogs—are descendants of the mastiff, they are generally large, powerful and fearless. Other dogs of the Arctic spitz lineage are sturdy dogs possessing enormous stamina. Most have an innate sense of responsibility, refined by selective breeding, and carry out their duties diligently. Given kind and consistent training, a working dog can make useful and reliable family friend.

Energetic, friendly, loyal

Regular brushing

Regular, moderate

Ideal for urban or apartment living, but needs plenty of exercise

Good watchdog

Male: 14-16 in (36-41 cm)
20-30 lb (9-14 kg)
Female: 13-15 in (33-38 cm)
18-28 lb (8-13 kg)

♂ red

SHIBA INU

Its convenient size and vivacious, outgoing personality has made the shiba inu the most common pet dog in its native Japan. It is now gaining popularity worldwide.

History The shiba inu is the smallest of the Japanese spitz-type dogs and was originally bred to flush birds and small game from brushwood areas. The name shiba possibly comes from a Japanese word for brushwood, or it may derive from an old word meaning small (*inu* means dog).

Description Agile and well proportioned, the shiba inu has a strong body and alert bearing. The waterproof, all-weather coat comes in red, sable or black and tan, with pale shadings on the legs, belly, chest, face and tail.

Temperament Lively and good-natured, this smart, independent dog can be somewhat difficult to train. It chooses which commands to obey, so it needs firm, consistent handling.

Although extremely sociable—regarding itself as part of the family—it can be aggressive to unfamiliar dogs. Prone to wreak havoc on your house as a pup, it digs and climbs with ease.

Grooming Groom the coarse, stiff, double coat with a firm bristle brush. Bathe only when absolutely necessary, as this strips the coat's waterproofing.

Exercise and feeding This active dog needs lots of exercise. There are no special feeding requirements.

Health problems The breed is generally hardy and healthy, with few genetic weaknesses. The coat protects it in both cold and hot conditions, so it can live outdoors in a secure yard of reasonable size.

CHOW CHOW

The unusual-looking Chow Chow is less exuberant than many of its fellows, but nevertheless is affectionate and loyal. It has a growing band of devotees.

History Physically very similar to fossilized remains of ancient dogs, this spitz-type breed probably originated in Siberia or Mongolia. Used as a temple guard and cart dog, it later became the favored hunting dog of Chinese emperors. It was almost unknown in the West until about 120 years ago.

Description Two distinctive features of the Chow Chow are its blue-black tongue and its almost straight hindlegs, which make its walk rather stilted. Its luxurious double coat comes in solid black, red, fawn, cream, blue or white, sometimes with lighter or darker shades, but never particolored. It can also be smooth-coated. The ears are small and rounded and there is a huge ruff behind the head, which gives the dog a lion-like appearance.

Temperament Although something of a challenge to train, the strong-willed Chow Chow makes a very good watchdog. Proud, aloof, and suspicious of strangers, it can be very territorial and a tenacious fighter if provoked.

Grooming The coat sheds heavily and should be brushed three times a week to maintain the lifted look. Dry shampoo when necessary.

Exercise and feeding The dog can be lazy and will benefit from a daily walk. There are no special feeding requirements, but don't overfeed.

Health problems Prone to eczema, joint problems and eye diseases, the breed is also unsuited to hot climates.

PET FACTS

Reserved, independent; a one-person dog

Regular brushing

Regular, moderate

Adapts well to urban living, but needs space

Very good watchdog

Male: 18-23 in (46-56 cm)
50-65 lb (23-29 kg)
Female: 18-22 in (46-53 cm)
45-60 lb (20-27 kg)

♂ black

PET FACTS

Brave, strong, alert

Regular brushing

Regular, moderate

Adapts well to urban living, but needs plenty of space and exercise

Excellent watchdog

Male: 21-24 in (53-61 cm)
90-110 lb (41-50 kg)
Female: 19-22 in (48-56 cm)
85-105 lb (38-48 kg)

♂ red and white

AKITA

The handsome Akita is renowned for its strength, courage and loyalty. The national dog of Japan, many champions of the breed are national treasures.

History The Akita has only recently become known outside Japan, where it was used for hunting deer, wild boar and black bears. In feudal times it was pitted in savage dog-fighting spectacles, but these are now outlawed. The dog has found work with the police and is a reliable guard dog.

Description The largest of the Japanese spitz-type breeds, it has a well-proportioned, muscular body and a waterproof coat that comes in all colors with clear markings. The thick tail is carried in a curl over the back. It has webbed feet and is a strong swimmer.

Temperament Despite the ferocity of many of its past activities, with diligent training the Akita can make an

excellent pet. Care should always be taken, however, around other dogs, as it may become aggressive. It is not suitable for first-time owners.

Grooming The coarse, stiff, double coat requires significant grooming and sheds heavily twice a year. Brush with a firm bristle brush and bathe only when absolutely necessary, since it removes the natural waterproofing of the coat.

Exercise and feeding The athletic Akita needs regular exercise. Avoid aggressive games like tug-of-war. There are no special feeding requirements.

Health problems Illness is rare in this robust breed, but there is some tendency to hip dysplasia, thyroid problems and genetic eye disease.

ALASKAN MALAMUTE

With its strong, powerful body and enormous stamina, this breed is ideal for work in the Arctic. Despite its wolf-like appearance, it also makes an affectionate pet.

History This sledding dog of the spitz family was named after the Malhemut, a nomadic Inuit tribe of Alaska.

Description The underbody and face masking of this compact dog is always white, while the remaining coat may be light gray to black, gold to red and liver. The plumed tail is carried over the back.

Temperament The malamute may look intimidating, but its exceptional friendliness toward people makes it an ineffective watchdog. However, its strong personality and tendency to dominate means it needs early, consistent training from an experienced owner. It may also become aggressive with other dogs and needs to be watched around them and other pets.

Grooming Brush the dense, coarse coat twice a week, and more often during molting, when the undercoat comes out in clumps. Bathing is mostly unnecessary, as the coat sheds dirt readily.

Exercise and feeding This dog enjoys an active lifestyle—a sedentary, bored malamute can become destructive. It needs a large yard with a high fence, but bury the base, as it is likely to dig its way out. This thrifty feeder needs less food than might be expected. However, it tends to wolf down whatever is offered, which can lead to bloat and obesity.

Health problems Subject to hip dysplasia, thyroid and eye disease, it is also unsuited to life in hot climates.

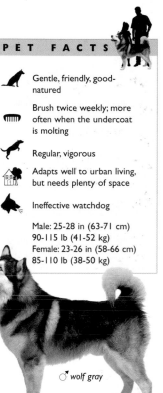

PET FACTS

Gentle, friendly, good-natured

Brush twice weekly; more often when the undercoat is molting

Regular, vigorous

Adapts well to urban living, but needs plenty of space

Ineffective watchdog

Male: 25-28 in (63-71 cm)
90-115 lb (41-52 kg)
Female: 23-26 in (58-66 cm)
85-110 lb (38-50 kg)

♂ wolf gray

229

PET FACTS

 Gentle, friendly, good-natured

 Brush twice weekly; more when molting

 Regular, robust

 Adapts well to urban living, but needs plenty of space

Ineffective watchdog

Male: 20-22 in (51-56 cm)
45-55 lb (20-25 kg)
Female: 18-20 in (46-51 cm)
40-50 lb (18-23 kg)

♀ *white*

SAMOYED

The Samoyed is almost always good-humored and ready for any challenge. Its pale, luxurious fur coat and black-lipped smiling face make it a spectacular pet.

History A member of the spitz family, this breed was used by the nomadic Samoyed tribe of Siberia to drive caribou herds, guard flocks, and as draft and sled dogs.

Description The compact muscular body of this hard-working breed is covered with a glistening thick, silver-tipped coat that comes in white, biscuit and cream. Its thick, perky tail curls over the back and to one side.

Temperament The Samoyed is independent and strong, so training should begin at an early age. While too friendly to be of much use as a watchdog, its high-pitched bark will indicate the presence of strangers. It willingly adapts to family life and loves children.

Grooming Brush two or three times a week to remove dead hair and keep the woolly undercoat from matting. This dog sheds heavily, so extra care is necessary when the undercoat falls out in clumps. Bathing is difficult and mostly unnecessary, as the coat sheds dirt readily. Dry shampoo from time to time by brushing unscented talcum powder through the coat.

Exercise and feeding This outdoor type needs robust daily exercise. There are no special feeding requirements, but the Samoyed is partial to fish.

Health problems This breed is particularly prone to hip dysplasia, skin and eye problems and diabetes. It is difficult to find ticks in the coat, and the dog does not tolerate hot climates.

SIBERIAN HUSKY

The Siberian husky's speed and stamina enable it to haul loads over vast distances in seemingly impossible terrain. It has served many polar expeditions.

History Originally from Siberia, this dog was bred by the nomadic Chukchi people to pull sleds and herd reindeer.

Description The face mask and underbody of this strong, compact dog are usually white. The remaining coat can be any color. Mismatched eyes are common. The feet have hair between the toes for grip on ice.

Temperament The friendly husky barks little, although its wolf-like appearance may deter intruders. An affectionate pet, dependable around children, it may also be hard to train and needs an experienced owner.

Grooming Brush the coarse, medium-length coat twice a week. The undercoat requires extra care during molting season. Bathing is difficult and mostly unnecessary, as the coat sheds dirt, but an occasional dry shampoo should help keep it looking clean. Clip the nails regularly.

Exercise and feeding Insufficient exercise may make this dog destructive, but it should not be excessively exercised in warm weather. It needs a large yard with a high fence, but bury the wire at the base so it can not dig its way out and go off hunting. A thrifty feeder, it needs less food than might be expected.

Health problems The breed is subject to hip dysplasia and skin, thyroid and occasional eye problems. It is unsuited to life in hot climates.

PET FACTS

Playful, friendly, good-natured

Brush twice weekly; more when molting

Regular, vigorous

Adapts well to urban living, but needs plenty of space

Ineffective watchdog

Male: 21-23 in (53-58 cm)
45-60 lb (20-27 kg)
Female: 20-22 in (51-56 cm)
35-50 lb (16-23 kg)

♂ gray and white

SAINT BERNARD

The Saint Bernard is universally admired for its feats of rescue in the Swiss Alps. For more than 200 years, its courage and skill have been the stuff of legends.

History The Saint Bernard is thought to have descended from the Molossi, the original mastiff stock introduced to the Alps by the Romans about 2,000 years ago. The breed is named after Bernard de Menthon, the founder of a hospice built in a remote alpine pass in Switzerland nearly 1,000 years ago to shelter mountain travelers. Bernardine monks developed the dog for guard, guide and draft work. It is not known when the dog started to be used for rescue work, although it is likely to have been during the seventeenth century. The breed has been credited for saving the lives of over 2,500 people—Barry, a Saint Bernard born in 1800, rescued 40 people in his 12 years of work.

Description This is an imposing dog: tall, broad and strong. It has a muscular neck, a deep chest, and a broad, powerful tail that curves slightly at the tip. The feet are large with well-arched toes, making the Saint Bernard sure-footed in snow and on ice. It has a highly developed sense of smell and also seems to have a sixth sense about impending danger.

Smooth- and rough-coated varieties are available. Both coat types are very dense and come in white, with tan, mahogany, red, brindle and black markings in various combinations. The rough coat is a modern development from crossing the dog with Newfoundland stock. The hair is slightly longer and there is feathering on the legs. However, since the hair ices up in extreme weather, the coat is less suited to the dog's original environment.

The short, square muzzle, face and ears are usually shaded with black. The dog's expression is benevolent.

Temperament Dignified and reliable, the Saint Bernard is generally good with children. It is highly intelli-

Smooth coat
♂ *red and white*

gent and easy to train although training should begin early, while the dog is still a manageable size, to quell any dominant tendencies. An unruly dog of this size presents a problem for even a strong adult if it is to be exercised in public areas on a leash, so take control from the outset.

The Saint Bernard does not bark a lot but makes a good watchdog, its size alone an effective deterrent.

Grooming Both types of coat need thorough combing and brushing with a firm bristle brush at least three times a week. During spring and fall, when there is considerable shedding, it will need daily brushing. Bathe only when necessary with mild soap—shampoo may strip the coat of its natural oils.

Since the breed drools, extra care is needed to keep the jowls and chest clean. The eyes, which may be inclined to water, also need special attention to keep them clean and free of irritants. Check the ears regularly and keep the nails trimmed.

Exercise and feeding A long daily walk will keep this dog in good condition. Like all large breeds, it grows rapidly and its diet requires careful attention. Do not to allow a puppy too much activity until the bones are well-formed and strong. Short walks and brief play sessions are best until the dog is about two years old.

This breed is highly susceptible to bloat, so give it two or three small meals a day. It is expensive to feed.

Health problems This giant dog is particularly prone to hip dysplasia and heart disease. It may also suffer from epilepsy, skin problems and an eye condition, called ectropion, that causes irritation and weeping because the eyelids don't close completely.

Male: 27 in (69 cm) or more
From 172 lb (80 kg)
Female: 25 in (63 cm) or more
From 160 lb (72 kg)

PET FACTS

Placid, affectionate loyal

Frequent brushing

Regular, moderate

Well-suited to urban living if given plenty of space and exercise

Good watchdog

Rough coat
red and white

PET FACTS

Calm, gentle, dignified

Regular brushing

Regular, extensive

Adapts well to urban living, but needs plenty of space and exercise

Very good watchdog

GREAT PYRENEES

A majestic dog that always impresses, the Great Pyrenees also requires a considerable commitment in space, patience and, most important, time to meet its needs.

History This breed has a long history in its native France as a guard of sheep and châteaux. It may also have been used for war in ancient times when it was less gentle than it is now.

Description This very large, muscular dog has a waterproof coat of solid white or white with patches of tan, pale yellow or wolf-gray. The long, coarse outer coat is either straight or slightly wavy; the fine undercoat is soft and thick.

○ white

Male: 25-32 in (63-81 cm)
100-130 lb (45-59 kg)
Female: 23-30 in (58-76 cm)
90-120 lb (41-54 kg)

Temperament Although it is calm, intelligent and has a natural instinct for guarding, this breed must receive consistent obedience training while young and small. It does not reach maturity until two years of age.

Grooming The outer coat doesn't mat, so care is relatively easy—just a couple of brushings a week; more when the dog is molting its dense undercoat. Bathe only when necessary.

Exercise and feeding This breed needs plenty of exercise. There are no special feeding requirements, although it has a relatively small appetite.

Health problems It may suffer from eye diseases, deafness and orthopedic problems including hip dysplasia.

NEWFOUNDLAND

A powerful swimmer, the Newfoundland has an outstanding record of sea rescues to its credit. It was prized by fishermen in its region of origin.

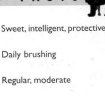

PET FACTS

Sweet, intelligent, protective

 Daily brushing

Regular, moderate

 Adapts well to urban living, but needs plenty of space

Good watchdog

History One of the few breeds native to North America, the Newfoundland did invaluable work for early settlers pulling sleds, hunting, guarding and helping fishermen with their catches.

Description The dog's thick, coarse double coat comes in black, browns, or black with white markings—this variant being known as the Landseer after its depiction in a painting by Sir Edwin Landseer. This water-loving breed has webbing between its toes.

Temperament Renowned for its gentleness with children, this breed is also adaptable, loyal and courageous, with great strength and endurance. Rather than bark or growl, it uses its massive body to deter strangers. It is easy to train and house-train.

Grooming Use a hard brush every day, and take extra care during molting. Avoid bathing unless absolutely necessary, as this strips the coat's oils.

Exercise and feeding Content to laze, it will benefit from moderate exercise and swimming. There are no special feeding requirements, but don't overfeed.

Health problems Prone to heart and orthopedic diseases, the dog is also unsuited to hot climates.

Male: 27-29 in (69-74 cm)
138-150 lb (63-68 kg)
Female: 25-27 in (63-69 cm)
110-120 lb (50-54 kg)

♂ black

Placid, cheerful, loving

 Daily brushing

Regular, moderate

 Adapts well to urban living, but needs plenty of exercise

 Excellent watchdog

BERNESE MOUNTAIN DOG

An all-around working dog in its native Switzerland, the Bernese mountain dog adapts easily to domestic life as long as it is given plenty of loving attention.

History Also known as the Bernese sennenhund, this is one of four Swiss breeds that are probably descended from the mastiff-type dogs of Roman times. It herds cattle, guards farms and pulls carts. It also shares the Saint Bernard's skill at finding people lost in snow.

Description The powerful, handsome Bernese is vigorous and agile. It has a glossy soft, wavy, medium-length black coat with distinctive white and chestnut markings.

Male: 24-28 in (61-71 cm)
85-110 lb (38-50 kg)
Female: 23-27 in (58-69 cm)
80-105 lb (36-48 kg)

♂ tricolor

Temperament This gentle, cheerful dog loves children. Very intelligent, it is easy to train and is a natural watchdog. Indeed, this family companion is so loyal that it may have trouble adjusting to a new owner after the age of 18 months.

Grooming Vigorous daily brushing of the thick coat is important, with extra care needed during shedding. Bathe or dry shampoo as necessary.

Exercise and feeding This large, active dog needs a regular exercise regimen. There are no special feeding requirements.

Health problems The breed is particularly prone to hip and elbow dysplasia, genetic eye diseases and cancer.

BULLMASTIFF

Despite its size and aggressive looks, the bullmastiff is a devoted pet and a watchdog par excellence. The strong, silent type, it rarely loses its temper and is easy to train.

History This powerful and intimidating dog was developed in Britain by crossing the fast and ferocious bulldog with the large and strong mastiff, an excellent tracker. It was widely used by estate gamekeepers to deter poachers.

Description Smaller and more compact than the mastiff, the bullmastiff has dense, coarse, water-resistant coat that comes in dark brindle, fawn and red shades. The face and neck are darker and deeply folded. There are sometimes white marks on the chest.

Temperament Although unlikely to attack, this dog will catch an intruder, knock him down and hold him. At the same time, it is even-tempered, calm and loyal. It is tolerant of children and craves human attention.

Grooming Use a firm bristle brush and shampoo when necessary. The coat sheds little and weekly rubdowns with a chamois will keep it shiny.

Exercise and feeding This dog tends to be lazy, so provide regular on-leash exercise. Feed it two or three small meals a day.

Health problems A robust breed, it is prone to bloat, hip dysplasia and some eye problems. It does not tolerate extremes of temperature well.

Male: 25-27 in (63-69 cm)
110-133 lb (50-60 kg)
Female: 24-26 in (61-66 cm)
90-110 lb (41-50 kg)

PET FACTS

Placid, gentle, loyal

Regular brushing

Regular, moderate

Adapts well to urban living, but needs plenty of space

Excellent watchdog

♂ fawn

237

PET FACTS

Reliable, valiant, but can be aggressive

Regular brushing

Regular, moderate

Adapts well to urban living, but needs plenty of space

Outstanding watchdog

MASTIFF

Few intruders would venture onto a property guarded by a mastiff. But this magnificent dog also has a gentle side and, if properly handled, is devoted to its people.

History References to mastiff-type dogs go back to antiquity. Ferocious and formidable fighters, they were used for military work as well as hunting. Today's mastiff is more correctly called the Old English mastiff, as its lineage can be traced to two surviving English strains.

Description This powerful dog is an imposing sight. The coat is dense and flat-lying and comes in shades of apricot, silver, fawn or darker fawn brindle. The muzzle and nose are black.

Male: From 30 in (76 cm)
From about 160 lb (72 kg)
Female: From 27 in (69 cm)
From about 150 lb (68 kg)

♀ fawn

Temperament An exceptional guard dog, the mastiff must be trained with firm kindness if it is to be kept under control. When properly handled, it is docile, good-natured and loyal.

Grooming Brush the coarse coat with a firm bristle brush and rub with a chamois for a gleaming finish. Bathe or dry shampoo when necessary.

Exercise and feeding Inclined to be lazy, the mastiff will be fitter and happier if given regular exercise. It's best to keep it leashed in public. As this breed is prone to bloat, feed two or three small meals a day.

Health problems In addition to bloat, the mastiff may suffer from hip dysplasia and genetic eye diseases.

ROTTWEILER

The Rottweiler is not a dog for the average home nor for inexperienced owners. An imposing and effective guard dog, it needs firm handling and proper training.

History Around the town of Rottweil, southern Germany, mastiff-type dogs left by the Roman army were crossed with sheepdogs to create a dog capable of herding and guarding butchers' cattle. It is now used in police, customs and military work.

Description This muscular dog has surprising speed and agility. The thick coat conceals a fine undercoat and is always black with rich tan markings. The tail is docked at the first joint.

Temperament Prized for its aggression and guarding abilities, the Rottweiler can, with kind, firm and consistent handling, also be a loving pet. Training and socialization must begin young, and great care should be taken to ensure that it is not made vicious.

Grooming A firm bristle brush will keep the medium-length coat glossy. Bathe only when necessary.

Exercise and feeding Provide lots of work and exercise, but avoid aggressive games like tug-of-war. There are no special feeding requirements, but don't overfeed pups.

Health problems It is prone to orthopedic, skin and eye diseases, bleeding disorders, diabetes and paralysis.

Male: 25-27 in (63-69 cm)
100-135 lb (45-61 kg)
Female: 23-25 in (58-63 cm)
90-120 lb (41-54 kg)

♂ black and tan

PET FACTS

Brave, intelligent, formidable

Weekly brushing

Regular, vigorous

Adapts well to urban living, but needs plenty of exercise

Excellent watchdog

GREAT DANE

Among the tallest of dog breeds, the Great Dane is not of Danish origin but was developed in Germany. It is surprisingly gentle for its size.

History Ancestors of this aristocratic breed have been known in Germany for more than 2,000 years. It was originally favored by the nobility for hunting wild boar and stags. It was also used in war and to guard estates. Its origins can be traced to fighting mastiffs brought to Europe possibly by the Romans, or by tribes from southwestern Asia. The first Great Danes were probably produced by crossing these dogs with greyhounds around the Middle Ages—Chaucer makes a reference to a massive, Great Dane-type dog in the 1200s. The breed is now the national dog of Germany.

♀ fawn (left) and brindle (right)

Description This dignified and noble-looking dog is large and muscular, with a deep chest and powerful hindquarters. It has long legs, cat-like feet with well-arched nails and a long, tapering, slightly curved tail. A surprisingly graceful, agile dog, it may owe its speed to its greyhound lineage.

The Great Dane has a dense, sleek, close-fitting coat that comes in fawn, black, blue, striped brindle and harlequin (white with black patches). The high-set ears may be cropped to a sharp point—making the dog look especially fearsome—although this questionable practice has fallen from favor in recent times.

Temperament Loyal, affectionate and playful, the Great Dane is well-behaved when properly socialized, trained and handled by an experienced owner. Training must begin before the dog grows too large. It can be territorial and aggressive with other dogs and makes a good watchdog—its size and deep bark are daunting for even the most determined intruder. However, it is usually even-tempered around its family and can be a gentle guardian for children and other animals. Supervision is required when the dog is around very young children, as it may inadvertently step on them or knock them over.

Grooming The smooth, thick short-haired coat is easy to groom. Comb and brush with a firm bristle brush every day, and dry shampoo when necessary. Bathing this giant is a major chore, so it pays to avoid the need by daily grooming. The nails must be kept trimmed if not worn down naturally by exercise.

Exercise and feeding The Great Dane needs plenty of exercise, at the very least a long daily walk or a run alongside a bicycle. Avoid games such as tug-of-war or wrestling. A puppy under ten months of age should never be given long or strenuous exercise sessions, as its bones are still forming and too much activity may cause abnormalities to develop. Instead, the pup should be given plenty of space to exercise freely on its own.

Slow to mature, the breed needs special nutritional requirements during its growing period, which can last 20 months. Due to its susceptibility to bloat, it should be fed two to three small meals a day and must never be exercised strenuously immediately after feeding. Ideally, the dish should be raised so that the dog can eat without splaying its legs. This giant breed has a food bill to match.

Health problems Being a very large and heavy breed, the Great Dane is particularly susceptible to hip dysplasia and some genetic heart ailments. Bone cancer and bloat are also common problems. Like many other giant breeds, such as the Great Pyrenees, it has a short life span of about ten years.

♂ fawn

Male: 30-32 in (76-81 cm)
100-125 lb (45-57 kg)
Female: 28-30 in (71-76 cm)
90-105 lb (41-48 kg)

PET FACTS

Gentle, loyal, affectionate

Daily brushing

Regular, moderate

Adapts well to urban living, but needs plenty of space

Very good watchdog

241

PET FACTS

Fun-loving, protective, loyal

Daily brushing

Regular, vigorous

Adapts well to urban living, but needs space

Excellent watchdog

Male: 22-24 in (56-61 cm)
60-70 lb (27-32 kg)
Female: 21-23 in (53-58 cm)
55-65 lb (25-29 kg)

brindle and white

BOXER

If your best friend is a boxer, you can rely on it to take care of your property and to be waiting with a boisterous welcome whenever you return home.

History Developed in Germany from mastiff-type dogs, the boxer was originally used in bull-baiting and eventually crossed with the bulldog to improve this ability. It was little known outside Germany until soldiers took some home after World War II. Intelligent and easily trained, it has been used in military and police work.

Description The body is compact and powerful and the shiny, close-fitting coat comes in fawn, brindle and various shades of red, with white markings. The tail is usually docked.

Temperament Training should start young and be firm and consistent—this exuberant dog should be handled by a strong adult. Reliable with children and intensely loyal to its family,

it makes an excellent watchdog and will restrain an intruder in the same way a bullmastiff does. However, it may be aggressive with other dogs.

Grooming Brush the smooth, short-haired coat with a firm bristle brush, and bathe only when necessary.

Exercise and feeding This playful, athletic breed needs daily work or exercise—a long, brisk, walk and lots of games. Since it is prone to bloat, feed two or three small meals a day.

Health problems A short-lived breed, at about ten years, it is subject to heart disease, cancer, stroke and skin problems. Sinus infections, heat-stroke and breathing difficulties are common due to the shape of the nose.

DOBERMAN PINSCHER

Developed to deter thieves, the Doberman pinscher is prized as an obedient and powerful watchdog. With proper training, it can also become a devoted pet.

History This intimidating dog was developed late in the nineteenth century by a German tax collector, Louis Dobermann. He drew on a number of breeds, including the Rottweiler, the German pinscher, the German shepherd and the Manchester terrier to produce the quintessential guard dog—obedient and courageous.

Description An elegant, muscular dog, it has a well-proportioned chest, a short back and a lean, muscular neck. Its close-fitting coat usually comes in black, or black and tan, but blue-gray, red and fawn also occur.

Temperament The reputation for aggression is generally undeserved, but firm and determined training from puppyhood is essential. Fortunately

the dog is easy to train, but it remains a powerful animal that should always be supervised around children.

Grooming The smooth coat does not shed much. Use a bristle brush and bathe only when necessary.

Exercise and feeding This agile and energetic breed requires plenty of daily exercise. It is not suitable for apartments or houses with small yards. Since it is prone to bloat, feed three small meals a day.

Health problems The Doberman is subject to heart disease, diabetes, liver dysfunctions, von Willebrand's disease, eye problems and orthopedic abnormalities including hip dysplasia. Do not expose it to extreme cold.

PET FACTS

Intelligent, loyal and fearless, but may be aggressive

Regular brushing

Regular, vigorous

Adapts to urban living if given enough space and exercise

Superb watchdog

Male: 25-27 in (63-69 cm)
55-75 lb (25-34 kg)
Female: 23-26 in (58-66 cm)
50-70 lb (23-32 kg)

○ black and tan

SCHNAUZER

Possibly a mix of spitz and ratting dog bloodlines, the schnauzer is an old breed that has been depicted in paintings and tapestries dating back to the 1500s. Although known outside its native Germany for less than a century, the dog's high spirits, cleverness and loyalty has now won it admirers worldwide.

History The schnauzer is an ancient German breed, or more correctly, three breeds, since the three sizes, Giant, Standard and Miniature (see p. 258), are considered separate breeds. In the US, where the schnauzer was introduced in the 1920s, the Giant and Standard are classified as working dogs while the Miniature is considered a terrier. Many countries class all three together in a group known as utility dogs. The name comes from the German word for muzzle, *schnauze,* a reference to the distinctive mustache of this breed, but the dog was once also known as the wirehaired pinscher. The Standard variety was valued as a herder, retriever, ratter and guard dog, and it often accompanied stage coaches and wagons. The most recent addition to the group, the Giant was developed by crossing rough-coated cattle dogs with smaller schnauzers and was first used for herding cattle and as a guard dog. It was later harnessed to pull small traps and served as a police and military dog in World War I.

Description This is an angular, square-looking dog—the height at the shoulders should be equal to its body length. It has a sturdy, heavy-boned, powerful body, with muscular forelegs. The feet are neat, round and cat-like, with well-arched toes and thick black pads. The tail is usually docked at the third joint. The ears are sometimes cropped too, to form an erect triangle, but this practice is illegal in Britain and Australia.

Giant
♂ black

Giant
Male: 26-28 in (66-71 cm)
60-80 lb (27-36 kg)
Female: 23-26 in (58-66 cm)
55-75 lb (25-34 kg)

Both varieties have a hard, wiry outer coat that comes in pure black or salt and pepper colors, sometimes with white on the chest, head, legs and under the tail. The undercoat is soft, short and dense. The thick, prominent eyebrows and long mustache are often trimmed to accentuate the dog's overall square-cut shape.

Temperament Animated but obedient, this breed is noted for its reliability and affectionate nature. The Giant variety is especially gentle and friendly with children. The schnauzer's bravery and highly developed senses also make it an excellent watchdog. Intelligent and independent, it is inclined to be headstrong and needs firm, consistent training. It may become aggressive with strangers or other animals and if left alone outdoors, will instinctively hunt rodents.

Grooming The wiry coat should be combed or brushed daily with a short wire brush or it will become matted.

Clip out knots and brush first with the grain, then against the grain to lift the coat. The dog should be stripped and clipped all over to an even length twice a year, but this is a job best left to an expert. Trim around the eyes and ears with blunt-nosed scissors, but keep the eyebrows bushy. The whiskers are only lightly trimmed, and they must be cleaned after meals.

Exercise and feeding This active, energetic dog will take as much exercise as it can get, and it relishes off-leash play sessions. At very least, it should be given a long, brisk daily walk. Don't overdo it with a young pup, though, until the bones are strong and mature. There are no special feeding requirements.

Health problems The Giant and Standard are relatively hardy, although the Giant may suffer from hip dysplasia and other orthopedic problems. Both are prone to genetic eye diseases.

PET FACTS

Spirited, lively, affectionate

Daily brushing

Regular, moderate

Adapts well to urban living, but needs plenty of exercise

Excellent watchdog

Standard
Male: 18-20 in (46-51 cm)
40-45 lb (18-20 kg)
Female: 17-19 in (43-48 cm)
35-40 lb (16-18 kg)

♂ Standard
salt and pepper

245

DOG BREEDS
TERRIERS

The name "terrier" is derived from the Latin *terra*, meaning earth, and is descriptive of the original purpose of this group: to hunt down small game and dig it out of burrows. Mostly small dogs with short legs and powerful jaws, terriers have distinctive personalities. Feisty, energetic, tenacious and brave, these quick little characters are alert to the slightest movement and typically have low tolerance for other animals, including other dogs. They are also highly inquisitive and enjoy exploring their surroundings. Their intelligence and attitude have gained them wide popularity as working dogs, and they make engaging companions for owners with playful, lively characters to match those of their pets.

PET FACTS

 Frisky, plucky, companionable

 Regular brushing

Regular, moderate

 Ideal for apartment living

Good watchdog

Male: 10-13 in (25-33 cm)
14-18 lb (6-8 kg)
Female: 9-12 in (23-30 cm)
13-17 lb (6-8 kg)

♀ red wheaten

CAIRN TERRIER

The vivacious little cairn terrier will steal your heart with its fun-loving ways and its courage. It makes an ideal pet: adaptable, friendly and alert.

History One of the oldest terrier breeds, the cairn has contributed to many other terrier varieties through cross-breeding. It originated in the Scottish Highlands where it hunted vermin among the cairns.

Description This compact dog has a thick, soft undercoat and a weather-resistant outer coat that comes in red, sandy, gray, cream, wheaten, brindle, black, pure white or black and tan. The ears and mask can be darker.

Temperament Intelligent and easily trained, this breed is devoted to its owner, almost to the point of jealousy. Strong, fearless and ever-alert, it is an effective watchdog. However, it may bark excessively, and some individuals are incorrigible diggers.

Grooming That shaggy "natural" look actually takes a lot of maintenance. Brush several times a week to avoid matting, being gentle with the undercoat. Bathe monthly and brush the coat while it dries. Trim around the eyes and ears with blunt-nosed scissors and clip the nails regularly.

Exercise and feeding This lively dog is always ready to play and will get enough exercise running in a fenced garden. If you live in an apartment, a daily walk or romp in the park will be necessary. There are no special feeding requirements.

Health problems While generally healthy, the cairn terrier is prone to skin allergies, dislocating kneecaps and hereditary eye diseases.

AUSTRALIAN TERRIER

Although its talents as a rat and snake killer are called on less frequently now, the playful Australian terrier still retains the best characteristics of a working dog.

History The cairn, Yorkshire and Norwich terriers are some of the several British terrier breeds that were combined to create this lively dog. Developed over the past 150 years as a working terrier, the Australian terrier is today kept mainly as a pet.

Description A sturdy, low-set dog, its shaggy, weather-resistant, double coat comes in blue and rich tan, clear reds or sandy shades. The topknot is lighter and there is a thick ruff. The tail is generally docked short.

Temperament Keen and smart, the Australian terrier responds well to training and makes a delightful pet. It is always eager to please and loves being around children. It remains an avid hunter.

Grooming Brush several times a week to bring the long, stiff coat to a high gloss. Be gentle with the soft undercoat. Bathe every month and brush the coat while it dries. The coat doesn't need clipping, but trim around the eyes and ears with blunt-nosed scissors and clip the nails regularly.

Exercise and feeding This adaptable dog will happily adjust to any amount of exercise you are able to provide—it is quite content in a garden of reasonable size. There are no special feeding requirements.

Health problems This dog may suffer from dislocating kneecaps, hip joint deterioration and skin problems. It is also prone to being bitten on the face by the small creatures it hunts.

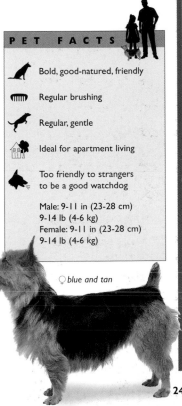

PET FACTS

Bold, good-natured, friendly

Regular brushing

Regular, gentle

Ideal for apartment living

Too friendly to strangers to be a good watchdog

Male: 9-11 in (23-28 cm)
9-14 lb (4-6 kg)
Female: 9-11 in (23-28 cm)
9-14 lb (4-6 kg)

♀ blue and tan

PET FACTS

Fearless, lively, loyal

Daily combing and brushing

Regular, moderate

Adapts well to apartment living, but needs plenty of exercise

Very good watchdog

Male: About 10 in (25 cm)
10-13 lb (5-6 kg)
Female: About 10 in (25 cm)
10-13 lb (5-6 kg)

♂ tan

NORWICH TERRIER

The feisty little Norwich terrier has a big heart and is happiest when looking after its human family. It makes a very good watchdog and devoted companion.

History The original Norwich terrier came from East Anglia in Britain. Until 1964, this breed comprised dogs with prick ears and dogs with ears that fell forward. After 1964, these virtually identical dogs became officially recognized as different breeds. Drop-eared Norwich terriers are now known as Norfolk terriers in Britain. US recognition followed in 1979.

Description These lovable dogs are among the smallest of the working terriers. Both breeds have short, sturdy bodies and short legs to match. Their wiry, medium-length, water-resistant coats come in red, tan, wheaten, black and tan, and grizzle, occasionally with white marks. Their faces sport jaunty whiskers and eyebrows. Their tails are usually docked.

Temperament These terriers are alert, smart and easy to train. Although good-natured and friendly with people, including children, they can be scrappy with other dogs.

Grooming Daily combing and brushing is important; take extra care during molting season. Little clipping is required and bathe or dry shampoo only when necessary.

Exercise and feeding Bred to work, these energetic dogs thrive on an active life. To avoid fights, keep them leashed while other dogs are around. There are no special feeding requirements.

Health problems These long-lived breeds may suffer from back problems and genetic eye diseases.

SCOTTISH TERRIER

The sturdy, distinctive Scottish terrier has become something of an unofficial emblem of its homeland. While a little stubborn, it makes a wonderful pet.

History Perhaps the best known of the Highland terriers, the modern "Scottie" hails from Aberdeen and was developed at least 100 years ago to hunt badgers, rabbits and rats.

Description Despite the short legs this is a strong, active and surprisingly agile breed. The rough-textured, weather-resistant coat comes in black, steel, iron gray, wheaten, or brindle of any color. The undercoat is short, dense and soft. Sharply pricked ears give the dog a thoughtful look.

Temperament Bold and self-possessed, the Scottie makes a good—and noisy—watchdog. It is also inclined to be stubborn, and can dominate the household if not handled firmly and consistently from an early age.

Since it is inclined to snap, it is better for homes with older children. It also likes to dig and go wandering.

Grooming Regular brushing is needed, especially when molting. The dog should also be trimmed twice a year. The body hair is left long, like a skirt, while the hair on the face is lightly trimmed and brushed forward.

Exercise and feeding Given a yard of reasonable size, the dog will exercise itself. It will also enjoy walks and play sessions. Beware of overfeeding or it will become fat and lazy.

Health problems It is prone to von Willebrand's disease, skin allergies, jawbone disorders and "Scottie cramp," making walking difficult.

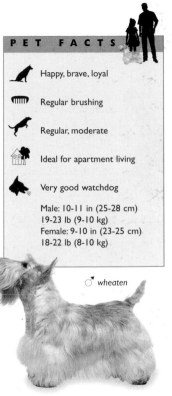

PET FACTS

Happy, brave, loyal

Regular brushing

Regular, moderate

Ideal for apartment living

Very good watchdog

Male: 10-11 in (25-28 cm)
19-23 lb (9-10 kg)
Female: 9-10 in (23-25 cm)
18-22 lb (8-10 kg)

♂ wheaten

JACK RUSSELL TERRIER

Admired for its courage and tenacity, the Jack Russell terrier will take on all challengers. A great watchdog, this clever and exuberant little dog will also keep your property free of small interlopers, such as rodents and snakes.

Smooth
♀ *tan and white*

History Although still not universally recognized as an official breed, the Jack Russell terrier was developed in Devonshire, in the southwest of England, in the mid- to late-1800s. The breed takes its name from English "hunting parson" the Reverend John Russell, an avid fox hunter and one of the first members of the British Kennel Club.

It is said that one day, as a young undergraduate on his way to college in Oxford, Russell noticed a white terrier that accompanied the milkman on his rounds. He was so taken by the appearance of the dog that he bought her, and she became one of the foundation dogs of his breed.

Description This terrier comes in two varieties: the Parson Jack Russell and the smaller and more popular Jack Russell. The Parson Jack Russell was specifically bred for the speed, stamina and agility required to follow the hunt, pursue the quarry underground or bolt it from its den. Its long legs enabled it to keep pace with the hounds.

Its shorter-legged cousin, the Jack Russell, was bred to hunt and kill rats—a task this feisty dog continues today with exceptional enthusiasm.

Both varieties are tough, compact and well-balanced. Their bodies are longer than they are tall, with strong, straight legs and muscular hind-quarters. The feet are round and cat-like, with thick pads, and the gait is free, lively and well-coordinated. The straight, high-set tail is docked, especially on working dogs, so that the tip is level with the skull. The small, V-shaped ears fold forward, with the tips pointing toward the eyes. The coarse, weather-proof double coat comes in two types: smooth and rough. The smooth, short coat is flat but dense and abundant. The rough or broken-coated variety has a short, dense undercoat covered with a harsh, straight, flat "jacket" of longer hair. This type also has a hint of eyebrows and a beard.

Regardless of coat texture, Jack Russells are predominantly white, or white with black, tan or lemon markings. The colors are well-defined and mainly confined to the head and tail, although grizzle is sometimes seen and is acceptable in the show ring.

Temperament Both varieties of Jack Russell are keen, excitable—almost hyperactive—dogs that make playful, overwhelmingly affectionate pets. Intelligent, quick-witted and full of life and fun, they settle well into family life if given firm training from an early age. Their hunting instinct remains strong, however, and they will chase just about anything that moves. Alert and confident, they make vigilant watchdogs, but are sometimes scrappy with other dogs.

Grooming This breed is supposed to have a "natural" appearance, so both smooth and rough coats require only minimal grooming. Comb and brush with a firm bristle brush, and bathe only when necessary.

Exercise and feeding These athletic dogs thrive on daily exercise and outdoor activity. Like other terriers, they get bored easily and are capable of inventing their own entertainment. They may be happy to exercise themselves in a small garden, but since they possess great endurance they are in their element with space to run, hunt and play. There are no special feeding requirements.

Health problems These long-lived, sprightly dogs have few genetic problems apart from dislocating kneecaps and some eye diseases.

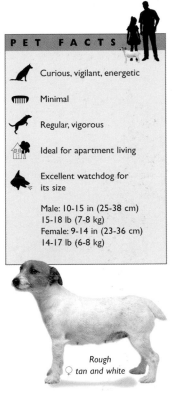

PET FACTS

Curious, vigilant, energetic

Minimal

Regular, vigorous

Ideal for apartment living

Excellent watchdog for its size

Male: 10-15 in (25-38 cm)
15-18 lb (7-8 kg)
Female: 9-14 in (23-36 cm)
14-17 lb (6-8 kg)

Rough
♀ tan and white

PET FACTS

Adaptable, bright, friendly

Daily brushing

Regular, gentle

Ideal for apartment living, but needs regular exercise

Good watchdog

Male: 10-12 in (25-30 cm)
15-18 lb (7-8 kg)
Female: 9-11 in (23-28 cm)
13-16 lb (6-7 kg)

♀ white

WEST HIGHLAND WHITE TERRIER

A perfect companion, the West Highland white has all the terrier charm and vitality, plus brains and beauty in one neat package.

History With similar ancestry to the other Highland working terriers, especially the cairn, the "Westie" was selectively bred for its white coat so as to be highly visible in the field. It was formerly known as both the Poltalloch and Roseneath terrier.

Description This sturdy little terrier has a harsh, all-white double coat and bright, dark eyes. The ears are small, pointed and erect, giving the dog a ready-for-anything look. The tail is carried jauntily and is not docked.

Temperament Friendly, playful, alert and self-confident, this dog just loves company and is suited for homes with older children. It is bold, strong and brave and makes a very good watchdog, despite its size. It will also

bark and dig a lot, but it is a little easier to train than most terriers. It remains an avid hunter.

Grooming Brushing several times a week should keep the coat clean, so bathe only when necessary. Trim around the eyes and ears with blunt-nosed scissors. The coat sheds little, but should be trimmed about every four months and stripped twice a year.

Exercise and feeding This dog enjoys daily walks and games but won't be upset if it misses a day. There are no special feeding requirements.

Health problems The breed is subject to allergic skin problems, copper toxicosis, jawbone disorders, hernias and deterioration of the hip joint.

BORDER TERRIER

A plain, no-nonsense little working dog, the Border terrier is game for anything. It loves being part of a family and is unrestrained in its displays of affection.

History Once known as the Reedwater terrier, the brave little Border terrier was used to hunt otters, foxes and vermin. Perhaps the toughest terrier, it evolved in the rugged country between England and Scotland.

Description This breed has a wiry body to go with its wiry double coat. It comes in reds, blue and tan, grizzle and tan, or wheaten. The muzzle and ears are usually dark. The loose skin, which feels thick, enables the dog to wriggle into tight burrows. The head looks different to those of other terriers and is described as being otter-like.

Temperament Reliable and intelligent, this breed is easily trained, obedient, sensible and bright. Start gentle training from a very early age.

Occasionally aggressive with other dogs, it may also hunt your cat and drive it crazy.

Grooming The coat is supposed to have a "natural" look and needs little grooming. Clip out any knots and brush occasionally with a slicker brush through to the dense undercoat. Bathe only when necessary.

Exercise and feeding The Border terrier was bred to hunt and has great vitality and stamina. If bored it can become destructive, so provide plenty of exercise. There are no special feeding requirements.

Health problems This hardy dog has few genetic problems but may suffer from dislocating kneecaps.

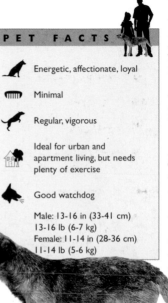

PET FACTS

Energetic, affectionate, loyal

Minimal

Regular, vigorous

Ideal for urban and apartment living, but needs plenty of exercise

Good watchdog

Male: 13-16 in (33-41 cm)
13-16 lb (6-7 kg)
Female: 11-14 in (28-36 cm)
11-14 lb (5-6 kg)

♂ grizzle and tan

FOX TERRIER

The look and stance of super-alertness and expectation are the hallmarks of the fox terrier. This breed is loaded with personality and ready for anything. Wire and smooth fox terriers are remarkably similar in nearly every way, except in their coats.

Wire
♀ tricolor

History Of British origin, fox terriers are among the oldest of the terrier breeds. They are reputed to have been developed by cross-breeding beagles, greyhounds, bulldogs and other terriers. The dogs were bred to accompany the hunt and to dig into burrows to flush out the fox after it had been run to ground by the hounds. They were also used to catch smaller animals in their powerful jaws and were highly prized as ratters. These versatile dogs also excelled as circus performers.

The wire-haired variety was developed for use in rough country, since the protective coat makes the dog less vulnerable to injury. One of the first of the terrier breeds to be imported to North America, the smooth variety quickly gained popularity as a family pet, perhaps aided by the use of the dog in the logo of a record company, listening to his master's voice.

While the two types are sometimes regarded as a single breed, since 1984 they have been classed as separate breeds in the US.

Description These are firm-bodied, squarely-built dogs. The flat, hard coat of the smooth variety is mainly white, with tan, black or ginger markings. The coarse, broken double coat of the wire variety comes in the same colors. It is dense, wiry and wavy, with longer hair on the eyebrows, muzzle, legs and chest and with a short, soft undercoat.

The feet of both varieties are small and neat. The V-shaped ears fold and fall forward. The tail is carried erect and is usually docked to three-quarters of its length.

Temperament Keen, alert and independent, fox terriers are always game and ready for fun. However,

Terriers

they can be obstinate and strong-willed and need to be firmly and persistently trained from an early age. They enjoy being part of the family and are quite reliable with children, although the wire variety can be snappish. Both varieties can also be argumentative with other dogs, even large ones. They make good watchdogs, although their high-pitched barking can be annoying and may cause problems with neighbors. The breeds may be too boisterous for elderly owners.

Grooming The coat of the smooth dog needs weekly brushing with a firm bristle brush. Bathe or dry shampoo when necessary. The coat of the more common wire variety presents a few more problems. If the dog is to look smart and shapely, the coat must be kept well-trimmed. Regular clipping is the easiest way to shape the coat, but hand-stripping four times a year is the only way to retain its texture. Professional groomers have many tricks to keep the wire looking well-tailored for the show ring, but if the dog is a family pet, the same straightforward care as for the smooth will suffice to keep it clean and looking neat.

Exercise and feeding These irrepressible, athletic dogs remain enthusiastic diggers. They will wreak havoc if they do not have an outlet for their energy, so they need regular long walks or romps in the park, off the leash if possible. However, keep them leashed if there are small animals about, as their urge to hunt is strong and they are likely to take off after cats. There are no special feeding requirements, but measure the amount of food against the level of activity.

Health problems These dogs are subject to few genetic weaknesses, although they are prone to eye diseases. Deafness can be a problem in predominantly white dogs. The breeds are also prone to skin allergies if they are kept indoors.

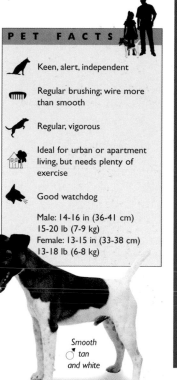

PET FACTS

Keen, alert, independent

Regular brushing; wire more than smooth

Regular, vigorous

Ideal for urban or apartment living, but needs plenty of exercise

Good watchdog

Male: 14-16 in (36-41 cm)
15-20 lb (7-9 kg)
Female: 13-15 in (33-38 cm)
13-18 lb (6-8 kg)

*Smooth
tan
and white*

PET FACTS

 Playful, smart, stubborn

 Daily brushing

 Regular, moderate

Ideal for apartment living, but needs plenty of exercise

Excellent watchdog

Male: 12-14 in (30-36 cm)
11-18 lb (5-8 kg)
Female: 11-13 in (28-33 cm)
10-15 lb (5-7 kg)

salt and pepper

MINIATURE SCHNAUZER

A dog of clean habits and neat size, the perky miniature schnauzer makes a delightful companion for someone without much living space.

History This is the smallest of the three schnauzer breeds, originally from Germany (see pp. 244–245). It is classified as a terrier only in the US; most countries classify all schnauzers as utility or working dogs.

Description The miniature schnauzer has a harsh, wiry double coat that comes in salt and pepper or any solid color, sometimes with white on the chest. The thick, prominent eyebrows and mustache are often trimmed to accentuate the dog's square-cut shape. The tail is usually docked.

Temperament Noted for its reliability and affectionate nature, this dog combines terrier behavior, such as excitability, barking, and digging, with the guarding instincts of its larger schnauzer relatives. Spirited and brave, it may be scrappy with other dogs, even those much larger than itself.

Grooming The coat will become matted unless it is groomed daily with a short wire brush. The dog should also be clipped all over to an even length twice a year. Trim around the eyes and ears with blunt-nosed scissors and clean the whiskers after meals.

Exercise and feeding This lively little dog enjoys long, brisk, daily walks and off-leash games. There are no special feeding requirements.

Health problems It may suffer from von Willebrand's disease, kidney and bladder stones, liver disease, diabetes and eye and skin disorders.

BEDLINGTON TERRIER

In full show trim, the Bedlington terrier looks more like a lamb than a dog, but it has retained its terrier qualities. It makes a good pet for people with allergies.

History Developed in Northumberland, England, during the 1820s, this dog was used for racing, hunting small game and ratting in coal mines and was very popular with poachers. It gets its speed from its whippet blood.

Description The body is graceful, flexible and muscular and covered in a slightly curly coat with a woolly undercoat. It comes in solid blue, liver and sandy beige, or particolored tan with any of these colors.

Temperament This affectionate terrier loves to be the center of attention. Although stubborn, it is relatively easy to train. It is an enthusiastic digger and, since it was once also used for dog fighting, can be scrappy with other dogs.

Grooming The thick coat does not shed and requires specialized clipping every six weeks. Thin and clip the coat close to the head and body to accentuate the shape. Shave the ears closely, leaving a tassel on the tips. The hair is left slightly longer on the legs. Brush the dog regularly and clean and pluck inside the ears.

Exercise and feeding This active dog needs plenty of exercise and will be bored and mischievous without it. There are no special feeding requirements.

Health problems Before acquiring a pup, check that the parents have been screened for copper toxicosis, a liver disorder. The breed is also prone to genetic kidney and eye diseases.

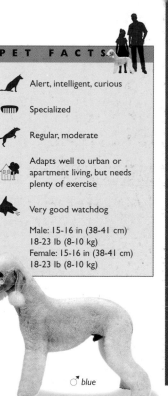

PET FACTS

Alert, intelligent, curious

Specialized

Regular, moderate

Adapts well to urban or apartment living, but needs plenty of exercise

Very good watchdog

Male: 15-16 in (38-41 cm) 18-23 lb (8-10 kg)
Female: 15-16 in (38-41 cm) 18-23 lb (8-10 kg)

♂ blue

Intelligent, loyal, brave

Regular brushing

Regular, vigorous

Adapts well to urban living, but needs plenty of exercise

Excellent watchdog

Male: 16-19 in (41-48 cm)
25-30 lb (11-14 kg)
Female: 15-18 in (38-46 cm)
23-28 lb (10-13 kg)

♀ red wheaten

IRISH TERRIER

Known for its fighting spirit, the game little Irish terrier is not for everyone. However, it is very adaptable and its courage and loyalty are unquestioned.

History Among the oldest of the terriers, this breed is only now regaining some of the immense popularity it once enjoyed. Admired for its pluck and unconquerable spirit, it was widely used as a ratter and a guard dog and for flushing out and retrieving foxes, badgers and otters. Later, it excelled in the dog-fighting ring.

Description This neat, work-manlike dog is closely related to the wire fox terrier (see pp. 256–257) but looks like a small version of the Airedale (right). It comes in solid red, yellow-red or red-wheaten colors.

Temperament While sociable with people and devoted to its owner, this dog, nicknamed "the Red Devil," has an often uncontrollable urge to fight other dogs. Although attentive and easy to train, it needs thorough socialization as a pup and may be unsuitable for inexperienced owners.

Grooming The hard, short, wiry double coat rarely sheds. Brush regularly with a stiff bristle brush and strip the loose, dead hair weekly with a fine-toothed comb or stripping comb. Bathe only when necessary.

Exercise and feeding Bred for active work, this dog needs plenty of regular exercise, including a walk twice a day. There are no special feeding requirements.

Health problems This robust dog is susceptible to a hereditary urinary problem and foot and eye diseases.

AIREDALE TERRIER

A lively, water-loving dog, the Airedale terrier fits in well with family life, as long as it has plenty of exercise and is not allowed to rule the roost.

History The largest of the terriers, this dog was developed in Yorkshire to hunt otters, badgers and wolves, becoming particularly popular in the Aire Valley. It has been used extensively in police and military work.

Description This strong dog has a jaunty, alert stance. The stiff, wiry coat comes in a combination of dark grizzle or black with red and tan markings, and the face is adorned with a beard, mustache and bushy eyebrows. The straight tail, usually docked to the same height as the head, is carried erect. The small, V-shaped ears fold forward and point to the sides.

Temperament The Airedale is intelligent and faithful; protective of its family and wary of strangers. It is a playful dog and loves children. However, it also has a strong personality and while not difficult to train, needs firm, kind and consistent handling.

Grooming The double coat is water-resistant and sheds very little. Remove the dead hair with a stiff bristle brush and bathe only when necessary.

Exercise and feeding This dog is an incorrigible digger and is easily bored, so keep it occupied with plenty of daily exercise. Extra oil in the diet is recommended if it suffers from dry, itchy skin.

Health problems The Airedale is susceptible to von Willebrand's disease, hip dysplasia, gastroenteritis and eye problems.

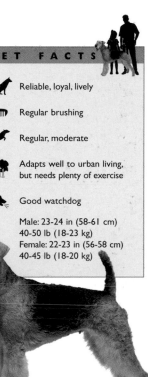

PET FACTS

Reliable, loyal, lively

Regular brushing

Regular, moderate

Adapts well to urban living, but needs plenty of exercise

Good watchdog

Male: 23-24 in (58-61 cm)
40-50 lb (18-23 kg)
Female: 22-23 in (56-58 cm)
40-45 lb (18-20 kg)

○ black and tan

BULL TERRIER

When the bull terrier bites with its large, strong teeth, it is unwilling to let go. Although surprisingly gentle with its family, this sturdy dog remains a powerful and determined animal and needs firm and careful handling. Even the miniature variety is not a pet for timid or inexperienced owners.

Miniature
♂ black,
brindle and white

History The bull terrier was developed in the mid-1800s by James Hinks of Birmingham, England. Its predecessors were the result of cross-breeding bulldogs with whippets and a variety of terriers, including the now-extinct English white terrier. The dogs were primarily employed in the ring to bait bulls and for dog-fighting, although they were also used to hunt badgers and rats. They proved formidable fighters and were prized for their strength, courage, tenacity, agility and speed. When these bloodsports were outlawed, the bull terrier was refined to its current, more benevolent, state.

The miniature has the same qualities of the standard bull terrier, but in a more manageable size. It evolved from a series of cross-breedings of small bull terriers.

Description The bull terrier is a thick-set, muscular, well-proportioned dog with a broad chest. Its most distinctive feature is its long head, which is almost flat at the top and curves down from the tip of the skull to the end of the nose. The face is oval, almost egg-shaped, and the small, thin ears are set close together and carried erect. The small, glinting eyes are also closely-set and almond-shaped. The gait of this heavy dog is surprisingly light, nimble and jaunty. The medium-length tail is carried horizontally and is left undocked.

Miniature
Male: Up to 14 in (36 cm)
Up to 20 lb (9 kg)
Female: Up to 14 in (36 cm)
Up to 20 lb (9 kg)

The dog's short, dense, tight-fitting and lustrous coat comes in pure white or black, brindle, red, fawn and tri-color with white markings.

Temperament A tenacious fighter, the bull terrier is more of a danger to other dogs than to people. However, when thoroughly socialized and properly trained it can be a devoted companion, usually sweet-natured, gentle and playful. The standard-sized dog is fond of children, although the miniature, which has perhaps more terrier blood, is feistier and does not tolerate teasing. Both varieties make good watchdogs.

Unfortunately, some dogs suffer from obsessive compulsive behaviors, such as tail-chasing. Owners should never reward this sort of behavior when it is first performed.

Grooming The smooth coat sheds little and is easy to groom. Brush with a firm bristle brush or a hound glove once a week, and bathe or dry shampoo as necessary. A rub with a piece of toweling or chamois will leave the coat gleaming.

Exercise and feeding The bull terrier needs a moderate amount of exercise to keep it in good health and good temper, but is often kept leashed in public places to avoid fights with other dogs. There are no special feeding requirements, but don't overfeed as it is inclined to become obese and lazy.

Health problems This breed may suffer from a fatal hereditary zinc deficiency. It can also occasionally suffer from allergic reactions such as interdigital dermatitis and hives. White dogs may be born deaf and are susceptible to heart disease, chronic skin inflammations and sunburn. Colored dogs are not so prone to these conditions, although kidney failure is a problem. Miniatures are subject to numerous eye conditions.

PET FACTS

Determined, fearless, playful

Regular brushing

Regular, moderate

Adapts well to urban living, but needs plenty of space to exercise

Excellent watchdog

Standard
Male: 15-19 in (38-48 cm)
60-70 lb (27-32 kg)
Female: 15-19 in (38-48 cm)
60-70 lb (27-32 kg)

Standard
♀ white

Terriers

PET FACTS

Tough, brave, trustworthy

Daily brushing

Regular, moderate

Adapts well to urban living, but needs plenty of exercise

Excellent watchdog

Male: 14-16 in (36-41 cm)
25-38 lb (11-17 kg)
Female: 13-15 in (33-38 cm)
23-35 lb (10-16 kg)

♂ brindle

264

STAFFORDSHIRE BULL TERRIER

The Staffordshire bull terrier is an affectionate all-purpose dog: very good with children and an excellent watchdog that will intimidate any intruder.

History A ferocious fighter, the Staffordshire was used in England for bull baiting and dog fighting until both of these pastimes were outlawed. It was also used to hunt badgers. Like the bull terrier, its bulldog blood gives it a broad-chested look of immovability.

Description This substantial, muscular dog has a short, dense coat that comes in white or solid reds, fawn, brindle, black or blue, or any of these colors with white.

Temperament Usually adored and adoring within its own family circle, the dog needs firm and consistent training and early socialization to curb its instinct to fight with other dogs. As a pup it tends to chew a great deal, so provide plenty of chew toys.

Grooming The smooth, shorthaired coat is easy to groom. Brush every day with a firm bristle brush, and bathe or dry shampoo as necessary. The coat will gleam if rubbed with a piece of toweling or a chamois.

Exercise and feeding The Staffordshire bull terrier must have plenty of regular exercise. Some owners prefer to keep their pets leashed in public places to avoid dog fights. There are no special feeding requirements, but don't overfeed.

Health problems This hardy dog is relatively free of genetic problems, although some individuals may suffer from cataracts. It is also susceptible to respiratory problems and can become overheated in very hot weather.

AMERICAN STAFFORDSHIRE TERRIER

The American Staffordshire terrier is a dog few strangers would mess with, yet with its own family, this powerful dog is devoted, gentle and loving.

History Developed independently after early Staffordshires were taken to the US during the nineteenth century, the American Staffordshire terrier has been recognized as a separate breed since 1936. The qualification "American" was added in 1972.

Description The American Staffordshire looks much like the British, although it is now larger and bigger-boned than its cousin. It probably bears an even closer resemblance to bulldogs of about a century ago, from which it is directly descended. The smooth, short coat comes in all colors.

Temperament This dog should never be confused with the notorious pit bull terrier. It is a brave and tenacious fighter if provoked, and needs firm, kind training to control this instinct, but its basic temperament toward people is gentle and kind.

Grooming Use a firm bristle brush every day, and bathe or dry shampoo as necessary. A rub with a piece of toweling or chamois will make the coat gleam.

Exercise and feeding This terrier must have plenty of regular exercise. Keep it leashed in public to avoid fights. There are no special feeding requirements, but don't overfeed as it is inclined to become fat and lazy.

Health problems While not long-lived, it is relatively free of genetic weaknesses. It may develop cataracts.

PET FACTS

Stoic, reliable, courageous

Daily brushing

Regular, moderate

Adapts well to urban living, but needs plenty of exercise

Excellent watchdog

Male: 17-19 in (43-48 cm)
40-50 lb (18-23 kg)
Female: 16-18 in (41-46 cm)
35-45 lb (16-20 kg)

♀ blue brindle

265

TOY DOGS

As human populations became more stable, leisure time increased and the concept of a dog as a pet, not a tool, took hold. The patronage of these "status dogs" by royal courts quickly brought toy breeds into public favor and they remain popular today, particularly in cities where their size suits them to apartment living. These breeds have personalities in inverse proportion to their tiny bodies; many make alert and courageous watchdogs and some, such as the Yorkshire terrier and even the Maltese, are ratters of renown. However, toy dogs are bred primarily for the pleasure of their owners. Since the dogs are unquestionably loyal and may become anxious when left alone, it seems that both species thrive on the other's devotion.

PET FACTS

Affectionate, alert, playful

Gentle, regular brushing

Regular, gentle

Ideal for apartment living

Poor watchdog

Male: 6-9 in (15-23 cm)
2-6 lb (1-3 kg)
Female: 6-8 in (15-20 cm)
2-6 lb (1-3 kg)

*Longhaired
♀ red and white*

CHIHUAHUA

The intriguing Chihuahua is prized for its tiny size. Although not the best dog for young children, this dainty creature is perfect for apartment dwellers.

History Little is known about this breed before its discovery in Mexico about 100 years ago, but it is believed to date back to the ninth century.

Description This, the world's smallest breed, comes in two coat types: smooth and short, or long and flat or slightly curly, with a ruffed neck and a plumed tail. The dogs are otherwise identical and can occur in the same litter, although in the UK they are considered separate and never interbred. Every color and combination occurs.

Temperament This intelligent and lively breed is intensely loyal and grows very attached to its owner, even to the point of jealousy. It responds well to training, although it may be difficult to house-train. When frightened it may bite; excessive barking can also be a problem. Its physique makes it unsuitable for active young children.

Grooming The short coat should be gently brushed regularly or wiped with a chamois. Use a soft bristle brush on the long coat daily. Bathe both types about once a month. Check the ears regularly and keep the nails trimmed.

Feeding and exercise It is tempting to carry this dog around but it will benefit from a short daily walk. A body harness is safer than a collar and leash. Feed small amounts twice a day.

Health problems This long-lived breed suffers from collapsing trachea, dislocating kneecaps, heart disease and eye, tooth and gum problems.

ITALIAN GREYHOUND

The graceful Italian greyhound is a perfect miniature of its larger forebear. A clean, odorless animal, it will adapt happily to any reasonably quiet, loving home.

History The Italian greyhound has been around since ancient Egyptian times. Whatever its original purpose—perhaps flushing birds, chasing small game or ratting—it has been bred for the past few centuries purely as a pet. In most countries the dog is classified as a toy breed.

Description Elegant and lithe, this dog is capable of short bursts of speed. The glossy, satiny coat comes in various shades of fawn, cream, white, red, blue, black and fawn, and white splashed with any of these colors.

Temperament The breed tends to be timid and easily stressed, so it must be handled very gently. It makes an ideal pet for a quiet household where there are no lively children.

Grooming All that is needed to keep the silky coat gleaming is a rubdown with a piece of rough toweling or a chamois. If absolutely necessary, the dog can be bathed, but make sure it is thoroughly dry and warm afterward.

Exercise and feeding A true hound, the Italian greyhound is an active little dog which loves daily outdoor exercise, be it walking, playing games or running free. There are no special feeding requirements.

Health problems This delicate dog is prone to broken legs and slipped kneecaps, especially when it is young. It is also susceptible to seizures and hereditary eye problems. Because of its fine coat, it should not be exposed to extreme weather conditions.

PET FACTS

Obedient, loving, sensitive

Minimal

Regular, moderate

Adapts well to urban living if kept in a quiet household

Not a good watchdog

Male: 12-15 in (30-38 cm)
6-10 lb (3-5 kg)
Female: 12-15 in (30-38 cm)
6-10 lb (3-5 kg)

♂ fawn

CHINESE CRESTED DOG

It is not known for certain how or even where this breed originated, but if you are looking for a novelty, this may be just the pet for you. However, choose a Chinese crested dog only if you are ready to provide the care the unusual coat requires, and to return the affection this merry, agile little dog is so eager to give.

Powderpuff
♂white

History Dogs of this type have been known in Central and South America for about 500 years but are no longer found in China, where they were once the favored pets of the mandarins. The similarities between this breed and the hairless African dogs (such as the Nubian dog and the African elephant dog) suggest that they may be distantly related. Perhaps the dog traveled to China with traders, who also took hairless dogs to the Americas. Since the Chinese crested does not tolerate cold climates, an origin in north or central Africa is a distinct possibility.

The Chinese crested dog was not exhibited in the West until the 1885 Westminster Show in New York. A breed club was first established in the US in the 1970s.

Description The smallest of the hairless breeds, the Chinese crested is a nimble dog with a prancing gait. It comes in two body types: one is fine-boned and graceful, while the other is heavier in body and bone.

The coat also comes in two varieties. One is hairless except for a flowing crest on its head, a plume on its tail and some fringing on the feet and erect ears. The other, called the powderpuff, is totally covered with an undercoat and flowing veil of soft, silky hair. The powderpuff's ears droop under the weight of the hair, which can grow up to five inches (12 cm) long. The long tail is also fringed.

The skin of both varieties is smooth, fine-grained and generally odorless. Many colors are seen, such as blue, pink, lilac, golden or spotted, and the color may darken or lighten with the seasons. The hairless dog's body temperature is no higher than any other dog's; it just feels warmer due to the lack of an insulating coat.

Since the hairless variety carries a gene for the powderpuff, the two types often occur in the same litter. The genetic makeup of the hairless is such that the dog can also lack a complete set of teeth.

Temperament Playful, entertaining and alert, this dog craves constant companionship. It tends to become very attached to its owner and has difficulty adjusting to a new one. Never vicious, it loves children and the company of other animals. It may be difficult to house-train, however.

Grooming The hairless variety needs careful weekly brushing and a weekly bath. Gentle use of a facescrub will remove dead skin cells, and an oil-free moisturizing lotion will keep the skin supple. Superfluous light body hair can be carefully shaved off. The powderpuff's fine double coat

requires daily attention; if neglected the woolly undercoat becomes matted. Provide extra care when the dog is molting. Some powderpuff owners prefer a clean-shaven face and a shaved V-shape down the throat (see picture). Ask a professional groomer about the clipping tools required.

Exercise and feeding This dog enjoys a walk or regular sessions of play. There are no special feeding requirements, but do not overfeed because it will easily become obese.

Health problems Both varieties have a high incidence of eye and skin conditions and some dogs have been known to suffer adverse reactions to the leptospirosis vaccine. The skin of the hairless reacts to contact with wool and is particularly vulnerable to sunburn. This variety is also unsuited to cold climates. Since it often lacks premolars or upper canine teeth, the hairless also merits regular dental check-ups.

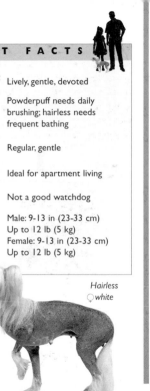

PET FACTS

Lively, gentle, devoted

Powderpuff needs daily brushing; hairless needs frequent bathing

Regular, gentle

Ideal for apartment living

Not a good watchdog

Male: 9-13 in (23-33 cm)
Up to 12 lb (5 kg)
Female: 9-13 in (23-33 cm)
Up to 12 lb (5 kg)

Hairless
♀ white

PET FACTS

Lively, friendly, playful

Regular brushing

Regular, gentle

Ideal for apartment living

Adequate watchdog

Male: 12-13 in (30-33 cm)
10-18 lb (5-8 kg)
Female: 12-13 in (30-33 cm)
10-18 lb (5-8 kg)

○ chestnut and white

CAVALIER KING CHARLES SPANIEL

A fearless, lively, sociable dog with a cheerful disposition, the cavalier King Charles spaniel has little of the fragility usually associated with toy breeds.

History Developed from cocker spaniel (see pp. 194–195) and King Charles spaniel bloodlines, the cavalier differs greatly from its forebears. Its breeders were trying to reproduce a toy dog similar to those seen in portraits from the Restoration. England's Charles II, who reigned from 1649 to 1685, is said to have doted on them.

Description Compact and handsome, the cavalier is slightly larger than the King Charles and has a longer muzzle, but comes in the same colors: solid reds, chestnut and white, black and tan, and tricolored black, tan and white. The long, silky coat is free of curls, although it is sometimes wavy. The pendulous ears are also silky and well-feathered (fringed). The tail may be docked to two-thirds of its length.

Temperament Easily trained, clean and sensible, the cavalier makes a delightful and diverting companion.

Grooming Use a firm bristle brush to groom the coat. Bathe or dry shampoo as necessary, making sure that the dog is dry and warm afterwards. Check the eyes and ears carefully—the ears are extremely prone to infection.

Feeding and exercise This adaptable dog will benefit from any amount of exercise, although it does enjoy a romp in the park. Avoid overfeeding or it will quickly become obese.

Health problems This breed is relatively hardy, but heart disease is common. It is also subject to hereditary eye diseases and dislocating kneecaps.

JAPANESE CHIN

Possibly a distant relative of the Pekingese, the lovely little Japanese Chin is a superlative lapdog favored by royalty and commoners alike.

History The pampered pooch of wealthy Japanese—including the imperial family—for centuries, the Japanese Chin was introduced to Japan from China in ancient times. It has been known in Western countries for only about 150 years. Britain's Queen Victoria was an aficionado of the dog.

Description Taller and lighter than the Pekingese (see p. 279), the Japanese Chin trots gracefully with its feet lifted high off the ground. The profuse, straight, longhaired coat comes in white with markings either of black or shades of red. The tail is plumed and carried over the back.

Temperament This happy, sweet-tempered dog is the perfect size for small living spaces. With its gentle ways and charming manners, it is perhaps best suited to homes in which there are no small children.

Grooming Comb out tangles every day and brush lightly, lifting the hair to leave it standing out a little. Clip any matted hair off the feet. Clean the eyes and check the ears for infection. Dry shampoo or bathe occasionally.

Exercise and feeding The Chin doesn't require a lot of exercise, but it will benefit from a daily walk or a chance to play in the open. It prefers to "graze" on small meals and tidbits.

Health problems The large and prominent eyes are vulnerable to damage and diseases such as cataracts and progressive retinal atrophy.

PET FACTS

Intelligent, lively, engaging

Daily brushing

Regular, gentle

Ideal for apartment living

Poor watchdog

Male: 7-11 in (18-28 cm)
Up to 9 lb (4 kg)
Female: 7-11 in (18-28 cm)
Up to 9 lb (4 kg)

○ black and white

PET FACTS

Animated, friendly, alert

Daily brushing

Regular, gentle

Ideal for apartment living

Not a good watchdog

Male: 8-11 in (20-28 cm)
3.5-10 lb (1-5 kg)
Female: 8-11 in (20-28 cm)
3.5-10 lb (1-5 kg)

♂ red sable and white

PAPILLON

A real charmer, the papillon steals hearts with its dainty elegance and amusing antics. It loves to be the center of attention and makes a delightful companion.

History The origin of the papillon (French for "butterfly" and pronounced pah-pee-yon) is uncertain, but by the sixteenth century this playful breed had become cherished among the European nobility.

Description Because of the tail, which is long and plumed and carried over the back in a curl, the papillon was once called the squirrel spaniel. Its long, lustrous coat is white with patches of any color, except liver. The "butterfly" ears are heavily fringed and there is a well-defined white noseband.

Temperament Smart and adaptable, this perky little dog does nevertheless tend to become possessive of its owner. Its usefulness as a watchdog is limited by its size, but it will alert you to

anything unusual. Note that the dog is small enough to wriggle through fences that might appear secure.

Grooming This breed is usually clean and odorless, and daily attention to its silky, single coat will keep it that way. Bathe or dry shampoo when necessary. Keep the nails clipped and have the teeth scaled regularly.

Exercise and feeding The papillon loves to run and play but won't fret too much if it misses the occasional daily jaunt. There are no special feeding requirements.

Health problems This fairly robust breed may suffer from eye and knee problems. It is also sensitive to some commonly-used anesthetics.

TOY POODLE

The toy poodle dislikes solitude and prefers to live indoors. It is a perfect pet for a less active person with time to pamper this clever little clown.

History This, the smallest version of the poodle (see pp. 290–291), may have been miniaturized after the breed made its way to France. Its wit and looks made it a star of the circus.

Description This active dog has a dense, woolly coat of springy curls that comes in solid red, white, cream, blue, brown, apricot, black and silver.

Temperament While the toy poodle is not fragile, it is not robust enough to be a small child's pet and can be snappish. Sensitive, highly responsive and very easy to train, it is demanding of affection and may bark a lot.

Grooming The toy poodle must be bathed regularly and clipped every six to eight weeks. Many pet owners opt for a simple lamb clip (the same length all over) which requires weekly brushing. Trim the hair between the pads to prevent matting. The nails should also be kept short to stop the toes from spreading. Clean and check the ears frequently for infection and pull out hairs growing inside the ear canal. The teeth need regular scaling.

Exercise and feeding Undemanding as far as exercise goes, the dog will be happier and healthier if given opportunities to run and play. There are no special feeding requirements.

Health problems Check pups to ensure there are no genetic disorders in the bloodline. The dog is prone to epilepsy, dislocating kneecaps, heart and eye diseases, cysts and diabetes.

PET FACTS

Very intelligent, excitable

Comb and brush daily

Regular, gentle

Ideal for apartment living

Very good watchdog for its size

Male: Up to 11 in (28 cm)
6-9 lb (3-4 kg)
Female: Up to 11 in (28 cm)
6-9 lb (3-4 kg)

♀ red

PET FACTS

Even-tempered, affectionate

Regular, extensive; be gentle with soft coat

Regular, gentle

Ideal for apartment living

Adequate watchdog

Male: 8-10 in (20-25 cm)
6-10 lb (3-5 kg)
Female: 8-10 in (20-25 cm)
6-10 lb (3-5 kg)

♂ white

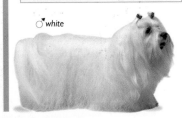

MALTESE

Celebrated since Roman times and perhaps even earlier, the main purpose in life of the glamorous Maltese has always been to lift the spirits of its doting owners.

History Possibly the oldest European toy breed, the gentle Maltese is featured in paintings and other artworks dating back 3,000 years. Its name may be derived from the island of Malta, or the Sicilian town of Melita.

Description The dazzling, profuse silky coat falls long and straight, parting along the spine and concealing the feet completely. It is always white, sometimes with lemony or beige markings. The tail arches gracefully over the back.

Temperament Intelligent and easy to train, the Maltese is generally good-natured. However, it can get snappy when handled roughly and is better off with older children. Lively and alert, it will bark if strangers are about.

Grooming Daily grooming is essential, but be gentle with the soft single coat. Check and wipe the eyes and beard daily to prevent staining. The fringe is often tied in a topknot to keep it out of the eyes. Bathe or dry shampoo regularly, making sure the dog is thoroughly dry and warm afterward. Pull out hairs growing inside the ear canal to increase air flow.

Exercise and feeding The Maltese enjoys walks or frolicking in the park and remains playful well into old age. Avoid overfeeding, and do not pander to a fussy or capricious appetite.

Health problems Generally hardy, this breed is subject to eye and joint problems, tooth and gum conditions, hypoglycemia and sunburn.

SHIH TZU

The entertaining shih tzu loves company and likes nothing better than to sit in a lap and be groomed—which is fortunate, as the coat demands extensive care.

History A number of similarities suggest that the shih tzu (pronounced shidzoo) is descended from Tibet's Lhasa apso, possibly as a result of being crossed with the Pekingese after it was introduced into China. It was a favorite of the Chinese imperial court.

Description The luxuriant coat of this proud-looking dog can be any color. A white blaze on the forehead and a white tail tip are very desirable.

Temperament The feisty, loyal shih tzu makes friends easily and responds well to training. Unlike some toy breeds, it does not snap or bark a lot.

Grooming Use a steel comb and a bristle brush on the soft double coat every day, with extra care during molting. The fringe is usually tied in a top-knot to keep it out of the eyes. Clip out any mats from the feet, dry shampoo as necessary and bathe monthly. Check the ears regularly for infection and clean the beard after meals.

Exercise and feeding If allowed, this dog will lounge about in its own particular spot. It should be encouraged to be active and will keep fitter with a daily walk. There are no special feeding requirements, but do not overfeed or it will quickly get fat.

Health problems The prominent eyes are prone to injury and tend to get dry from exposure, causing ulceration. The dog is also subject to respiratory conditions, heatstroke, kidney disease, joint and dental problems.

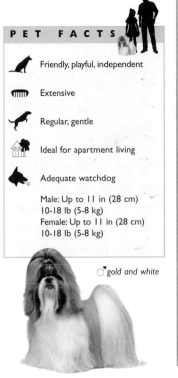

PET FACTS

Friendly, playful, independent

Extensive

Regular, gentle

Ideal for apartment living

Adequate watchdog

Male: Up to 11 in (28 cm)
10-18 lb (5-8 kg)
Female: Up to 11 in (28 cm)
10-18 lb (5-8 kg)

♂ gold and white

277

PET FACTS

Lively, inquisitive, friendly

Frequent brushing

Regular, gentle

Ideal for apartment living

Good watchdog despite its size

Male: 7-9 in (18-23 cm)
3-5 lb (1.5-2 kg)
Female: 7-9 in (18-23 cm)
4-6 lb (2-3 kg)

♂ orange and sable

POMERANIAN

While the Pomeranian adores pampering, it also loves to play and be active. It is a most accommodating creature, ready to fit in with the needs of any owner.

History Named for a region in central Europe, the Pomeranian resembles the much larger sled-pulling spitz-type dogs from which it is descended. It was deliberately miniaturized during the nineteenth century, when toy breeds were very popular.

Description This breed looks like a walking powderpuff of dense black, gray, blue, orange, cream, shaded sable or particolored hair. Its cheeky, fox-like face peers out from an outsize ruff. The spectacular tail curls over the back.

Temperament Easily trained, this bold, extroverted dog makes a good watchdog, calling attention to anything unusual with a frenzy of barking. The barking may become a problem if not curbed from an early age.

Grooming Frequent brushing of the very long double coat—and the tail— is recommended. If you work from the head, parting the coat and brushing it forward, it will fall back in place. The cottony undercoat is shed once or twice a year. Dry shampoo when necessary. Clean the eyes and ears daily and schedule regular dental check-ups.

Exercise and feeding Special provision for exercise is unnecessary if there is a small area for the dog to play in. Otherwise, occasional outdoor games will suffice. There are no special feeding requirements.

Health problems The breed is subject to diabetes, dislocating knees and eye and heart problems. Tooth loss may occur if they are not cared for.

PEKINGESE

Venerated since ancient times by the Chinese, the tiny Pekingese is, perhaps, the ultimate toy dog: a devoted companion quite content to loll on a cushion or a lap.

History This fabled breed once led a pampered life in the Imperial Court of Peking, where the smallest specimens were sometimes carried around in the sleeves of royalty.

Description The extravagant, flowing coat has profuse feathering and comes in all colors except albino and liver. The flat face has a dark, wrinkled muzzle and the drooping ears are heart-shaped. This tiny, heavy-boned dog has a characteristic rolling gait.

Temperament The loyal Pekingese is affectionate with its owner but aloof with strangers. Although it can be hard to train and house-train, it is an alert and courageous watchdog. Like many toy breeds this dignified dog is better for homes without young children.

Grooming Daily grooming of the long, straight double coat is essential. Care is needed around the hindquarters, which can become soiled and matted. Females shed the undercoat when in season. Dry shampoo regularly. Clean the face and eyes daily and check the feet for trapped debris.

Exercise and feeding Disinclined to exercise, the Pekingese will stay in better health if given short, regular play sessions. It will quickly become obese if overfed.

Health problems The pushed-in face makes the dog subject to breathing problems (which may require surgery to correct) and skin infections. The prominent eyes are sensitive and prone to corneal ulcers and injury.

PET FACTS

Intelligent, devoted, determined

Special care is needed

Regular, gentle

Ideal for apartment living

Excellent watchdog for its size

Male: 7-10 in (18-25 cm)
7-11 lb (3-5 kg)
Female: 7-10 in (18-25 cm)
8-13 lb (4-6 kg)

♂ silver-gray brindle

279

PET FACTS

 Brave, alert, affectionate

Daily, extensive

Regular, moderate

Ideal for apartment living, but needs plenty of exercise

Excellent watchdog for its size

Male: 9-10 in (23-25 cm)
8-18 lb (4-8 kg)
Female: 9-10 in (23-25 cm)
8-18 lb (4-8 kg)

♀ gray-blue and tan

SILKY TERRIER

Bred purely as a lively companion, the dainty silky terrier exhibits the best traits of its several forebears. A confident, entertaining dog, it has a charm all its own.

History Derived from several toy and terrier varieties, including the Yorkshire terrier, which it resembles, the silky terrier was developed in New South Wales, Australia in very recent times. It is also known as the Sydney silky. It was never intended to work, but in spite of its tiny size, it is an excellent watchdog.

Description This small, strong breed has a silky coat that falls straight down from a spinal parting. The coat is long except on the face and ears, and comes in either blue or gray-blue with tan. The tail is usually docked.

Temperament Alert and intelligent, this dog is easy to train. It can become jealous, however, and may pick fights with other dogs. It also enjoys digging.

Grooming A big commitment is required to keep this dog's lustrous hair in top condition. Daily combing and brushing and a regular shampoo are necessary. After bathing, make sure the dog is dry and warm. The coat must be trimmed occasionally, and the hair below the knees is often cut short. To improve the dog's vision, the fringe is usually tied in a topknot.

Exercise and feeding This energetic dog delights in extended play sessions and has surprising stamina. It needs regular exercise and activity to stay fit and happy. There are no special feeding requirements.

Health problems Generally hardy, it may suffer from a collapsing trachea and genetic eye diseases.

YORKSHIRE TERRIER

The Yorkshire terrier was originally pressed into service as a ratter, a job it did very well. With its unusual appearance it later became a favored breed as a pet.

History   Developed just over a century ago, the Yorkshire terrier is a mysterious blend of English, Scottish and Maltese terriers. Today's toy breed is much smaller than its forebears.

Description   The long, fine, silky single coat parts along the spine and falls straight down on either side. It is steel-blue on the body and tail, and tan elsewhere. The tail is usually docked to half its length.

Temperament   Alert, indomitable and spirited, this tiny terrier is also admired for its loyalty. It makes an excellent watchdog, defending its territory in no uncertain manner. However, its barking may disturb the neighbors. It can also become snappish and is unsuitable for young children.

Grooming   For a show dog, strict grooming guidelines must be adhered to. The pet owner may opt for a natural shaggy look, but daily combing and brushing and regular shampooing are still necessary to keep the lustrous hair in top condition. This involves a commitment in time and effort. There is little shedding, however.

Exercise and feeding   This lively little warrior doesn't need much exercise but it will benefit from regular opportunities to run and play. Meat intake should be restricted, and fussy eaters should not be indulged.

Health problems   The dog is prone to eye, hip and gum problems, a collapsing trachea and dislocating knees. The teeth should be scaled regularly.

PET FACTS

Courageous, clever, feisty

Daily, extensive

Regular, gentle

Ideal for apartment living

Good watchdog despite its size

Male: 7-9 in (18-23 cm)
4-7 lb (2-3 kg)
Female: 7-9 in (18-23 cm)
3-7 lb (1.5-3 kg)

♂ dark steel-blue

PET FACTS

Smart, sociable, mischievous

Daily brushing

Regular, moderate

Ideal for apartment living if given enough exercise

Good watchdog

Male: 12-14 in (30-36 cm)
13-20 lb (6-9 kg)
Female: 10-12 in (25-30 cm)
13-18 lb (6-8 kg)

♂ fawn

PUG

Not at all pugnacious, this lovable softie relishes company and is good with kids. It seems always to have been a pet rather than bred for a particular task.

History The pug was first thought to have originated in Holland, since William of Orange brought some to Britain when he ascended the throne in 1689. But the appearance of pug-like dogs on Chinese porcelain and paintings suggests that it is an older, Oriental breed—perhaps a smooth-coated, long-legged version of the Pekingese.

Description This strong dog has a square, thickset body and a sleek coat that comes in fawn, apricot, silver and black, all with a black muzzle and velvety ears. Moles on the frowny face are considered beauty spots. The tail lies in a tight curl or even, in the best specimens, a double curl on the back. The jaunty, rolling gait of the short straight legs is quite distinctive.

Temperament Intelligent and with a big bark for its size, the pug makes a good watchdog. It is playful and affectionate and not inclined to snap.

Grooming The soft short coat only needs a weekly brushing and doesn't shed much. Clean the face regularly.

Exercise and feeding The pug enjoys energetic games. It also loves to eat, but don't overfeed or it will quickly become obese.

Health problems The pug's muzzle contributes to chronic breathing problems. It may suffer allergies, and it is stressed by both hot and cold weather. Its prominent eyes are prone to injury, while the screw tail and crinkled face are susceptible to skin-fold infections.

MINIATURE PINSCHER

This very active terrier-type has undoubted courage. It was valued in Germany, where it originated, as a ratting dog of outstanding vigilance and tenacity.

History This is not a miniaturized version of the Doberman pinscher but a much older breed known in Germany for at least 300 years. It may be a cross between the German smooth-haired pinscher and the Italian greyhound or the dachshund.

Description A neat dog with a high-stepping gait, this breed makes a lively pet. The smooth hard coat comes in black, blue and chocolate, all with well-defined tan markings on the face and matching patches on the chest and above the eyes. Solid reds are also seen. The tail is usually docked short.

Temperament This self-possessed, bold and stubborn little dog will bark and nip at intruders and makes an excellent watchdog. However, it is not so easy to train and is unsuited to homes with small children because, if handled roughly, it can react aggressively. It may also become aggressive with other dogs.

Grooming The coat is easy to groom and sheds very little. Use a firm bristle brush or wipe over with a chamois. Shampoo only when necessary.

Exercise and feeding Provide regular opportunities for running and play, and ensure that the yard has a fence high enough to foil any attempts to escape and explore. There are no special feeding requirements.

Health problems A robust breed, it is subject to eye and joint problems and does not tolerate cold weather.

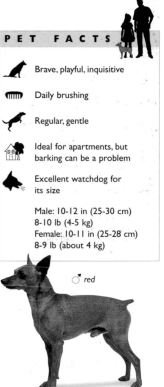

Toy Dogs

PET FACTS

Brave, playful, inquisitive

Daily brushing

Regular, gentle

Ideal for apartments, but barking can be a problem

Excellent watchdog for its size

Male: 10-12 in (25-30 cm)
8-10 lb (4-5 kg)
Female: 10-11 in (25-28 cm)
8-9 lb (about 4 kg)

♂ red

DOG BREEDS

NON-SPORTING DOGS

This is a catch-all group for breeds that, although officially recognized by kennel clubs, don't fit neatly into any of the other breed categories. Some belong to the group because the task for which they were developed no longer exists—the bulldog, for example, was bred for bull-baiting and then for dog-fighting, pastimes that are now outlawed. Others are included because of their unique looks or characteristics, such as the shar pei and the Lhasa apso. Breeds such as the poodle and the Dalmatian are familiar sights, while others, like the schipperke, are rare in most neighborhoods. While the members of this group have little in common, they are some of the most beautiful, intelligent and popular pets today.

PET FACTS

Charming, friendly, playful

Extensive

Regular, gentle

Ideal for apartment living

Good watchdog

Male: 9-11 in (23-28 cm)
11-16 lb (5-7 kg)
Female: 9-11 in (23-28 cm)
11-16 lb (5-7 kg)

♂ white

BICHON FRISE

It's easy to see why people are enchanted by the fluffy bichon frise. It loves to be the center of attention and is always eager to please—a delightful and amusing pet.

History Although it first came to notice as the darling of French royalty during the sixteenth century (*bichon* is French for lapdog; *frisé* means curly), the bichon frise is thought to have descended from French or Belgian dogs taken to the Canary Islands by sailors. The breed was once called the Teneriffe.

Description This sturdy, confident little dog has a lively, prancing gait and a puffy white coat, sometimes with cream or apricot markings. The eyes and nose are large, round and dark.

Temperament This gregarious, merry breed is intelligent and easy to train. Good for first-time owners, it is generally even-tempered and sociable among family and strangers.

Grooming The coat quickly becomes a matted mess, so daily brushing is essential. The hair falls in curls and is usually cut to follow the contours of the body and brushed out to a soft cloud. Bathe once a month. Trim around the eyes and ears and clean the eyes meticulously to prevent staining.

Exercise and feeding Play will take care of most of its needs, but it loves to walk and romp in the open. There are no special feeding requirements.

Health problems A fairly sturdy breed, the bichon frise may suffer from epilepsy and dislocating knee-caps. It is also subject to eye problems including cataracts and blocked tear ducts, which can cause the eyes to run, staining the white coat.

DALMATIAN

Exuberant and fun-loving, the Dalmatian always turns heads. Much more than a fashion accessory, it's an ideal choice for anyone with the time to exercise and train it.

History The handsome Dalmatian's origins are obscure, but in nineteenth-century Europe its main task was to run beside carriages—either to protect the travelers inside or merely for appearance. It was also used to kill rats.

Description This elegant breed has the lean, well-muscled lines of the pointer, to which it may be related. Born with a white coat, the dog develops the well-defined, black or liver-colored spots (see p. 285) during the first year. The nails are either the same color as the spots or white.

Temperament Boisterous and energetic, this protective dog adores children. It is rather sensitive, so training takes patience and gentle but firm handling from an experienced owner.

Grooming This breed is a heavy shedder. Daily brushing with a firm bristle brush is required to keep the lustrous, short-haired coat smooth. Bathe only when necessary.

Exercise and feeding Athletic by nature, the Dalmatian is not an ideal dog for apartment dwellers unless it can be taken out for a brisk walk or run several times a day. When bored, it becomes destructive, so it must be kept busy. Be careful not to overfeed it as it easily becomes obese.

Health problems The breed has problems with hip dysplasia, urinary bladder stones, skin allergies and sunburn. It is also prone to deafness, so make sure your pup's hearing has been checked before purchasing.

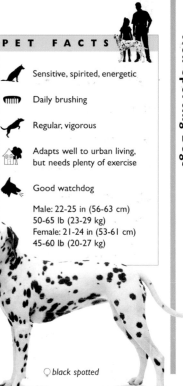

⚲ black spotted

PET FACTS

Sensitive, spirited, energetic

Daily brushing

Regular, vigorous

Adapts well to urban living, but needs plenty of exercise

Good watchdog

Male: 22-25 in (56-63 cm)
50-65 lb (23-29 kg)
Female: 21-24 in (53-61 cm)
45-60 lb (20-27 kg)

PET FACTS

Playful, devoted, fearless

Daily cleaning

Regular, moderate

Ideal for apartment living

Excellent watchdog

Male: 11-15 in (28-38 cm)
15-25 lb (7-11 kg)
Female: 11-15 in (28-38 cm)
15-25 lb (7-11 kg)

○ brindle and white

BOSTON TERRIER

Besides being an excellent watchdog, the popular
Boston terrier has much to recommend it—easy-care,
handy size and a delightful disposition.

History The Boston terrier's direct
forebears are English and French bulldogs and the English white terrier. It
was developed in the US only about
150 years ago as a fighting dog, a pas-
time that has since been outlawed.

Description This well-muscled dog
has an unmistakable face: a short,
wide muzzle, prominent wide-set eyes
and short, erect ears. The coat is black
or brindle, with white markings.

Temperament While this dog is still
likely to scrap with other dogs, it is
affectionate toward people and reliable
with children. Intelligent and easy to
train, it adapts to both an active family
or a more retiring owner and may
become anxious if left alone. Despite its
size, it makes an excellent watchdog.

Grooming The shorthaired, glossy
coat is easy to groom with a firm
bristle brush. Wipe the face with a
chamois every day and clean the
prominent eyes carefully. Check both
the ears and eyes for grass seeds. Ticks
may also lurk in the ears. The nails
should be clipped from time to time.

Exercise and feeding Regular
walks or play sessions in a fenced yard
will keep a Boston terrier fit. There
are no special feeding requirements.

Health problems This short-faced
dog may have breathing difficulties
when stressed by exertion and hot or
cold weather. Heart conditions, skin
tumors, eye injuries and skin-fold
infections are common. Whelping the
large-headed pups is often difficult.

BULLDOG

This stalwart has come to epitomize determination and the broad-chested stance suggests immovability, if not downright stubbornness. Yet the bulldog is a loving pet.

History In earlier times this breed would fight bulls, bears, badgers, or even other dogs in the ring. When such bloodsports became outlawed, breeders concentrated on developing the bulldog's non-ferocious traits.

Description With its stocky legs set squarely at each corner of its compact, muscular body, the bulldog's deliberate gait has become a waddle. The coat comes in reds, fawn, brindle or fallow, or white pied with any of these colors.

Temperament Despite its history the bulldog is now among the gentlest of breeds and can make a particularly kind playmate for children. Although it does not bark a lot, its somewhat intimidating appearance makes it an effective deterrent against intruders.

Grooming The short, fine coat does not shed much. Comb and brush with a firm bristle brush, and bathe only when necessary. Wipe the face with a cloth every day to clean the wrinkles.

Exercise and feeding The bulldog will stay fitter with regular, not overly strenuous activity, such as walking. Be careful not to overfeed it as it easily becomes obese. It can also be some- what possessive of its food.

Health problems This short-lived breed suffers eye and heart problems and skin infections. Its short muzzle and narrowed nostrils cause breathing difficulties and heatstroke. It is also stressed by exertion and hot or cold weather. The large-headed pups are often delivered by cesarean section.

PET FACTS

Reliable, calm, sweet

Regular brushing

Regular, moderate

Adapts well to urban living

Very good watchdog

Male: 14-16 in (36-41 cm)
55-70 lb (25-32 kg)
Female: 12-14 in (30-36 cm)
48-60 lb (22-27 kg)

♂ brindle and white

POODLE

Once a poodle owner, always a poodle owner—fanciers of this breed seldom become attached to another. The winning ways of this clever dog captivate almost everyone. Bright, good-natured and versatile, it is comfortable in the show ring, the field or the home and makes an animated, fun-loving companion.

Standard
◯ *cream*

History The poodle's name derives from the German word *puddelin* ("to splash in water") while in France it is known as the *caniche*, or duck dog. Both titles are descriptive of its original purpose: a retriever of waterfowl. Known since the thirteenth century, the poodle was originally used in Germany and France as a gundog, while in Russia it was also used to pull milk carts. First miniaturized in France, it became the darling of the eighteenth-century European aristocracy and remained a fashion accessory until recent times. Its trainability and comic appearance also made it the mainstay of traveling circuses and vaudeville.

Despite the claims of several other countries, France has been officially recognized as its country of origin. Its ancestors probably include the Portuguese water dog, the Hungarian water hound and the Irish water spaniel.

Description The poodle comes in three officially recognized sizes, Standard (the largest), Miniature and Toy (the smallest, see p. 275). The Standard is the oldest breed, from which the other two varieties were developed.

This active, sure-footed dog has excellent balance and moves lightly at a bouncing trot. Its dense, woolly coat of springy curls are either brushed out to a soft cloud and clipped, or simply combed for a more natural look. The fine hair is not shed, and for this reason the poodle is often recommended as a pet for people

Standard
Male: 15-24 in (38-61 cm)
45-70 lb (20-32 kg)
Female: 15-22 in (38-56 cm)
45-60 lb (20-27 kg)

with allergies. The coat comes in solid white, black, cream, brown, apricot, silver and blue.

In the Standard dog the high-set tail is usually docked at birth to half its length. The tail of the Miniature variety is docked to two-thirds of its length.

Temperament Considered by many the most intelligent of all breeds, the poodle is particularly easy to house-train. The Standard is exuberant and independent, whereas the Miniature can be sensitive and demanding of attention. However, the breed is normally full of fun and eager to please. It makes a great playmate for children—often feeling slighted if left out of family activities—and a good watchdog.

Grooming The dog must be bathed regularly and clipped every six to eight weeks from puppyhood. The show clips are stylized versions of the traditional clip developed to lighten the weight of the coat for swimming and to protect the joints and major organs

from cold and thorns. However, a lamb clip (the same length all over) is easier and cheaper to maintain.

Special care must be taken to ensure that the long, feathered ears do not become infected. They must also be checked frequently for mites. The teeth need regular scaling.

Exercise and feeding The poodle adores water and will keep fit and in better spirits if given regular opportunities to swim, run and play. The Miniature needs a few walks a week, while the sporty Standard has great stamina and needs daily activity. To prevent bloat, feed two or three small meals a day and avoid exercise after meals.

Health problems Check pups carefully. This long-lived breed is subject to eye diseases, allergies, cysts and other skin conditions. Miniatures are prone to von Willebrand's disease, diabetes, heart disease, epilepsy and bladder problems, while Standards also get hip dysplasia and bloat.

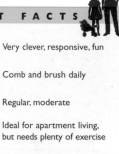

PET FACTS

Very clever, responsive, fun

Comb and brush daily

Regular, moderate

Ideal for apartment living, but needs plenty of exercise

Very good watchdog, particularly the Standard

Miniature
Male: 11–15 in (28–38 cm)
15–17 lb (7–8 kg)
Female: 11–15 in (28–38 cm)
15–17 lb (7–8 kg)

Miniature
♂ black

PET FACTS

Curious, brave, independent

Minimal

Regular, moderate

Adapts well to urban living and is ideal for an apartment if given plenty of exercise

Excellent watchdog

Male: 10-13 in (25-33 cm)
12-16 lb (5-7 kg)
Female: 9-12 in (23-30 cm)
10-14 lb (5-6 kg)

♂ black

SCHIPPERKE

The agile and hardy little schipperke is remarkably self-sufficient and backs down for no one. But it is also sociable and affectionate, and adapts well to family life.

History The name possibly derives from the Flemish for "little boatman," because the schipperke (pronounced skipper-key) was a popular watchdog and ratter on Belgian barges. It may be related to the Groenendael, a Belgian shepherd dog (see pp. 310–311).

Description The schipperke's harsh double coat is usually black, but gold and some other solid colors do occur. Smooth on the fox-like head, the hair is off-standing elsewhere, and the male has a ruff around the neck. It is often born without a tail, but if a tail is present it is docked a few days after birth.

Temperament This plucky little dog is alert and very curious—nothing escapes its attention. Very suspicious of strangers, it makes an excellent watch-dog. It is also an undemanding family pet, devoted to its owner and good with children if treated with respect.

Grooming This very clean dog pretty much takes care of its own grooming. It does not shed much and only needs weekly care with a firm bristle brush. Shampoo when necessary.

Exercise and feeding Some individuals will be content with games in a yard or park, while others will want at least a long daily walk. There are no special feeding requirements.

Health problems The schipperke is a hardy breed relatively free of genetic problems, apart from eye diseases, occasional cases of hip dysplasia and skin infections.

TIBETAN TERRIER

While it is treasured in its native land as a symbol of good luck, you will probably cherish your appealing Tibetan terrier more for its joyous zest for life.

History Still something of a rarity in Western countries, the Tibetan terrier was little known outside Tibet until about 70 years ago. It is not a true terrier as it does not dig prey out of burrows. In its homeland it is something of an all-purpose farm dog.

Description Compact, nimble and sure-footed, this dog will stand on its hindlegs and jump to see what is on a table, especially if it senses food. The shaggy double coat falls over the face and comes in white, gray, gold, cream, silver, black, particolor and tricolor. The tail is well feathered and carried in a proud curl over the back.

Temperament This gentle, lively, engaging dog is easy to train, alert and full of bravado. It will certainly let you know if strangers are around. It is also a good jumper, so make sure your yard is secure.

Grooming Comb the long, fine coat every second day with a metal comb to keep it free of tangles. Extra attention is needed when the dense, woolly undercoat is shed twice a year. Bathe or dry shampoo as necessary. Trim about the eyes with blunt-nosed scissors and check the ears regularly.

Exercise and feeding Regular play and walks will keep this energetic breed healthy. There are no special feeding requirements, but if allowed it can become a finicky eater.

Health problems This fairly robust dog is prone to eye diseases.

PET FACTS

Loving, alert, playful

Regular combing

Regular, moderate

Ideal for apartment living

Good watchdog

Male: 14-16 in (36-41 cm)
18-30 lb (8-14 kg)
Female: 13-15 in (33-38 cm)
16-25 lb (7-11 kg)

♂ black, silver and white

LHASA APSO

This bewitching creature seems to be composed entirely of hair, but the Lhasa apso is neither a toy nor a lapdog. It is a rugged little animal that earns its keep as a companion and watchdog in the chambers of Tibetan monasteries. A Lhasa apso is the traditional gift of the Dalai Lama.

♂ slate (left), ♂ cream (right)

History Seldom seen outside Tibet until the 1920s, the Lhasa apso was bred in monasteries as a temple and palace sentinel. The breed is said to be regarded as the reincarnations of lamas who have not yet reached Nirvana. To present the gift of a Lhasa apso was to bestow great distinction, an honor reserved only for society's most esteemed. Chinese emperors enjoyed the companionship of this little dog in the palaces of the seventeenth-century Manchu dynasty.

Since Buddhism prohibits the trade of living things, the dog was never sold. Only males were given away as gifts, so that breeding remained under Tibetan control.

The breed takes part of its name from the Tibetan capital, Lhasa. *Apso* may be derived for the Tibetan word for "goat-like," or from the dog's alternative name, *apso seng kyi*, which very loosely translates as "barking lion sentinel dog." It was accepted for registration by the American Kennel Club in 1935.

Description To protect against the Himalayan climate, this breed has a long, luxurious yet coarse coat that parts along the spine and cascades over its entire body, including its eyes, pendulous ears and round, cat-like feet. The tail is well feathered and carried high over the back in a screw. The dog also has a beard and mustache. The most popular colors are gold, cream and honey, but smoke, slate, dark grizzle, and particolors of black, white or brown are also seen.

Temperament The cuddly look of this dog belies a bold temperament. Its hearing is acute, and in the monasteries and palaces where it stood guard against intruders, it was said to be more terrifying than the Tibetan mastiffs who guarded the entrances. It continues to be a fine watchdog and will bark aggressively at unusual sights and sounds.

Wary of and aloof around strangers, the Lhasa apso tends to be a one-person dog that does not change loyalties easily. Adaptable, playful and affectionate, it thrives on human companionship and doesn't like to be left alone. Since it does not tolerate rough handling, it is better suited to families with older children. It can be stubborn and resistant to strict or harsh discipline, so it needs patient, firm handling from an experienced owner.

Grooming This high-maintenance dog requires fastidious attention. Daily combing and brushing of the heavy topcoat is important to prevent matting. The thick undercoat will also become matted if neglected. Some owners opt for easier care with a short

all-over clip, which has no less appeal than the full coat. Dry shampoo as necessary, but bathe no more than three times a year. Check the feet for matted hair and trapped debris, and clean the eyes and ears meticulously. The beard must be washed clean of dribbles of food after every meal to prevent staining and matting.

Exercise and feeding The Lhasa apso does not demand exercise, although it loves to scramble about and will be healthier and happier if given regular opportunities to run free and play. There are no special feeding requirements.

Health problems Slow to mature, the Lhasa apso does not reach its prime until three or four years of age. It is relatively free of health problems, although it may suffer from genetic kidney conditions, eye injuries and blocked tear ducts. Poor ventilation of the ears may lead to ear infections.

PET FACTS

Clever, devoted, very alert

Daily, extensive

Regular, gentle to moderate

Ideally suited to apartment living

Very good watchdog

Male: 10-11 in (25-28 cm)
14-18 lb (6-8 kg)
Female: 9-10 in (23-25 cm)
12-16 lb (5-7 kg)

○ cream

PET FACTS

Gentle, intelligent, devoted

Daily brushing

Regular, moderate

Ideal for apartment living, but needs plenty of exercise

A natural watchdog

Male: 17-19 in (43-48 cm)
55-65 lb (25-29 kg)
Female: 16-18 in (41-46 cm)
50-60 lb (23-27 kg)

♂ silver-gray

KEESHOND

The keeshond is a great favorite in its native Holland, in spite of not being considered a purebred. A long-lived dog, it becomes deeply attached to its owners.

History Originally used as a watchdog on barges in Holland, the keeshond (pronounced kays-hond) is sometimes called the "smiling Dutchman" for its perpetual good-natured grin. A member of the spitz group of dogs, it has the tightly curled tail typical of this group and a spectacular ruff.

Description A compact, muscular dog, the keeshond has a cream or pale gray undercoat and a luxurious, off-standing outer coat that comes in shades of gray with definite black tips. There are distinctive pale "spectacle" markings around the eyes.

Temperament Reliable, adaptable, easy to care for and loyal to its family, the keeshond is a natural watchdog and easy to train for other tasks.

Grooming The dense undercoat sheds twice a year, but grooming is not especially onerous. Use a stiff bristle brush to brush with the grain, then lift the hair with a comb, against the grain, and lay it back in place. Bathe or dry shampoo only when necessary.

Exercise and feeding This dog will readily adapt to any exercise regimen, be it demanding or easy, but will keep fitter with regular activity. There are no special feeding requirements, but beware of overfeeding as it puts on weight quickly.

Health problems While generally robust, the keeshond may be subject to hip dysplasia, heart defects and eye diseases. Ticks are difficult to locate in the thick coat.

SHAR PEI

Also known as the Chinese shar pei, this breed is thought to be about 2,000 years old. Its loose, wrinkled skin gives it a worried, forlorn look.

History Once the world's rarest dog, this ancient Chinese breed was on the brink of extinction until a resurgence of interest in the 1960s.

Description Two varieties occur: a heavily wrinkled dog with a large head and a smaller-headed dog with tighter-looking skin. The bristly coat comes in red, fawn, cream, apricot and black (see p. 285), often with lighter tones on the hindquarters and the curled tail. The dog has a blue-black tongue.

Temperament Once used for fighting, the shar pei is a one-person dog with a strong guarding instinct. It can be aggressive with strangers and other animals and needs firm training from an early age. In experienced hands it can be friendly and devoted pet.

Grooming Shedding is not a big problem and regular brushing will keep the unusual coat in good condition. Dry shampoo or bathe when necessary, taking care to dry the skin folds completely. Watch for mites.

Exercise and feeding Daily walks and an occasional run are beneficial, but keep it leashed in public. There are no special feeding requirements.

Health problems Sadly, the shar pei suffers from chronic skin problems and inflammatory bowel disease. It may also need corrective eye surgery.

Male: 18-20 in (46-51 cm)
40-55 lb (18-25 kg)
Female: 18-20 in (46-51 cm)
40-55 lb (18-25 kg)

PET FACTS

Independent, intensely loyal

Regular brushing

Regular, moderate

Adapts well to urban living, but needs plenty of space

Good watchdog

♂ apricot

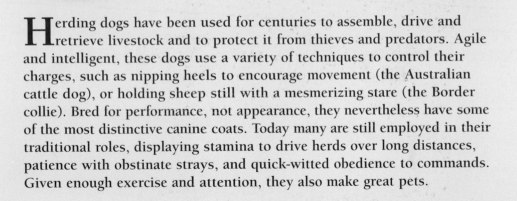

Dog Breeds
HERDING DOGS

Herding dogs have been used for centuries to assemble, drive and retrieve livestock and to protect it from thieves and predators. Agile and intelligent, these dogs use a variety of techniques to control their charges, such as nipping heels to encourage movement (the Australian cattle dog), or holding sheep still with a mesmerizing stare (the Border collie). Bred for performance, not appearance, they nevertheless have some of the most distinctive canine coats. Today many are still employed in their traditional roles, displaying stamina to drive herds over long distances, patience with obstinate strays, and quick-witted obedience to commands. Given enough exercise and attention, they also make great pets.

PET FACTS

Affectionate, loyal, independent

Regular brushing

Regular, gentle

Ideal for apartment living, but needs plenty of exercise

Very good watchdog

Male: 10-12 in (25-30 cm)
20-24 lb (9-11 kg)
Female: 10-12 in (25-30 cm)
18-22 lb (8-10 kg)

♀ sable

PEMBROKE WELSH CORGI

Long associated with royalty, especially the British monarchy, this breed is widely recognized. Its neat size and affectionate nature make it a popular pet.

History Thought to have been brought to Wales by Flemish weavers about 1,000 years ago, the Pembroke has been considered a breed separate from the Cardigan for only about 70 years. It was valued for herding sheep and cattle in the steep Welsh hills.

Description The long, powerful body is set on short, well-boned legs. The medium-length coat comes in red, sable, tan, fawn and black, all with or without white. The tail is quite short or docked very close to the body.

Temperament This is a clever little dog with a big personality. Easy to train and house-train, it is wary of strangers and makes a very good watchdog. It also loves children, but because it moves herds by nipping at

their heels, it has a tendency to also nip people. This trait should be firmly discouraged from an early age.

Grooming The thick, soft, water-resistant coat sheds heavily twice a year and drops hair all year round. Use a firm bristle brush every week and bathe only when necessary.

Exercise and feeding This active breed should be encouraged to run and play. There are no special feeding requirements, but don't overfeed or it will become obese and lazy.

Health problems The short legs and long back of this breed make it prone to slipped spinal disks. It may also suffer inherited eye disorders, bleeding disorders and hip dysplasia.

CARDIGAN WELSH CORGI

Although it has not attained the widespread popularity of its cousin, the Pembroke, the Cardigan Welsh corgi predominates in many rural communities in Wales.

History The Cardigan Welsh corgi may have arrived in Wales from Scandinavia, but whatever its origins, it has become indispensable for the herding of cattle in parts of that country's rugged terrain. The dog nips at the heels of the beasts, then ducks out of the way of vengeful kicks.

Description This tough, fearless dog can move very quickly on its short legs. The face is quite fox-like and the coat comes in any color, except pure white. Slightly longer in the body than the Pembroke, it also differs by having a long, thick tail and larger, more widely spaced ears.

Temperament Intelligent and easy to train, the Cardigan is an obedient little worker. Like the Pembroke it has a tendency to nip, so it is not well suited to households with young children. Wary of strangers, it makes a very good watchdog.

Grooming The wiry, medium-length, water-resistant coat sheds twice a year. Groom with a firm bristle brush, and bathe only when necessary.

Exercise and feeding Even more active than the Pembroke, this dog must have regular exercise. There are no special feeding requirements, but don't overfeed or it will become obese and lazy.

Health problems Like the Pembroke, this generally hardy breed is subject to spinal problems and eye diseases. It is also prone to epilepsy.

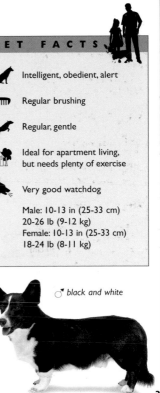

PET FACTS

Intelligent, obedient, alert

Regular brushing

Regular, gentle

Ideal for apartment living, but needs plenty of exercise

Very good watchdog

Male: 10-13 in (25-33 cm)
20-26 lb (9-12 kg)
Female: 10-13 in (25-33 cm)
18-24 lb (8-11 kg)

♂ black and white

PET FACTS

Diligent, courageous, loyal

Minimal

Regular, vigorous

Adapts well to urban living, but needs plenty of exercise

Excellent watchdog

Male: 17-20 in (43-51 cm)
32-35 lb (15-16 kg)
Female: 17-19 in (43-48 cm)
30-35 lb (14-16 kg)

blue, black and tan

AUSTRALIAN CATTLE DOG

The Australian cattle dog, also known as a heeler, has the best characteristics of its several antecedents. If you need a working dog, this is as good as they get.

History A potent cocktail of blood runs in the veins of the Australian cattle dog: blue merle collie, Old English sheepdog, Dalmatian, Australian kelpie, the little-known Smithfield and the native dingo. The result is a worker with few equals, used to drive cattle across vast distances in hot, dusty conditions.

Description The coarse, shorthaired, weather-resistant coat is well-suited for a tough dog bred for hard work. There are two coat colors: speckled blue, with tan or black markings, or speckled red, with dark red markings.

Temperament Absolutely loyal and obedient to its master, this is something of a one-person dog. Its guarding and herding instincts are very strong and may extend to people and other pets. It may also feel compelled to establish dominance over other dogs.

Grooming The coat needs minimal care—just brush occasionally and bathe when necessary.

Exercise and feeding Exercise is of paramount importance with this breed. It has incredible stamina and without enough activity it will become bored and destructive. There are no special feeding requirements.

Health problems The Australian cattle dog is extremely hardy, but may suffer from eye problems and hereditary deafness. Check pups for any signs of deafness before purchasing, and ask the breeder about the parents.

COLLIE

Instantly recognizable to generations of children who were brought up watching the television series "Lassie," the collie is now one of the world's most popular dogs.

History This hard-working sheep-dog was first used in the Scottish Lowlands. Its name is derived from the term for the local black sheep, colleys.

Description There are two types, identical but for the length of the coat: the rough collie and the smooth collie. The more popular rough variety is often referred to simply as the collie.

A white collar, chest, feet and tail tip are typical of this strong dog. The coat comes in sable, blue merle (blue-gray streaked with black) and tricolor.

Temperament This very sociable dog is family-oriented and good with children, but it can also be high-strung and aloof with strangers. Smart and easy to train, it makes a good watchdog but can be a terrible barker.

Grooming A thorough weekly brushing will keep the double coat in good shape. Take extra care when the soft, dense undercoat is shedding. Clip out mats and bathe as necessary.

Exercise and feeding The collie needs plenty of daily jaunts, preferably off the leash. There are no special feeding requirements.

Health problems The dog is subject to epilepsy, hip dysplasia, skin and eye problems, including a condition known as collie eye anomaly. It is sensitive to some heartworm preventatives, and dogs with little or no pigment in their noses are prone to "collie nose"—severe sunburn and scarring. Due to its thick coat, it is unsuited to hot or humid climates.

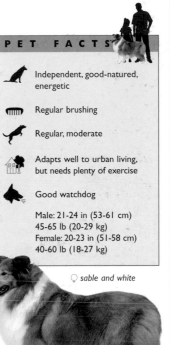

PET FACTS

Independent, good-natured, energetic

Regular brushing

Regular, moderate

Adapts well to urban living, but needs plenty of exercise

Good watchdog

Male: 21-24 in (53-61 cm)
45-65 lb (20-29 kg)
Female: 20-23 in (51-58 cm)
40-60 lb (18-27 kg)

♀ sable and white

PET FACTS

Brave, responsive, playful

Daily brushing

Regular, vigorous

Adapts well to urban living, but needs plenty of exercise

Good watchdog

Male: 21-22 in (53-56 cm)
45-55 lb (20-25 kg)
Female: 20-21 in (51-53 cm)
40-50 lb (18-23 kg)

♂ slate

BEARDED COLLIE

The friendly, even-tempered bearded collie is an attractive—and fairly long-lived—family pet. It needs a lot of exercise and care.

History A working sheepdog for most of its known history, the bearded collie is thought to have developed from Polish lowland sheepdogs taken to Scotland about 500 years ago.

Description The breed resembles a small Old English sheepdog with an undocked tail. It has a shorter muzzle than other collies. The harsh coat comes in gray, red, slate, black, brown and fawn, with or without white markings. It has a silky beard and abundant feathering (fringing).

Temperament This is an intelligent and willing worker with great endurance. It is friendly and loves children, but due to its size and herding instinct it may scare a small child.

Grooming Daily brushing is vital to prevent matting—mist the double coat lightly with water before beginning, then use the comb sparingly. Give extra care when the dog is molting. The coat can also be clipped every two months. It is hard to find ticks in the thick undercoat, so check regularly. Bathe or dry shampoo when necessary.

Exercise and feeding This active, energetic dog needs lots of exercise, preferably running free. There are no special feeding requirements.

Health problems The breed has few genetic weaknesses, although hip dysplasia and eye defects do occasionally occur. It may react badly to some heartworm preventatives, so consult your vet before administering tablets.

BORDER COLLIE

Ready, willing and able sums up the Border collie asleep at your feet. You think you've tired him out, but move a muscle and he'll be instantly alert and raring to go.

History Developed for herding sheep in the Scottish border country, the speed and stamina of the Border collie has made it an outstanding worker and now a favorite worldwide.

Description This well-proportioned dog has a lean, muscular body. The medium-length double coat comes mainly in black with white, but tri-colored with tan and blue merle with white markings are also seen. There is often lavish feathering on the legs, underbody and tail, and a thick ruff.

Temperament Highly intelligent and eager to please, the dog makes a wonderful pet, especially in homes with energetic children. However, it may bark excessively and be scrappy and jealous with other dogs. It is easily obedience trained, but harsh or overbearing training can make it submissive.

Grooming Regular grooming will keep the coat gleaming, with extra care needed when the soft, dense undercoat is molting. Bathe or dry shampoo only when necessary. Check the ears and coat frequently for ticks.

Exercise and feeding Destructive when bored, this athletic dog has boundless energy and thrives on hard work and play. There are no special feeding requirements, but don't let it become fat and lazy.

Health problems Generally hardy, the breed is subject to some joint problems and genetic eye diseases.

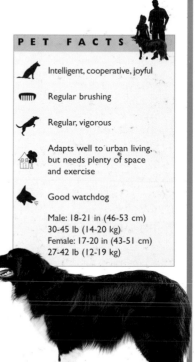

PET FACTS

Intelligent, cooperative, joyful

Regular brushing

Regular, vigorous

Adapts well to urban living, but needs plenty of space and exercise

Good watchdog

Male: 18-21 in (46-53 cm)
30-45 lb (14-20 kg)
Female: 17-20 in (43-51 cm)
27-42 lb (12-19 kg)

♀ black and white

305

Obedient, intelligent, loving

 Regular brushing

 Regular, moderate

 Ideal for apartment living, but needs plenty of exercise

 Good watchdog

Male: 13-15 in (33-38 cm)
14-18 lb (6-8 kg)
Female: 12-14 in (30-36 cm)
12-16 lb (5-7 kg)

tricolor

SHETLAND SHEEPDOG

The "Sheltie" is well endowed with both beauty and brains. It is intuitive and responsive to its owner's wishes, and becomes deeply attached to its family.

History This beautiful dog looks like a small version of the collie (see p. 303), but it has developed over centuries on the Shetland Islands where it was used for herding sheep. Other Shetland animals, notably ponies and sheep, are also miniaturized.

Description Strong, nimble and lightly built, the dog is a fast runner and can jump well. The most common colors for the long, shaggy coat are sable, blue merle and tricolor, but it also comes in black with white or tan.

Temperament Alert and remarkably intelligent, the sensitive Sheltie likes to feel like part of the family. It is easy to train, but may be shy or nervous and is better suited to older children. Excessive barking can be a problem.

Grooming The coat readily sheds dirt and is easier to care for than might be expected, but regular brushing is important. Mist the coat with water before beginning and tease out mats, using the comb sparingly. The dense undercoat sheds heavily twice a year. Bathe or dry shampoo only when absolutely necessary.

Exercise and feeding This graceful dog loves to frolic outdoors. It is prone to obesity, so avoid overfeeding it.

Health problems The breed is susceptible to von Willebrand's disease, epilepsy, liver, heart, eye and skin diseases and "collie nose." It is also sensitive to some heartworm preventatives. Blue merles should be checked for any signs of deafness.

OLD ENGLISH SHEEPDOG

If you have the patience and time to spend exercising and grooming the Old English sheepdog, your reward will be the love of a faithful and handsome companion.

History Commonly called bobtails, Old English sheepdogs were developed for herding livestock, both sheep and cattle, in England's West Country.

Description This large, thickset, muscular dog has a distinctive low-pitched, loud, ringing bark. The long shaggy coat is free of curls and comes in gray, grizzle, blue or blue merle, with or without white markings.

Temperament Playful and clever, the dog learns quickly, but training should be started while it is still of a manageable size. If bored it may become mischievous.

Grooming If the coarse coat is not groomed through to the dense, water-resistant undercoat at least three times

a week, the dog may develop skin problems or be plagued by parasites. Clip out any mats; if you prefer, the coat can be clipped every two months. (In former times the dog was shorn with the sheep.) Trim around the eyes and rear with blunt-nosed scissors.

Exercise and feeding This dog was developed for hard work and loves a good run. There are no special feeding requirements.

Health problems Subject to hip dysplasia and eye diseases, the breed is also unsuited to hot climates.

Male: 22-24 in (56-61 cm)
From 65 lb (29 kg)
Female: 20-22 in (51 cm)
From 60 lb (27 kg)

○ gray and white

PET FACTS

 Keen, obedient, energetic

 Minimal

 Regular, vigorous

 Adapts well to urban living, but needs plenty of space and exercise

Good watchdog

Male: 19-23 in (48-58 cm)
40-70 lb (18-32 kg)
Female: 18-22 in (46-56 cm)
35-65 lb (16-29 kg)

♂ black tricolor

AUSTRALIAN SHEPHERD

Highly regarded in ranching circles long before its official recognition as a breed, the Australian shepherd is not yet widely appreciated beyond this sphere.

History This breed is not Australian, but was developed in the US to work as a herding dog. The name was possibly derived from one of the dog's ancestors, since its principal forebears were most likely Spanish dogs that accompanied the herds of Merino sheep exported to the US and Australia in colonial times. At some point, it was probably crossed with collie stock.

Description The medium-sized "Aussie" has a lean, muscular body and a coarse coat. The ears, chest, underbody and the tops of the legs are well feathered and there is a thick ruff. The coat color and pattern are remarkably varied, but red merle, blue merle (see p. 299), red or black are common. The tail is either very short or missing. If present at birth, it is usually docked.

Temperament Intelligent, easily trained, obedient and very responsive, this dog seems to know exactly what is required of it.

Grooming The medium-to-long coat needs very little attention. Groom occasionally with a firm bristle brush, and bathe only when necessary.

Exercise and feeding The dog needs plenty of vigorous exercise, such as running free in a field, or better yet some real work to do. There are no special feeding requirements.

Health problems This hardy breed may suffer from hip dysplasia, eye problems and "collie nose." It is also sensitive to some heartworm preventatives. Merles are prone to deafness.

GERMAN SHEPHERD

Originally a herding dog, it seems the German shepherd can be trained to do any job. Police, search and rescue, military and guide work—it thrives on a life of service.

History Standardized in Germany in the 1890s, the breed was imported to the US in the early 1900s and became popular largely due to the screen exploits of Rin Tin Tin. This versatile dog now performs a variety of tasks.

Description The handsome German shepherd has a dense double coat that comes in black with tan, fawn or gray markings. Other colors also occur.

Temperament This intelligent, confident dog is both loved and feared. Ever-vigilant and inclined to be aggressive toward other dogs, it requires firm, kind and consistent handling from a strong, experienced adult. It is inclined to be reserved and its friendship must be won, but from then on its loyalty is unquestioned.

Grooming Daily grooming is necessary. During molting periods, the dead woolly undercoat must be removed with a slicker brush. Bathe or dry shampoo only when necessary.

Exercise and feeding The dog revels in strenuous activity, preferably combined with obedience training. Without a daily walk it will become restless and destructive. Feed two or three small meals a day.

Health problems This dog suffers from von Willebrand's disease, hip and elbow dysplasia, skin, heart and eye ailments, diabetes, epilepsy, spinal paralysis, inflammatory bowel disease and bloat. Insufficient digestive enzymes may lead to chronic diarrhea.

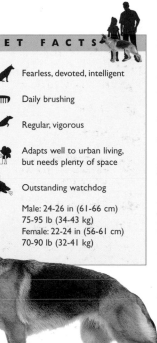

PET FACTS

Fearless, devoted, intelligent

Daily brushing

Regular, vigorous

Adapts well to urban living, but needs plenty of space

Outstanding watchdog

Male: 24-26 in (61-66 cm)
75-95 lb (34-43 kg)
Female: 22-24 in (56-61 cm)
70-90 lb (32-41 kg)

♂ black and tan

BELGIAN SHEPHERD DOG

The picture of power and grace, the Belgian shepherd makes its appearance in several guises. But beneath its beauty is a reliable, hard-working and adaptable dog.

History These dogs were used in Belgium mainly to guard and herd sheep and cows. All are closely related but in recent times have evolved into one basic type with four distinct varieties distinguished by coat coloration, length and texture. They are the Groenendael, Laekenois, Malinois and Tervuren (or Tervueren). In the US, the rare Laekenois has not yet been officially recognized. The other varieties are classified as separate breeds. The popular Groenendael is known simply as the Belgian sheepdog.

Description Belgian shepherds are similar in body type to German shepherds. The Groenendael has an abundant, glossy, slightly rough coat, black with occasional white markings. The muscular Tervuren is identical to the Groenendael—the mating of two Groenendaels can result in the birth of a Tervuren pup. It too has a long, off-standing coat and feathered tail but comes in fawn, mahogany and gray. The hair is tipped with black and the mask and ear tips are also black. Both varieties have a generous ruff, and the male's coat is longer than the female's.

The Malinois is the only variety with a short coat. It comes in fawn to mahogany with the same black overlay and shaded areas as the Tervuren. The Laekenois has similar coloring to the Malinois, but the short hair is thick, harsh and wiry—but never curled—with dark shading on the tail. The muzzle is bristly, with some feathering.

Temperament Like most herding dogs, Belgian shepherds are independent thinkers. Their training should be thorough, and firm, patient and consistent—if it is harsh they will become uncooperative. Once trained, these resource-

Groenendael
♂ black

Malinois
♀ fawn

ful dogs are reliable and diligent, with a strong sense of responsibility. They adore children and thrive on loving companionship. Ever-alert and wary of strangers, they make good watchdogs. Police and service work is currently their primary duty; the Tervuren is also used to assist the disabled.

Grooming The grooming needs of the Malinois are minimal. Brush weekly and bathe only if absolutely necessary as bathing strips the coat

of its natural oils. Care of the Groenendael and Tervuren is more demanding. Their coarse, straight outer coats are long and heavy; the undercoats are very dense. Groom daily and give extra care during molting. Clip out mats, particularly in the ruff and on the legs, and clip hair from between the toes and on the outer ears. Bathing is not recommended, but dry shampoo if necessary.

The Laekenois's rough, wiry coat needs only occasional brushing. Again, bathing is not recommended.

Exercise and feeding These high-energy dogs are bred for an active outdoor life. They need as much exercise as possible, preferably running off the leash. There are no special feeding requirements, but do not overfeed as they can become obese and lazy.

Health problems These dogs suffer few genetic diseases, although some get hip dysplasia and eye problems.

Laekenois
♀ *fawn*

Tervuren
♂ *fawn*

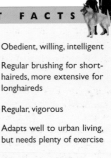

PET FACTS

Obedient, willing, intelligent

Regular brushing for short-haireds, more extensive for longhaireds

Regular, vigorous

Adapts well to urban living, but needs plenty of exercise

Very good watchdog

Male: 24-26 in (61-66 cm)
65-75 lb (29-34 kg)
Female: 22-24 in (56-61 cm)
60-70 lb (27-32 kg)

PET FACTS

 Kind, reliable, intelligent

 Regular brushing

Regular, vigorous

 Adapts well to urban living, but needs plenty of exercise

Very good watchdog

Male: 23-27 in (58-69 cm)
70-80 lb (32-36 kg)
Female: 21-25 in (53-63 cm)
65-75 lb (29-34 kg)

♂ fawn

BRIARD

The gentle Briard is now becoming better known and appreciated outside its native France, where it is a working shepherd dog and devoted pet.

History The Briard's lineage goes back more than 1,000 years, although today's dog is more refined than those of earlier times. Long regarded as a shepherd dog, it impressed soldiers in World War I with its abilities as a messenger and as a hauler of supply wagons. It first appeared in the US in the late eighteenth century.

Description A large, muscular dog, the Briard's gait is smooth and appears almost effortless. The long, shaggy coat comes in solid colors, especially black and fawns, the darker the better. The hind legs have double dewclaws.

Temperament A long history of working with humans has made the Briard sweet-natured and gentle. Intel-ligent and easy to train, it makes a wonderful family pet and a very good watchdog. However, the herding instinct remains strong, even in pets.

Grooming If the dog is kept outside, the hypoallergenic coat seems to largely take care of itself. If the dog spends a lot of time indoors, you may wish to brush the coat regularly and bathe or dry shampoo as necessary.

Exercise and feeding This working dog requires plenty of vigorous exercise. There are no special feeding requirements.

Health problems This breed is generally hardy, although hip dysplasia and eye problems such as cataracts and progressive retinal atrophy do occur.

BOUVIER DES FLANDRES

The bouvier des Flandres conveys dependability—from its workmanlike body to its calm, steady manner. Today, it works for the police and as a guide for the blind.

History The bouvier des Flandres, or ox-drover of Flanders, originated in pastoral regions around the Franco-Belgian border. Initially a herder and guard dog, in World War I it was used as a messenger and an ambulance dog.

Description First and foremost a working dog, the bouvier is powerful and compact. The rough, long, shaggy double coat comes in black, gray, salt and pepper, brindle and fawn, sometimes with a white mark on the chest. There is also a thick beard and mustache. The tail is usually docked.

Temperament Adaptable and even-tempered, the bouvier goes about its business quietly and calmly. It is easy to train and, being suspicious of strangers, is an excellent watchdog.

Grooming If the dog is kept outdoors, the harsh, long coat seems to look after itself, shedding dirt and water easily. If the dog lives indoors, the appearance of the coat will be improved with regular brushing. It may benefit from an occasional trim. Bathe or dry shampoo as necessary.

Exercise and feeding Energetic and active, the bouvier needs plenty of daily exercise. There are no special feeding requirements.

Health problems This hardy breed was developed to work in harsh conditions and is rarely ill. However, some dogs may suffer from hip dysplasia and genetic eye problems, including cataracts.

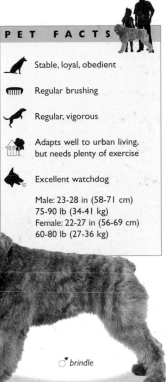

PET FACTS

Stable, loyal, obedient

Regular brushing

Regular, vigorous

Adapts well to urban living, but needs plenty of exercise

Excellent watchdog

Male: 23-28 in (58-71 cm)
75-90 lb (34-41 kg)
Female: 22-27 in (56-69 cm)
60-80 lb (27-36 kg)

♂ brindle

INDEX

Page numbers in *italics* indicate illustrations and photos.

INDEX continued

Index

ACKNOWLEDGMENTS
The publisher would like to thank all the people who kindly brought their dogs to photo shoots.

TEXT Lowell Ackerman, D.V.M., Ph.D., Janine Adams, Kim Campbell Thornton, Lynn Cole, Susan Easterly, Bette LaGow, Debra Horwitz, D.V.M., Amy Marder, V.M.D., Susan McCullough, Paul McGreevy, B.V.Sc., Ph.D., M.R.C.V.S., Arden Moore, Kristine Napier, Jacqueline O'Neil, Liz Palika, Audrey Pavia, Puddingburn Publishing Services (index), Brad Swift, Elaine Waldorf Gewirtz, Christine L. Wilford, D.V.M.
ILLUSTRATIONS Christer Eriksson, Richard Hook/Bernard Thornton Artists UK, Virginia Gray, Janet Jones, David Kirshner, Frank Knight, Iain McKellar, Keith Scanlon, Chris Wilson/Merilake
PHOTOGRAPHS Ad Libitum/Stuart Bowey, Auscape International, The Photo Library
CONSULTANT EDITOR Dr. Paul McGreevy is a veterinarian and lecturer in animal behavior at the University of Sydney, Australia